INSTITUTIONAL RACISM IN
HIGHER EDUCATION

INSTITUTIONAL RACISM IN HIGHER EDUCATION

Edited by
Ian Law, Deborah Phillips and Laura Turney

A Trentham Book
Institute of Education Press, London

Institute of Education Press
20 Bedford Way
London
WC1H 0AL

First published 2004

British Library Cataloguing-in-Publication Data
A catalogue record for this book is available from the
British Library

ISBN-10: 1 85856 313 5
ISBN-13: 978 1 85856 313 8

Designed and typeset by Trentham Print Design Ltd, Chester and
printed by CPI Group (UK) Ltd, Croydon, CR0 4YY

Acknowledgements

We would like to express our gratitude to all the contributors to this volume
who both helped to make the Institutional Racism in Higher Education
Conference such a successful event and who have invested their efforts in
producing the chapters for this collection. Thanks also to Gillian Klein at
Trentham for her support and efforts on this project. We would also like to
thank HEFCE for supporting our Innovations Fund Toolkit Project which
facilitated the Leeds conference.

Contents

Introduction

Racism is a part of everyday life in higher education institutions in Britain. We face a future where university racisms are likely to be highly durable, protean and impervious to intervention. They are likely to co-exist alongside a wide range of progressive, antiracist, multicultural and inclusive ideas, programmes, practices and initiatives. These conflicting forces are the subject of this collection. This book seeks to promote debate over the nature and extent of institutional racism in higher education and how we can move effectively towards fundamental institutional antiracism in this sector. It is based upon a collection of papers originally presented at a national conference organised by the Centre for Ethnicity and Racism Studies, University of Leeds with the assistance of the Equality Challenge Unit and held at Leeds in July 2002. This was the culmination of a HEFCE funded Innovations Project led by Ian Law, Deborah Phillips and Laura Turney examining the evidence of institutional racism in the sector and in their own institution and preparing a web based toolkit to promote and assist institutional change (see www.leeds.ac.uk/cers/toolkit/toolkit.htm). In a context of legal and government pressure for the sector to deliver credible race equality plans by May 2002, these papers provided an opportunity to assess structural constraints on change, the nature and extent of racism in higher education institutions (HEIs) and evidence of innovative responses to these issues. The relative lack of research and publications in this field further prompted this collection and the associated activities.

Our call to arms here is to highlight the urgent need to scrutinise and research the historical and contemporary processes by which racism has operated and continues to operate in higher education institutions.

Debates about racism and universities remain, at present, limited mainly to contemporary matters with little if any connections made between contemporary issues and the racial formation of ideas and institutions in modern British society – an example of what Barnor Hesse and Stuart Hall have called 'white amnesia'. We need to understand why almost forty years since the first Race Relations Act higher education institutions are only now beginning to develop race equality strategies, and that is primarily because they have been forced to do so by the imposition of legal statutory duties.

The history of the role of British universities in the development of race thinking has yet to be written, and there are many questions to ask. For example, one could draw some links with recent debates on slavery and reparations and raise some historical questions about British universities, which have been little researched and rarely exposed to scrutiny. What exactly were the links between British involvement in slavery and the foundation, funding and development of universities? What role did they play and what acknowledgement should be given to their activities? The analysis of the role of universities and the nature of their links and involvement with slavery, colonialism and Empire may assist our understanding of the ways in which white superiority has been secured. In his chapter Sharma emphasises the need to shed historic patterns of elitism and Eurocentrism. Where we do see this story unfolding is in the critical analysis of academic work which has promoted race thinking in various ways, in different subject areas. But the focus has been more on the individual scholar than on the significance of institutional contexts in which the work was produced. A key shift needs to be made. The concept of institutional racism was developed in the 1960s primarily to serve the purpose of moving our gaze from individual attitudes to the collective impact large organisations have in maintaining white privilege.

It may be too simple to suggest that this heritage of an active role in the promotion of race thinking is part of the explanation why universities have never pursued antiracist and racial equality interventions nor developed positive action initiatives. It is also necessary to consider the myths of academic liberalism, the strength of professional academic autonomy, hostility to external policy and prescription, and complacency in the face of inequality. In their contributions to this collection Andrew Pilkington and Jacques Rangasamy highlight issues of academic complacency and academic hostility which may account for institutional inertia in this sector.

When we compare progress in this sector to other public services we find significantly less in universities than almost any other major public sector. If we look at the track record of research on racism much of which has been carried out by the Commission for Racial Equality (CRE) in schools but also on housing estates, we have a wealth of detailed local and national evidence. But where is the comparable evidence on racism in universities? Why is it that higher education has remained for so long absent from the growing literature on race and ethnicity in the British educational system?

Higher education has been less able to hide its activities from scrutiny and debate in the US. In September 2001 the *Guardian* carried an article exposing the controlling influence of a white racist group called the 'Machine' at the University of Alabama. This group of white students and alumni are reported as acting like a 'shadow government on the University campus', influencing access to student housing and promoting white only professional networks of career advancement. It would be naïve to propose that there are identical networks to the Machine in UK universities. But strong, closed, white-led, informal networks may well be promoting white privilege both inside and outside universities. The audit of Cambridge University highlighted elements of these aspects of senior and middle ranking managerial cultures, as did our qualitative research at Leeds University.

The exposure of racist organisational cultures across a range of institutions continues to be a central component of news media coverage of race-related issues. In Britain, the overall picture of institutional racism that emerges from news coverage is wide but selective. Racism in the immigration service, criminal justice organisations, football clubs, health authorities and trusts, the armed forces and private employers like Ford have been in the news. Attention has also been given to racism in churches, schools, Fire Services, the entertainment and fashion industry and airlines. But news coverage of debates about racism in higher education institutions is recent and still rare. This may have less to do with the decisions of news producers and more to do with the producers of race-related research. The new programme of research into Equal Opportunities in HE funded by HEFCE may improve matters.

This book includes a range of different voices and approaches and aims to give space both to those in differing institutional positions and disciplines and to those engaged with differing constituencies.

Part One brings together four strong voices who seek to challenge institutional racism in higher education. Chapter One presents the text of a speech given by Les Back at the opening plenary session of the Institutional Racism and Higher Education Conference at the University of Leeds on July 3rd, 2002. In this challenging presentation he contrasts the 'multicultural drift' of many HEIs with their inability to shed white resentment and racist thinking. He urges white intellectuals to engage in a 'troublesome and uncomfortable' dialogue with their own racism and with that of their colleagues and institutions.

Chapter Two provides a highly critical account of the emergence of debates about race and race equality in higher education. Drawing on the experiences of the AUT Black Network, and in particular primary research on Vice Chancellor's perceptions of race issues in the sector, William Gulam highlights the clash between white and black perspectives. He calls primarily for greater inclusion, dialogue and negotiation with black staff in these debates.

In Chapter Three, Andrew Pilkington draws strong parallels between institutional racism in the police and HEIs, and examines the responses of organisations operating in Midshire to race equality imperatives. He establishes that, in both institutional settings, action and initiatives taken have failed to affect core activities and that both institutions exhibited complacency and perpetuated institutional racism through the marginalisation of race equality issues. This chapter reveals the ease with which legislative, policy and political interventions around race equality and antiracism can be deflected and ignored by key figures, such as Departmental Heads, in higher education institutions.

This deep concern over the strength of opposition to institutional change is further explored by Jacques Rangasamy in Chapter Four. Rangasamy brings debates from linguistic anthropology to bear on the understanding of institutional racism. He argues for greater awareness of cultural contexts and the codes of institutional language. He highlights the failures of simplistic attempts to pursue institutional change or adequately consult black staff, and notes differential treatment of foreign students. He argues that the use of institutional power in constructing racial divisions, 'race-making', is evident in the suppression of criticism and opposition, and also in the differential constraints on career progression for non-white staff. Rangasamy identifies four key features of higher education institutions which he argues are important barriers to effective intervention in patterns of institutional racism: institutional defensiveness, conservatism, active discrimination and the legacy of colonialist thinking. And he makes an impassioned call for enlightened, compassionate institutional leadership.

Part Two presents accounts of the ways in which different groups and constituencies encounter higher education. Chapter Five discusses the spread of institutionalised Islamophobia in British universities. David Tyrer argues that fears surfaced during the mid-1990s of a distinct threat to campus harmony in British universities from radical Islamists. Despite the lack of empirically reliable research into the nature of this assumed problem, it was regularly reported in the press, and gave rise to organised campaigning against fundamentalism by a number of bodies including the National Union of Students. At the heart of these campaigns was the idea that bound up in the question of Islamist activities on campus were a range of concerns directly relating to equal opportunities and the rights of minority groups to be protected from victimisation and harassment. Despite an established literature identifying stereotyping of Muslims as fundamentalists with Islamophobia, little consideration was given to the rights of Muslim students as a minority group on campus, or to the reliability of reports about Islamic 'fundamentalism' in universities. These difficulties were illustrated by the report on *Extremism and Intolerance on Campus* produced by the Committee for Vice-Chancellors and Principals in 1998 which, despite being widely welcomed as a tool for combating the spread of Islamism, did not name a single Muslim organisation among its list of groups consulted. Still more alarming, the report acknowledged that the CVCP's aim was not to produce 'a different kind of study of, for example, how to promote multicultural, inter-racial and inter-religious harmony and mutual respect' (CVCP, 1998: 5). So, notwithstanding the equal opportunities issues, pluralist principles were suspended in the context of fears about an Islamist assault on the very fabric of the academy. Tyrer critically examines debates about Islamic fundamentalism on campus in order to explore just what goes into characterising student political activities as extremist or fundamentalist. His research in four universities reveals that, contrary to widespread fears, Muslim students were frequently the victims of extremism and intolerance on campus.

In Chapter Six, drawing on Bourdieu's concept of 'habitus', Nirmal Puwar explores the racialised social spaces of academia and the positions of black bodies in institutions of higher education. She weaves a tale of feeling out of place in the whiteness of the academy. She reveals tensions between the ability of people of colour to gain limited access to HEIs as members of staff and their experience of racialisation. This process generates feelings of marginalisation, ethnic pigeon-holing, infantalisation and hyper-surveillance of black academics. Puwar argues that while 'academia prides itself in being an open space', it is characterised by systems of racialised patronage, networking and social cloning, which renders black academics at variance with the somatic norm in positions of authority in academia.

Chapter Seven gives voice to South Asian female students and explores how higher education has provided a space for the complex and shifting construction of their cultural and religious identities. Shirin Housee uses in-depth interviews with students at the University of Wolverhampton to reveal how higher education for these women has helped them to be more assertive and confident about their religion, culture and identity. Although some women have to overcome significant family resistance to higher education, the South Asian students displayed agency in their decision making and were able to use the spaces of academia for their personal and cultural development. The identity construction process was sharpened for all Asians, but Muslims in particular, by the events of September 11th 2001.

In Chapter Eight, Colin Clark presents an historical and contemporary overview of the long term challenges facing Gypsy/Travellers in accessing formal education. This chapter alerts us to the silence of most mainstream educationalists, policy makers and academics on Gypsy/Traveller rights and access to HE; this group is simply excluded from consideration in most discussions about cultural diversity, race equality and widening participation. As Clark reminds us, there are very few Gypsy/Travellers in HE, for reasons of institutional racism, individual prejudice and cultural difference, and there has been scant systematic research on those who have entered this sector. Drawing together the available evidence, Clark advocates a holist approach encompassing the barriers associated with access to schooling as well as HE, and emphasises the need to look at the problems of accessing the right kind of education; that is, education that is inclusive, relevant, participatory, appropriate and responsive to the needs of Gypsy/Traveller communities.

Chapter Nine considers the intersection of race and disability for access to employment in higher education. Ozcan Konur draws on a number of case studies to examine how implementation of the RRA (1976) and DDA (1995) can prove ineffective in helping the progress of minority ethnic and disabled people. The hurdles to be overcome in challenging decisions about access are illustrated through analysing the processes of jurisdiction and procedural testing, disability/race tests, discrimination tests and enforcement tests.

Part Three moves from perceptions and experiences of hostility, exclusion and discrimination to consider the prospects and opportunities for building institutional change in the HE sector. Chapter Ten presents a new framework for promoting debate about the operation of institutional racism in higher education. This toolkit brings together conceptual and organisational ideas which seek to go beyond the boundaries of mechanistic racial equality guidelines and discuss fundamental and practical questions about the contemporary role of higher education institutions. Concepts of racism, Eurocentrism and whiteness are employed to consider what issues and questions need to be raised if we are to build antiracist strategies across employment, student access, teaching and learning, research, contracts and purchasing and external affairs in the HE sector. Almost all HEIs are now implementing various policies, initiatives, training and other activities in the name of equality. Many have used this toolkit to help them engage with the question of what is to be done. Greater debate and openness about the depth of racism in HEIs is a vital precondition to organisational change.

In Chapter Eleven, Sanjay Sharma moves beyond the likely impact of the Race Relations (Amendment) Act 2000 on staffing and student recruitment to consider the challenges of curriculum development in the multicultural university. His chapter focuses on the intersections between cultural difference, 'otherness', knowledge and power in educational praxis in order to argue that so-called 'multicultural curriculum' developments are rarely transformative. Although multicultural projects in higher education aim to 'acknowledge and value' cultural difference, Sharma argues that institutions usually end up regulating and containing these differences through their hegemonic practices. Cultural differences are thus often addressed through a process of inclusion (e.g. by including black authors on reading lists) rather than through a more radical process of transformation. The outcome, Sharma argues, is a 'domesticated otherness' that cannot challenge or disrupt white, Eurocentric frameworks of knowledge.

In Chapter Twelve, Joyce Hill and Emmanuell Kusemamuriwo outline the remit of the Equality Challenge Unit (ECU), in which they work, and discuss the challenges and opportunities faced by the Unit in helping implement the Race Relations (Amendment) Act 2000 in the higher education sector. The ECU was established in 2001 to promote action on equality issues in HEIs across the UK and to help them respond to the new legislative demands of the 2000 Act. It has engaged in developmental work with individual institutions and the dissemination of general guidance on implementating race equality initiatives across the sector. Hill and Kusemamuriwo present a picture of significant activity in the establishment of new structures for the promotion of race equality in HEIs. Their evaluation of developments to date suggests progress across the sector, although it is erratic. They leave us with the warning that, 'The Race Relations (Amendment) Act is a ground-breaking piece of legislation. It requires major changes to be made in all our public bodies, a process which is invariably difficult and often disturbing.'

Part Four explores the wider nature of the disturbing process required of higher education by challenging fundamental positions and assumptions that underlie contemporary debates over institutional racism and urges us to reflect and re-think our core ideas. Barnor Hesse and Salman Sayyid argue that we can only understand the persistence and durability of racism in higher education and elsewhere in Western states by revealing the colonial inheritance of racialised governance and by interrogating post-colonial conditions.

In Chapter Thirteen Hesse considers the construction of Western concepts of racism, examining debates within the League of Nations and the United Nations. He challenges a dominant view contained in these Eurocentric positions which treats racism as exceptional, or as principally a radical deviation from the enlightened institutions of the West. He seeks to re-connect the cultural relations between colonialism, racism and liberalism by elaborating how racial rule is exercised by the powerful racial majority in the UK and US. Institutional racism is thus revealed as only what the racial majority is prepared to indict, and good race relations become mechanisms for perpetuating the norms of white rule by covert means while overtly presenting an 'antiracist show' and appeasing the perceptions of subordination amongst racial minorities. Hesse reveals the matrix of ideas which underlie many of the ahistorical and decontextualised contemporary debates over institutional racism.

In Chapter Fourteen Salman Sayyid also explores the importance of developing a post-colonial analysis of ethnic relations in the UK. He identifies the discursive tools used to talk about, manage, regulate and discipline immigrants. This old and pervasive grammar of ethnic relations he terms the 'immigrant imaginary'. Ideas of assimilation, exoticism and generational differences are some of the lexicon that he identifies. Contemporary ways of addressing people who have been marked as being of different colour and ethnicities demand redeployment of colonial discourse. The task is challenging: to build accounts, policies, research and teaching which move beyond the privileging of the Western enterprise and instead construct a clearer understanding of postcolonial conditions and dilemmas.

PART ONE
CHALLENGING RACISM IN HIGHER EDUCATION

CHAPTER ONE

Ivory Towers?
The Academy and Racism

Les Back

oni Morrison observed that the genesis of higher education is centrally implicated in an 'unabashedly theological and consciously value-ridden and value-
seeking' moral project.[1] What she exposes are the fallacies of impartiality and
neutrality that are often invoked in the debate about education and social inequalities.
Universities are not value-neutral places. In Britain the traces of this theological scheme
survives in the ways that universities speak of themselves in Mission Statements. Now
the sermon from the secular pulpit has changed to embrace themes like Widening Participation and Social Inclusion. Thinking of universities as both value-ridden and value-
seeking begs a number of questions: what kinds of values do universities embody today?
how close are we to realising a multicultural university?

I want to suggest that two sets of antagonistic forces are at play. First, there is a deep resistance in the academy to reckon with – what might be called the sheer weight of whiteness.[2] These are the value-ridden maxims that govern seemingly neutral ideas like
academic freedom, objectivity and fairness. Second, some universities in Britain and
elsewhere in Europe have moved a long way – perhaps without much conscious direction
– towards what Stuart Hall calls a 'species of multicultural drift'[3]. This is certainly true
of my own work place, Goldsmiths College in London. For all its problems, the College
is certainly a more international and cosmopolitan place than it was twenty years ago
when I first encountered it as a student. These two impulses, that is the drift towards
multiculture and the wall of white resistance and resentment that seeks to block cultural
diversity, are set on a collision course in the universities.

Making universities more democratic and inclusive is not just about developing a more
multicultural curriculum, or ensuring fair and respectful treatment of black and ethnic
minority staff. It also involved raising issues of ethics and responsibility in intellectual
life. A series of incidents in recent years have brought into focus the culpability of intellectuals in reproducing and legitimising racism.

Two Faces of the Academy

In the British media much ink has been spilt over the now notorious outburst of Geoffery Sampson, a Professor of Natural Language Computing at the University of Sussex. He claimed in a paper published on his website that racialism – i.e. the preference for people who appear genetically similar – is inevitable and universal and that 'yellow-skinned Orientals tend to be brighter than whites and Negroes tend to be rather less bright'. Ian McDonald concluded that Sampson had violated his right to academic freedom,

> Outside the academy, Sampson's article represents little more than a footnote in the out-pouring of racist myths and lies of the past few years. But, if unchallenged, its potential power lies in the rationalisation of an intuitive sense that many people will hold, namely that pre-ference for racial familiarity is 'natural'.[4] (*Times Higher Education Supplement*, 24.6.02)

In aftermath of McDonald's article a debate is being hosted on the THES website. It made for interesting reading. A host of liberal-minded academics lined up – shoulder to shoulder with right wing libertarians and pernicious racists – to defend Sampson's academic freedom. By turns 'antiracist academics' are accused of 'lacking confidence' in their own arguments, 'political correctness' and of not being 'tough enough to defend principles'. In short, we are charged with being too thinned skinned, and unable to take the raciological knocks. What is significant about all of this is that such accusations are launched from within the armature of an assumed – perhaps even invisible to those pro-tected by it – whiteness that stakes out the terms of the argument. As Ben Carrington pointed out, those involved have, 'virtually nothing to say about racism and how it might be challenged'. The whole incident 'reveals just how deeply entrenched racism, in its various guises, still is within the HE Sector'.[5]

The second face of the present to note is the shocking endorsement of racist immigration policies in *The Guardian* by a professor of sociology: that the Right can be fought on the Centre Left through developing policies that are 'tough on immigration, but tough on the causes of hostility to immigrants'[6]. Tony Blair has said that Anthony Giddens is his favourite sociologist. Flattery can evidently be blinding. Professor Giddens' defence of the Third Way in tackling the Extreme Right is certainly sightless when it comes to identifying the complicity of the Centre Left in a context where there is a resurgence of popular racism and anti-immigrant politics. At a time when the Extreme Right is seeking to mobilise support by popularising anti-immigrant sentiments, it is shocking that a sociologist of Giddens's standing uses language that can at best confuse debate and at worst accepts the argument that immigration is a cause of racism. What Giddens does is in effect take the current popular debate about immigration for granted and ignore the whole history of racism in immigration policy over the past fifty years. Even the term 'immigrant' is over-determined by the legacy of the racial coding of movements of labour.

So we need to look critically at what is happening in both immigration and racism in British society. Giddens says nothing about the behaviour of New Labour on im-migration and asylum over the past five years. Rather his call for New Labour to be 'tough on immigration' simply apes the language of the right. Far from countering the politics of extremism, such a stance can be seen as allowing the political agenda to be dominated by what Giddens calls 'people's anxieties' – meaning white people's anxieties. It is hard to see how this strategy defeats the Far Right, since by and large it seems to accept the argument that immigrants are a problem.

A columnist on the *Muslim News* wrote about this: 'What is disturbing now is that leading ethically sensitive intellectuals are today not only vying with crude racists in vilifying Islam and Muslims, but sometimes leading the way'[7]. The two examples above, in different ways, address the culpability of intellectuals in reproducing raciology and racism. They also show how invocations of academic freedom allow and normalise these acts of speech. Intellectual complicity in racism points to the urgent need to create a response on campuses and in faculties. This process is already underway.

Significant in the debate about racism and academic ethics is that the issue of individual culpability is conflated with heady invocations of academic freedom, censorship and free speech. So raising these issues of racism is immediately reduced to a stifling political correctness. The consequences of the ideas that are being expressed are sidestepped. What would it mean for students to hear or read Geoffrey Sampson's outpourings? What consequences do they have in the classroom? In a brilliant act of doublethink, those who advocate academic freedom in this context are trying to re-assert the *status quo* that silences and inhibits a serious discussion of the relationship between racism and knowledge production. But vigorous dissenting voices are countering such arguments, and this must be nurtured if the universities are to play a role in creating a more inclusive society.

Hideously white?

It is over ten since black teenager Stephen Lawrence was murdered by a racist gang in south east London. The failure of the police to bring his killers to justice and the report into the causes of these failures have done more than any single event to put the issue of institutional racism on the social agenda. The Stephen Lawrence Inquiry, published in 1999, defined institutional racism as:

> the collective failure of an organisation to provide an appropriate and professional service to people because of their colour, culture or ethnic origin. It can be seen or detected in processes, attitudes and behaviour which amount to discrimination through unwitting prejudice, ignorance, thoughtlessness, and racist stereotyping which disadvantage minority ethnic people.[8]

Yet although institutional racism is on the agenda in Britain, there is still no effective language to name the ways institutions like universities police their boundaries. The invocations of 'witting' and 'unwitting racism' in the Stephen Lawrence Report have done little to help us name and identify the allusive forms of racism that haunt the academy.

It has become almost routine for high profile figures in institutions to make public admissions of guilt with regard to racism in their institutions. In January 1991 Greg Dyke, then Director General of the BBC, told a journalist that it was 'hideously white'[9]. Sir David Calvert-Smith, the Director of Public Prosecutions, told Radio 4's *On the Ropes*: 'It is my firm belief that British society is institutionally racist. I come to this with the idea that the whole of society has a problem'[10]. There is something in the blanket assertions of institutional racism that is somehow comforting for its speakers. This can be found also in police responses after the Stephen Lawrence Inquiry. It seems that these blanket admissions say 'it's not just about us' as if somehow this mitigates their responsibility as the 'carriers of the problem'. I am not sure how helpful such assertions are as they produce such easy material for the counter-blast. Alternative, the unwitting notion of racism some how abrogates responsibility like a racist playground spat 'I didn't mean anything by it'.

A more sophisticated way must be found to talk about and name implicit forms of exclusion. Zygmunt Bauman has argued in the context of the experience of European Jewry that the emancipation of migrants was haunted by a perverse paradox. In order to gain entry to any sense of universal humankind, Jews had to renounce Jewish particularity. Bauman observes that: 'exit visas were a collective matter, whereas entry tickets had to be obtained individually'[11]. This illustrates how boundaries of inclusion and exclusion are mediated through cultural terms. One way forward may be to try and identify the kinds of cultural passports that are required to gain entry to the academy and the embodied and implicit knowledge necessary to attain academic forms of distinction. It seems that institutional racism is too often unwritten, embedded and embodied within the academy's sheer institutional weight. These are surely the palpable – if not articulated – values Toni Morrison was speaking of. The ways in which academic value is calculated needs to be scrutinised. Implicit hierarchies that define particular theoretical proclivities, fashionable or specific areas that are seen as the leading edges of academic disciplines may serve to entrench the dominant culture.

Reckoning with whiteness

Lastly, I want to foreground the fraught responses by white faculty to the issue of racism on campus. Most white academics consider it unreasonable that an accusation of racism should be levelled at them. For many academics the face of racism is that of the moral degenerate, the hateful bigot. So it is unthinkable that such an ugly word could be directed at a genteel, educated and liberal don such as themselves. Even raising the issue of institutional racism tentatively produces responses like 'how could you' or 'how dare you' make such accusations? This reaction goes deeper than a response to being accused of something. What raises their blood pressure is that something is being taken away. It is the theft of all that is mannerly about liberalism, knowledge and educational progress. To accuse educators of racism is – in their minds – tantamount to taking their education away from them. And this is why it is so difficult to have a measured and open debate about racism in the academy.

The framing of the problem of racism has become part of the problem itself. I suggest that there is another way to argue with its consequences. Rather than simply hide in the refusal to acknowledge the problem with the white rebuff 'Don't look at me!', the open question that white academics need to embrace is 'why not me?' Not that I am suggesting that the addiction to white supremacy should be countered by some kind of AA (Alcoholics Anonymous) meeting approach:

'Hi. My name's Les Back – I am a Recovering White Person'.

What I want is to acknowledge that racism has damaged reason, damaged academic and civic freedoms and damaged the project of education itself. Admitting this means pursuing a kind of resolute and ongoing reckoning with whiteness. This is not a matter of an end point, or an achievement; rather it is an ongoing questioning that strives to step out of whiteness' brilliant shadow.

There is another danger here. The temptation to present the persona of an exceptional 'alright white person' needs also to be resisted. I have seen others indulge in pieties of this sort and recognise it in myself. It is another version of a political masquerade where bad white academics can be denounced roundly by those adopting the comfortable position of exception-to-the-rule. There is something deeply disingenuous about this move because it forecloses critical reflection rather than opening it up. It can be manifest in a number of academic settings, particularly those concerning staff appointments. 'Alright Whites' can castigate new white colleagues for their complicity in benefiting from exclusionary employment practices without ever questioning the status of their own tenure. The logic is that 'racism couldn't have been applicable to me and my employment fortunes because I am an exception – I am an alright white person!'. Delusions of this kind give false comfort and they are vulnerable to attack from anyone who pays them close attention.

The kind of reflexivity I am arguing for should be troublesome and uncomfortable because as John Dewey[12] pointed out, it demands a 'willingness to endure a condition of mental unrest and disturbance'. This is a reckoning with ethical judgements driven by shame and not guilt. It is shameful to read in recent research that black colleagues in British universities are routinely undermined, 'cut out' of the loops of academic communication and subjected to crude racism inside and outside the classroom.[13]

This brings me back to Toni Morrison. At the end of her lecture on values and education, she warns:

> If the university does not take seriously and rigorously its role as a guardian of wider civic freedoms, as interrogator of more and more complex ethical problems, as servant and preserver of deeper democratic practices, then some other regime or ménage of regimes will do it for us, in spite of us, and without us.[14]

Her warning is timely because despite the difficulties this challenge presents there is something precious to be cherished and fought for. In response to her essay, Denis Dutton argued that universities should not try to promote values:

> Open, uncommitted inquiry and intellectual independence is simply not compatible with unquestioning obedience to officially sanctioned and sponsored moral values in the university. You can have the University of Michigan as we understand it, or you can have Taliban U. You can't have both.[15]

My quarrel with this line of argument is that uncommitted inquiry and intellectual independence can foster moral values at the very moment it is disavowing them. Consequently racism cannot be countenanced as part of a wider commitment to independent thinking because it stands in the place of thinking; it stands for easy quick answers of the kind discussed above – 'yellow-skinned Orientals tend to be brighter than whites and Negroes tend to be rather less bright'.

I do not want to gloss over the real challenges, dilemmas and difficulties in achieving something that comes close to a multicultural university. It is possible to imagine what it would be like now but twenty years ago it would have been unthinkable. The values we need to be arguing for are precisely those which foreground the role of the university arguing for wider civic freedoms. Higher Education offers a place where complex ethical problems can be interrogated in a democratic atmosphere. So it is important to hold on to the bloodless revolutions in thinking that can happen almost routinely in the seminar room. Once exposed to the intoxication of thinking it can seem as if mere ideas will change everything. I remember that sense of wonder all too well and recognise it in today's students, particularly those who are the first in their families to go to university. The realisation that books and education have only limited power can lead to disappointment and disillusion, rather as if they have been let down by a friend. Those most dazzled by the vertigo of ideas – I am speaking from experience – can quickly come down: if it is not everything, it is nothing.

The view that 'nothing has changed' and that 'racism wins out at every turn' damages our understanding as much as our will. Real shifts are taking place and we need look no further to see this than across the lectern and into the faces of our students. But first there has to be recognition of what Hannah Arendt called the 'banality of evil'[16], that education and sophistication produce no immunity from racism and white supremacy. The sheer weight of whiteness that bears down on the academy can only be lifted through the open acknowledgement, however difficult, of the damage that racism has done to it. Then, and perhaps only then, will universities be ready to play a role in producing a post-imperial society that is at peace with itself.

Notes

1   Toni Morrison How Can Values be Taught in the University, lecture given at the Center for Human Values, Princeton University, April 27, 2000. http://www.umich.edu/~mqr/morrison.htm p. 1

2   Echoing Stephen Lukes, *Power: A Radical View* (London: Macmillan, 1974)

3   Stuart Hall 'The Multicultural Question' in Barnor Hesse (ed.) *Unsettled Multiculturalism* (London: Zed Books, 2001) p. 231

4   Ian McDonald 'No Refuge for Racists within the Academy' *THES* June 7th 2002 p. 17

5   Http://www.thes.co.uk/common_room/ thread.asp June 24th 2002

6   *The Guardian* May 3rd, 2002 p. 18

7   Abdulwahab El-Affendi European racism and the 'Third Way' between xenophobia and neo-fascism, *Muslim News*, 28th June 2002 p. 4

8   *The Stephen Lawrence Inquiry report by Sir William Macpherson of Cluny*, February 1999 Section 6.34

9   *The Observer*, January 7th 2001

10   *Daily Express*, June 24th, 2002

11   Bauman, Z. (1998) 'Exit visas and entry tickets: the paradoxes of Jewish assimilation', *Telos*, 77 p. 51

12   John Dewey *How We Think* (Amherst, New York: Prometheus, 1991) p. 37

13   Laura Turney, Ian Law and Deborah Phillips *Institutional Racism in Higher Education, Building the Anti-Racist HE: A Toolkit* (Leeds: University of Leeds, CERS, 2002)

14   *Ibid.* p. 4

15   Denis Dutton 'Dare to think for yourself: a response to Toni Morrison' http://www.umich.edu/~mqr/dutton.htm

16   Hannah Arendt *Eichmann in Jerusalem: a report on the banality of evil* (New York: Viking Press, 1963)

CHAPTER TWO

Black and White Paradigms in Higher Education

William A. Gulam

The racial dynamic in Higher Education has for many years been a secret garden. However, intermittent public angst periodically generated research initiatives and well-meaning dialogue. Various committees were established, numerous conferences held, papers published and race-oriented programmes established and soon abandoned as the funny money ran out.

Recently though, there have been slight, and probably transitory, indications that HE may yet be compelled to consider the multi-faceted dimensions of race within overall operational life. The drivers for this intrusion into the sector are various. The main driver has certainly been the murder of Stephen Lawrence and the Macpherson Inquiry report identifying the institutional racism surrounding the event. Politicians and society at large could no longer openly ignore racism. Yet we inhabitants of HE, tried to keep somewhat aloof and detached from the issues it raised. Witness the question from the Registrar of a Yorkshire university at a Committee of Vice Chancellors (CVCP) sub group meeting held under the auspices of their former equality spearhead Commission on University Careers Opportunity (CUCO). During a round table discussion on the issue of employment and equality within the sector which focused on race and ethnicity and the concept of institutional racism, the Registrar asked without the slightest embarrassment, 'What is this Macpherson report?' (Gulam and Hapeshi, 2000). This from someone whose institution is not far from the recent racial disturbances in the county.

Nevertheless, the societal momentum generated by the murder of Stephen Lawrence could not be too overtly diverted. The issues surrounding race and ethnicity began to percolate into our sector. It originated from what many would now regard as a most unlikely source – David Blunkett, in 1999 Secretary of State for Education. Blunkett wrote an open letter to the chair of the Higher Education Funding Council in which he said:

> I am particularly concerned to see that all institutions make progress on race equality for staff. I therefore ask Council to encourage institutions to give proper emphasis to race in their statements. (DfEE, 1999a)

This letter was seminal in more ways than one. It was the first indication of formal recognition by the Government of the issue of race in HE, the first suggestion that there might be some dysfunction regarding race in this sector. Blunkett had personally inserted the sentences and the emphasis. But this was – in politics – a long time ago.

To the sceptic this 1999 clarion call might have had greater impact had it emphasised action rather than statements. However, his symbolic intervention was soon followed by two events that added weight to this move. Malcolm Wicks, then DfEE minister, observed that: 'There are too few ethnic minority staff in our universities – especially in senior positions' (DfEE, 1999b).

This was followed by a request from Mr Blunkett that the head of the CVCP and other CVCP officers, as the representatives for the Vice Chancellors, should attend a meeting convened by DfEE to discuss the issues that had been flagged. A hastily convened meeting was called at CVCP's London headquarters. It involved CVCP officers and selected people who were seen as race activists and experts. The session was memorable in that it recorded comments and commentaries from the gathering which presumably helped to provide a steer for the meeting with the DfEE. With hindsight, it is interesting that after the Lawrence murder, there was a need even to call such a meeting. Be that as it may, the process had begun to place race, however temporarily, on the HE agenda.

The Government might have been motivated by its determination to widen participation in HE. Their stated aim was to ensure that some 50% of the eligible population would soon enjoy the benefits of HE. If this objective were to be attained, some attention had to be accorded to the issue of race and ethnicity. Ethnic minority communities were the fastest growing sector of the population – then some 7.1% of the total population, increasing some fifteen times faster than the white population. In the ten years between the census counts of 1991 and 2001, this cohort had increased by one million. If this pool of potential students were to be tapped into to help meet targets for entry into HE there had to be some consideration of the issue of race. The overt signs of a racially dysfunctional situation highlighted by the DfEE pronouncements were difficult to ignore. To persuade this burgeoning population to enlist and remain within the HE ranks as both students and staff required action.

The construction of a scenario in which race became part of the legitimate discourse in HE was a long time coming. It could be argued that from its inception, a racialised and divided sector had been consolidated as the operational and institutional norm. Some educational commentators had characterised the sector as akin to those 'incredible islands' (Major, *Guardian*, 9, 15/1/2002) where people, especially teaching staff, were positioned and defined by racial and ethnic criteria. As early as 1999 Hague in the *Times Higher Education Supplement* (18 June 1999) asked simply: How many Vice Chancellors are black? She replied in a word: None.

Examples supporting the contention that HE is racialised and divided were and are easily found. On many of the indices that could signify a pattern of institutionalised and inequitable treatment a racialised pattern can be discerned across the whole HE continuum.

- The apex of the HE system, where Vice and Pro Vice Chancellors remain a white enclave

- At professorial level, there are 261 black professors out of a sector total of over 11,000 (HESA, 1999/2000)

- White staff are more likely to be senior lecturers – 17.8% compared to 10.1% Asian staff and 9.3% black staff (Gulam, Hapeshi and Wilkinson, 2001)

- On the matter of job permanency, fewer white academic staff are on fixed term contracts – 39% compared to 45.2% black academic and 65.3% Asian academic staff (HESA, 1999/2000)

- With some 14% of 2001 first year UK domiciled undergraduates coming from ethnic minority communities, it is still notable that 'ethnic minority groups are less likely than white applicants to gain admission to the traditional universities' (Home Office, 2001)

One is moved to conclude that accusations of institutionalised racism in the HE sector are valid. Perversely, however, the dominant view is otherwise. Experience and research indicate that the contention of institutionalised racism would not be accepted by the majority of the overwhelmingly white key decision-makers in the sector, nor by most of the white workers in it.

A study run by the sector's teaching union illustrates this. Following the successful resolution moved by the black members of the Association of University Teachers (AUT) at the annual conference of May 2000, it was agreed to set up a scoping study concerning race in the sector. The objective of the research was to discover the workplace situation and positional circumstances of black staff in HE. A postal questionnaire was sent out to all members of the AUT and some 10,000 useable responses were returned (roughly just under a quarter of total membership; it must also be noted that 96% of the 10,000 returns were from white respondents). What can be teased out of the returns are that two paradigms regarding race in the HE sector seemed to be operating. The critical factor which decided which paradigm a respondent ascribed to was largely determined by their race or ethnic affiliations. Among white respondents the operational paradigm was as follows:

- 90% rejected the possibility of institutional racism in their own institutions

- 40% believed their institution was committed to the concept of equality

- only 2% had ever reported an incident of harassment

- only 1% felt that they had been unfairly treated in job interviews and promotion

- only 2% felt that race equality was an important concern in their work place.

This benign paradigm was contrasted with the one that emerged from the responses of black staff who had returned the questionnaire. Their experiences differed considerably from that expressed and perceived by their white colleagues in the same institutions. The operational paradigm of black staff was less benign:

- 42% identified institutional racism operating within their work place

- 33% had experienced harassment at their institution

- 25% felt they had been unfairly treated in the rounds of job interviews and attempts at securing promotion

- only 20% felt their institution was committed to the concept of equality (AUT, 2002).

There are clear perceptional differences amongst these workers in HE. The AUT research suggests that the contrasting paradigms betray a racial fault line at operational level.

Interestingly, the existence of dual paradigms regarding the racial dynamic is replicated at the strategic and decision making level (Gulam, Hapeshi and Wilkinson, 2001). It appears to exist also at the Vice Chancellors level either as individuals or collectively, as indicated in the *Report on interviews with heads of institutions on racial equality issues* (CUCO, 2000). The Committee of University Careers Opportunities (CUCO) was set up by the Committee of Vice Chancellors (CVCP – the forerunners of the Vice Chancellors collective the Universities UK – UUK). This subsequent report followed on the heels of *Ethnicity and Employment in HE* (Carter, Fenton and Modood., 1999), so they had prior warning about a fraught and dysfunctional sector. During four months in 2000, thirteen heads of universities and HE institutions volunteered to be interviewed with regard to their own perceptions of the race dynamic in the sector and their own institutions. They were drawn from both old (pre 1992 universities, n=3) and new (post 1992 universities, n= 10) institutions across the United Kingdom, and they represented a 'varied mix of universities and colleges; institutions located in urban and rural areas' (CUCO, 2000:1).

The interviewers were officers from CVCP in tandem with black members drawn from the Association of University Teachers (AUT) Black Network. The AUT presence on the interview round had been negotiated at earlier CUCO meetings on grounds that any report which involved white employees of the CVCP interviewing their own white pay-masters about the racial dynamic within the sector might lack credibility. The interviews were carried out using a set of common research instruments.

In regard to the view from the top, apart from the universal pledge of a 'commitment to equality' (CUCO, 2000, 6) and commitment to the Commission for Racial Equality's (CRE) Leadership Challenge initiative whereby leaders in respective fields pledged to champion race equality in their institutions, what came across was a sophisticated and impressive defence of the HE sector. First, they implied that there was insufficient public recognition for current race-related achievements: 'achievements and successful initiatives instigated by HE institutions were not always noted' (CUCO, 2000, 7). Next came an attempt to water down criticism: 'failures tend to be highlighted' (CUCO, 2000, 7). There followed two old chestnuts: firstly that there were 'difficulties in the recruitment of academic and senior staff from ethnic minorities' (CUCO, 2000, 3), and second the explanation for so little specific staff training on race: '(This) can only be offered on a voluntary basis and in some institutions low attendance figures for this type of training has limited its development" (CUCO, 2000, 3). One could also detect an overall defense of the sector in relation to race: 'racial equality and the achievement of progress is a long term issue for institutions as the composition of the student and staff body evolves' (CUCO, 2000, 7) and that this is largely dependent on: 'long term planning subject to the changing age and racial profile of society as a whole' (CUCO, 2000, 3).

Some attempts have been made to rationalise what the VCs meant by all this. They maintained that:

> We, as VCs are trying; we have done a lot that you refuse to recognise as you are only interested in faults; but what can we do as we cannot seem to recruit 'them' for the really well paid/high status jobs and also we cannot force our people to attend courses on racial issues as it imperils academic freedom; really all that can be done is to wait until the overall age and racial composition of society changes and then this, in turn, will eventually effect us; then the situation will change in our sector'. (quoted by Gulam, Hapeshi and Wilkinson, 2001)

The CUCO report is interesting in many respects. Apart from the studied defence of the status quo by the VCs, what is also of concern is what did not appear in the final draft of the report. There is also the issue of what the AUT Black Network members who took part in the exercise felt about the narrative and the paradigm relayed by the official CUCO document.

Of the thirteen institutions visited, members of the AUT Black Network were present on six occasions as part of the agreed interview team. The six institutions visited by the joint teams comprised of two old and four new universities in Lancashire, Yorkshire, the Midlands, the Home Counties, London and Scotland. Extensive communication before hand via email and a series of meetings amongst black network members had helped determine a strategy for the interviews. The Network believed that this initiative was important and should not be allowed to go wrong. Accordingly any network member taking part was mandated to keep duplicate copies of their interview notes and their reflections on the interview. This was to be additional to any contribution to the overall CUCO agenda and report. This may have seemed unnecessarily paranoid but, as events transpired, their caution and strategy turned out to be of value. When the CUCO report was published the strategy of keeping duplicate notes of the interviews and the personal reflective notes made by Black members as soon as possible after each interview was vindicated. Many of their observations and reflections they made at interviews and which were collated by the CVCP/CUCO officer either did not appear in the report or were watered down in the editing process.

This editing and whitewashing may be explained by the two separate and racially determined paradigms regarding the race dynamic that exist in HE. For some, especially those who took part in the exercise, the editing proved this contention. The Black Network members of the AUT themselves operated from within a paradigm also. Their own experiences as educators in the HE system meant that their observations were shaped by a particular perspective and personal history. Their notes and reflections were at variance with the tenor of the official and final CUCO document. The observations and commentaries made by these authors tended to concentrate on the structural issues and the macro shortcomings of the sector itself. For them, what the visits highlighted as the key incidents of good practice or as dysfunctional issues diverged somewhat from the emphasis and perceptions of the VCs and CUCO. Issues revealed by their involvement included:

- the impression that concerns around the race dynamic were not high on the sector's priorities nor on their funding agenda

- that race initiatives were marginal to institutional life. This often meant that institutional commitment rarely extended beyond the celebration of cultural diversity and specific cultural events; that the oft quoted emphasis of training to know the Other frequently constituted a superficial steel band, sari and samosa approach

- the reluctance of VCs to challenge established structures, including devolved management and the concept of academic freedom, which in turn militated against the establishment of institutional wide and remediative processes or race specific training

- the tendency to emphasise generic equality issues and development rather than race as this was felt to be a more comfortable and less contentious option

- that VCs projected a low level of awareness and sophistication regarding race and the race dynamic operating in their sector compared to other equality issues

- that VCs were, however, politic and astute enough to be able to exploit the absence of a larger political will and national race strategy in order to maintain the status quo.

That two operational paradigms exist in HE can explain the genesis and rationale behind the emergence of the Black Network that operates from within the AUT. Like its counterpart in the Further Education sector, the Black Managers Network, the HE network members had a collective and frequently disaffected view of life as workers in the sector. Their experience, and the effects of a dominant paradigm that appeared to be subscribed to by most others in the sector, prompted reaction. To counter the dominant paradigm and its effects on their lives and prospects the black network was established. Its functions are defensive: it seeks to provide practical support for members, to raise issues as perceived from within the dominant paradigm and to apply pressure for change. Finally, it aims to highlight the centrality of the issue of race and racism within the sector and society by bringing in the voice and perceptions of black members from the wilderness and striving towards a synthesis of the dual paradigms that presently prevail.

Notes

Following the definition suggested by G. Jantes in Lavrijsen, R (ed) Cultural diversity in the arts, (Amsterdam: Royal Tropical Institute, 1993), the term black has been used to describe those who face cultural and racial discrimination and those who have a cultural / racial root that differs from the European mainstream.

Members of the AUT collective referred to in the text also refer to their network as the AUT black network (blackaut).

References

AUT (2002) *Initial findings of the AUT race and higher education survey*, London: AUT

Carter J, Fenton S and Modood T (1999) *Ethnicity and employment in Higher Education*, London: Policy Studies Institute

CUCO (2000) *Report on interviews with heads of institutions on race equality issues,* London: CUCO 00/191

DfEE (1999a) *David Blunkett's letter to Sir Michael Checkland of the HEFCE*, London: DfEE 1/99/211 para 27, p 5

DfEE (1999b) *Press release of Ministers speech following the Stephen Lawrence conference,* London: DfEE press release 535/99 dated 26/11/99

Guardian (2002) Report of a question asked in the House of Lords by Lord H Ouseley, 22/1/2002

Gulam WA and Hapeshi D (2000) 'Rediscovering the lost tribes in Higher Education', *Multicultural Teaching,* 18, 2

Gulam WA, Hapeshi D and Wilkinson V (2001) 'The apologist's syndrome and other modern tales', *Multicultural Teaching*, 19, 2

HESA (1999/2000) statistics obtained by E Halvorsen of the London AUT research unit and collated with statistics from PCEF, UAP, Clinical, CSCFC and 'locally determined' sources. Personal correspondence to author

HESA (2001) *Individual academic staff records for 1999-2000*, (Quoted in the AUT circular LA/ 7115 sent to AUT Local Associations nationally)

Major L (2002) Incredible islands, *Guardian,* 15/1/2002, 9

Performance and Innovation Unit (2001) *Improving labour market achievements for ethnic minorities in British society*, London: Home Office, 7/2001, 14

Times Higher Education Supplement (2001) Britain's universities, 21/9/2001

CHAPTER THREE

Institutional Racism in the Academy? Comparing the Police and University in Midshire

Andrew Pilkington

Institutional racism: the rebirth of an idea

The revival of the concept of institutional racism is primarily a result of the Macpherson's report's promulgation of the idea in the official inquiry into the police investigation into the murder of Stephen Lawrence. The concept is not new. Initially coined by Stokely Carmichael in 1967, it has since had consistent advocates such as the Institute for Race Relations. Until Macpherson resurrected the idea however, most social scientists found the concept of little analytical utility. Previous official inquiries had either ignored the concept or, as in the case of the Scarman report (1981), explicitly rejected its relevance.

While the concept has been variously defined it is now generally seen as 'the collective failure of an organisation to provide an appropriate and professional service to people because of their colour, culture or ethnic origin' (Macpherson, 1999, para 6.34). The term sensitises us above all to processes in organisations which, however unintentionally, disadvantage members of minority ethnic groups. Two inter-linked processes in particular tend to be highlighted: the 'institutional culture', which 'is racist if it constitutes a climate of assumptions which are hostile to outsider groups, racially or ethnically defined', and 'routine practices', which are racist if they entail unfair treatment of members of minority ethnic groups (Carter, Fenton and Modood, 2000: 3-4).

Despite the widespread use of the term since the publication of the report, the value of the concept remains hotly disputed, both within and outside the academy (Green, 2000). To its advocates, the acceptance of Macpherson's definition and subsequent acknowledgement of its applicability to key organisations in British society represents a huge step forward. It involves a recognition 'that, to thrive, racism does not require overtly racist individuals, and conceives of it rather as arising through social and cultural processes' (Parekh, 2000:71). For its critics, institutional racism represents a form of 'conceptual inflation' (Miles, 1989): the concept of racism loses any specificity and its value as an analytical tool diminishes as important distinctions such as that between beliefs which legitimise racial inequality, racially discriminatory practices and patterns of racial disadvantage are obscured.

While there is real danger of institutional racism becoming a blunderbuss concept (Pilkington, 2001; 2003), it is nonetheless valuable to use the concept as a sensitising device in order to investigate whether institutions exemplify what have been conceptualised as 'the various interacting components of institutional racism' (Parekh, 2000:73). Is there evidence of indirect discrimination in the services provided for members of minority ethnic groups? Are employment practices racially inequitable? Is the occupational culture ethnically inclusive? Is the staffing structure one in which senior staff are disproportionately white? Is there a lack of positive action in involving members of minority ethnic groups in major decision-making? Do management and leadership consider the task of addressing institutional racism a high priority? How widespread is professional expertise in intercultural communication? Is there evidence of relevant high quality training? How much consultation is there with representatives from minority communities? Is there a lack of information on the organisation's impact on minority communities? (Parekh, 2000:74-75).

This chapter compares the responses of two organisations in Midshire – the police and a university – to the charge of institutional racism. Previous investigations have identified these organisations in Midshire as 'exemplifying good practice' (HMIC, 2001) in the case of the police, and having an 'advanced policy' in the case of the HEI (Carter, Fenton and Modood, 1999). First I examine the initiatives taken in the handling of racist incidents to establish whether these signify serious reflection on the institutional culture of the police and significant change in routine practices. I found that the apparent flurry of activity camouflages significant continuity in the institutional culture and the persistence among the vast majority of police officers of routine practices that continue to provide an inappropriate service to members of minority ethnic groups. Promoting race equality has effectively been marginalised by making it the responsibility of a special unit. In the second part, I consider how Midshire University has responded to two government imperatives and initiatives: the widening participation agenda and the Equality Challenge. The implementation of strategies in these areas has apparently paid scant regard to race equality and has entailed little change in either the institutional culture or routine practices. The issue of promoting race equality has been marginalised by delegating it to one department, Human Resources, and a special committee, the equal opportunities committee, that lacks teeth and is marginal to the workings of Senate. In both organisations the initiatives that have occurred have had little impact on personnel in mainstream and core activities.

Combating institutional racism: a new imperative?
The Macpherson report has imbued greater public legitimacy to tackling racism and the government has recognised the limitations of its earlier colour and culture blind approach (Parekh, 2000). One indication of this is the government's decision to amend the 1976

Race Relations Act so as to bring all public bodies within the scope of the act. In addition the amended act not only declared it to be unlawful for public bodies, including the police and HEIs, to be discriminatory but also placed a duty on them to be proactive in promoting race equality. Although we cannot ascertain the long term impact of the Act on the policies and procedures of public organisations yet, the Act does signal the increased significance attached by the state to combating racism and confirms that the Stephen Lawrence case has indeed served as a catalyst for change.

The police have been placed under greater pressure than the academy to address issues relating to race. The Home Office has developed an action plan, which has significant implications for the police, and Her Majesty's Inspectorate of Constabulary (HMIC) have conducted regular audits to check on the performance of each force in relation to race and community relations. A plethora of recommendations has flowed from these audits, many of them echoing Macpherson. On the specific issue of racist incidents, the imperative to change has been reinforced by the development of good practice guides: a code of practice on reporting and recording racist incidents (2000) has been published by the Home Office and the Association of Chief Police Officers (ACPO, 2000) have produced a guide to identifying and combating hate crime. In contrast to the pressure exerted on the police, the academy has been let off lightly. With the exception of the Race Relations (Amendment) Act, which applies to all public organisations, government initiatives in this area have not specifically addressed race but have instead enjoined HEIs to address more general issues such as widening participation and equal opportunities, with race merely one component.

Policing in Midshire: handling racist incidents

Unlike in areas which have witnessed outright conflict between the police and members of minority ethnic communities, the policing of plural communities in Midshire has been relatively consensual. Credit is due to the proactive leadership of senior officers in the force, who incorporated racist incidents along with domestic violence and homophobic incidents in a Special Crimes Unit (SCU) in 1985 and took the initiative in 1990, along with other local public bodies, of setting up Multi Agency Groups against Racist Attack and Harassment (MAGRAHs) across much of the country. The creation of the SCU testified to the force's recognition that racist crimes, like other hate crimes, have specific characteristics which set them apart from other crimes, while the advent of MAGRAHs signalled an acknowledgement that racist incidents could not be tackled effectively by one institution alone.

In response to the Macpherson report, the Midshire police set up a task force under the Chief Constable and devised a Stephen Lawrence action plan. This culminated in a three-year race equality strategy. Published in April 2000, the strategy represented a response not only to the recommendations of the Macpherson report and the first two HMIC reports (1997; 1999), but also to a consultation process with approximately seventy community representatives. It is noteworthy that the strategy commits itself to prioritising racist incidents, harassment and victimisation, sets out its objectives for doing so and indicates the timescale for fulfilling them.

New procedures were established for reporting and recording racist incidents, while at the same time the Special Crimes Unit was used to follow up and support repeat victims. The Macpherson definition of a racist incident has been adopted; a victim pack has been produced in tandem with MAGRAH to encourage reporting; procedures have been adopted which require the review of all reported cases of racist incidents; and a new recording system for racist incidents has been adopted 'to identify underlying trends and build up a picture of racism in the local area' (Home Office, 2000).

The creation of these new procedures for reporting and recording racist incidents, coupled with the continuing employment of a Special Crimes Unit to follow up repeat victims and identify underlying patterns, suggest that senior officers have taken the re-commendations of the Macpherson report seriously and that they are committed to im-prove the way they deal with racist incidents. The question still remains, however, of the impact of policies and procedures on the ground.

A research study on Midshire's handling of racist incidents led by the author (Pilkington, 2002) identified four factors which challenge the efficacy of the force's policies and procedures in practice

- evidence of continuing under-reporting

- evidence of some reluctance on the ground to record racist incidents

- evidence that not all recorded incidents come to the attention of the Special Crimes Unit

- evidence that underlying trends are not in practice identified

Doubts about the practical efficacy of the force's policies and procedures were reinforced by a survey of victims. It is helpful to compare the overall satisfaction rating in our survey of victims of racist incidents with those of victims of crimes in other surveys. The Equality of Service Monitoring Report (ESMR) for April-September 2000 points locally to variable satisfaction ratings by victims of four ethnic groups. They range from 85% for White victims to 57%, 83% and 73% for Black, Asian and Other victims (see Pilking-ton, 2002). By comparison, the data from our survey of victims of racist incidents indicate that the overall satisfaction rating of victims is 46.9%, a figure markedly lower than even that for Black victims in the ESMR. Nationally, the British Crime Survey for 2000 points to a satisfaction rating for victims overall as 58% (Sims and Myhill, 2001), which again is a markedly higher rating than that in this survey.

Few studies have measured the levels of satisfaction of victims of racist incidents. One national study, however, 'found that about half of those respondents who had reported being subjected to some form of racial harassment were dissatisfied with the police res-ponse' (Modood *et al*, 1997:279). This study suggests that victims of racist incidents tend to be more dissatisfied than victims of other crimes. The finding that only 41% of res-pondents were at all satisfied with the way the police dealt with their cases and only 46.9% were at all satisfied with the overall response of the police becomes less sur-prising. Placing the findings of the victim survey in Midshire in this context does not, however, make them less disturbing. What is more, not only are repeat victims particularly dissatisfied but also there is a significant ethnic differential in satisfaction rating. While White and Other victims express a satisfaction rating of 65% and 66.6% respectively, Black and Asian victims express a satisfaction rating of 41.2% and 38.1%. The ratings are in all cases below those for victims generally reported by the EMSR, but what stands out is the ethnic differential and especially the extremely low level of satisfaction of Asians – 38.1% – compared to 83% in the EMSR. Nationally there is an ethnic differential in satisfaction ratings of police work but the differentials tend to be lower and the overall level of satisfaction higher. When the 1994 BCS asked respondents reporting a crime in a twelve-month period about their level of satisfaction with the police response, 75% of Whites expressed satisfaction but 61% of both Black and Asians expressed satisfaction (Bucke, 1997). If the relatively high levels of dissatisfaction of victims of racist incidents give cause for concern, the ethnic differentials reinforce it.

Despite its new policies and procedures it cannot be said that the force ensured that officers were appropriately prepared to handle racist incidents effectively or that the main mechanism for supporting repeat victims was adequately resourced. The research revealed that none of the officers on the ground had received training in handling racist incidents or any recent training on community and race relations. While the role of the Special Crimes Unit (SCU) and the Racist Incidents Officer (RIO) in particular is to pay specific attention to repeat victims by supporting them, liasing with other agencies and participating in further investigations, the SCU is seriously under-staffed and reliant on a single officer to act as RIO. When the SCU was first set up and the post of the RIO created, there were only seventy racist incidents a year and it was possible to follow up all victims and discover the extent of repeat victimisation, and provide appropriate support and assistance. In 2000, there were 302 incidents, making it impossible for one officer to contact all victims in person. Consequently, the level of repeat victimisation is underestimated and, as one of the officers who has taken on the role of RIO recognises, 'It is difficult to now give perhaps the same quality of service from one officer'.

This created particular problems in 2000 because the RIO became ill and had time off work. Although a very able officer replaced her she was by her own admission only able to 'do the bare minimum' as she was carrying another role. So the sickness of one officer caused 'a big gap and a big problem'. 'You have a problem when you have just got one officer dealing with an issue' said the replacement. The SCU is rightly not expected to deal alone with racist incidents but it clearly has an important part to play, especially with repeat victims. Unless steps are taken to improve the way racist incidents are dealt with, there is the danger that the public will become disillusioned – as evident to some extent in our survey – and the reporting of incidents will drop.

The persistence of institutional racism in the police

This chapter has so far examined the response to the Macpherson report of one police force, renowned for its proactive approach to dealing with racist incidents. Although senior officers have established a range of appropriate policies and procedures for handling racist incidents, their implementation has not been as smooth as anticipated. There is evidence that significant under-reporting persists, that some officers are still reluctant to record racist incidents, that not all incidents are communicated to the unit responsible for supporting repeat victims and that underlying trends are not routinely identified. An analysis of victims of racist incidents reveals their comparatively low overall satisfactory rating of the police response, especially among victims from minority ethnic groups. This low rating becomes explicable once it is recognised that there has been a dearth of training for officers in this area and that the unit responsible for supporting repeat victims is so under-staffed.

Despite the considerable activity of the Midshire force in responding to the Macpherson report, these significant lacunae have meant that their initiatives have not delivered demonstrably successful outcomes. Why were such obvious lacunae not addressed? Interviews conducted with officers from minority ethnic communities in Midshire suggest that the institutional culture remains strongly impervious to change (see also Holdaway, 1996). Among other things, these interviews reveal that white officers in general are still reluctant to take action against the racism that minority officers routinely experience from the public, and they exhibit derisory attitudes towards an organisation that represents a lifeline for many minority officers, the Black Police Association. So it is not surprising that laudable initiatives have had so little impact on routine practices in the force.

The Academy's response to race

While the police have paid considerable attention to race, especially since the early 1980s, the same cannot be said of the academy's response. Until very recently, no connection was made between the transition from an elite to a mass system of higher education which produced an increasingly diverse student population, and the growing proportion from minority ethnic communities. There is evidence that minority ethnic groups as a whole are over-represented among admissions compared to their proportion of the 15-24 age group (Modood and Shiner, 1994). While it is true that, after controlling for differences in achievement, social class and other background factors, some minority ethnic groups, notably Black Caribbeans, Pakistanis and Bangladeshis, continue to be significantly less likely to be admitted to university, minority ethnic groups are generally over-represented in higher education and form an increasing proportion of the student body. This is especially evident in the new universities, such as Midshire, partly because of the ethnic bias found in 'old' universities (Modood and Ackland, 1998; Mortimore *et al.*, 1997; Shiner and Modood, 2002).

The increase in pupils from minority ethnic groups in schools in the latter half of the 20th century generated a range of policy responses and a significant research programme, initially into the underachievement of African Caribbean pupils (Rampton 1981) and less specifically Swann, 1985 and recently Gillborn and Mirza, 2000; but also see Pilkington, 1997). Although the response of schools, local education authorities and central government to issues relating to race and education was variable and by no means followed a linear pattern, we can distinguish a number of policy phases – 'assimilation, integration and cultural pluralism' (Troyna and Carrington, 1990:20). While we need to recognise both the lack of explicit reference to race and ethnicity in much policy formulation –

seen by some as 'doing good by stealth' (Kirp, 1979) and others as 'spurious deracialisation' (Troyna and Williams, 1986) – and 'an enduring commitment to assimilation' arguably evident throughout the seemingly distinct policy phases (Grosvenor, 1997:50), what is incontrovertible is that both practitioners and policy makers have recognised the need to address issues relating to race and schooling. Educational researchers have not side-stepped the ensuing debates and on occasions 'passionate disagreements in the wider society' over race and schooling have been 're-played inside the academy' (Pilkington, 1999:411).

The lack of attention paid to race and ethnicity in relation to higher education is therefore extraordinary. Especially as equal opportunity policies were initially developed during the 1980s, mainly in some polytechnics, partly in response to pressure from local authorities (Jewson et al, 1991). With the Committee of Vice-Chancellors and Principals' (CVCP's) establishment of the Commission on University Career Opportunity (CUCO) in 1994, external stimulus was given to developing policies in both the 'new' and 'old' universities. Thus by 1996 equal opportunities policies had become almost universal across the sector (CUCO, 1997). But most of these policies pay far less attention to race and ethnicity than to gender, focus almost exclusively on staffing issues and have had limited impact (Farish et al, 1995; Neal, 1998). A recent study confirms that race equality initiatives still lag behind those concerned with gender. A third of institutions have equal opportunities policies that do not specifically address issues of race equality (Carter et al, 1999).

Aware of the limitations of such equal opportunities policies, the Commission for Racial Equality issued a leadership challenge in 1997. Both CVCP and the Standing Conference of Principals (SCOP) were early signatories. As part of their response to this challenge, research was commissioned on ethnicity and employment in higher education, culminating in a report published in June 1999, which pointed to disadvantages experienced by academic staff from minority ethnic groups (Carter et al, 1999). This was the year Macpherson reported. Although it focused on the police, the report suggested that all major organisations in British society were characterised by institutional racism and that it was therefore incumbent on all organisations, including HEIs, to examine their practices and procedures to promote race equality. This report, coupled with the findings of the Carter report (and the Bett report 1999) which highlighted in particular the disadvantages faced by female academics) raised the profile of equal opportunities, and especially the issue of race equality, within higher education.

A flurry of activity followed. The leaders of the major academic unions (Paul Makney of the National Association of Teachers in Further and Higher Education (NATFHE) and David Triesman of the Association of University Teachers (AUT)) publicly accepted the charge that higher education institutions were characterised by institutional racism. A major conference was mounted by NATFHE in collaboration with other agencies to discuss future strategies within the context of the recommendations of the Stephen Lawrence inquiry and the Carter report. The CVCP, SCOP, the Universities and Colleges Employers Association (UCEA) and CUCO, along with the unions, agreed in their formal response to the Macpherson report to a partnership approach whereby individual institutions would be encouraged to review their equal opportunity policies in the light of the recommendations of the Bett, Macpherson and Carter reports and effect real cultural change (NATFHE, 2000). Urged on by the Secretary of State for Education and Employment in his funding letter to the Higher Education Funding Council for England in November 1999, CVCP, SCOP, UCEA subsequently pledged to take equal opportunities further by placing the partnership approach within a new national framework agreed with HEFCE. This framework is known as the Higher Education Equality Challenge Framework and was launched in 2001.

The above analysis indicates not only the increased impetus being given to equality initiatives within the sector but also widespread recognition that by themselves equal opportunity policies have not produced real cultural change. And this is not the first time that the unions have expressed concern about race equality and this is not the first time that managers have highlighted race issues as part of a generic equal opportunities agenda (Gulam and Hapeshi, 2000).

Before the Race Relations (Amendment) Act the two major levers used by the government to expedite change in HEIs involved financial incentives to encourage widening student participation and also to implement the imperatives of the Equality Challenge in relation to staff. The sector's funding body, HEFCE, reduced the block grant in order to allocate specific monies to institutions relating to widening participation and the development of a human resources strategy. Although government is concerned to push HEIs in a particular direction, neither focuses on race. Confirmation that other government priorities for higher education are more significant is evident in its 2003 White Paper, *The Future of Higher Education*, where race is scarcely mentioned.

The University in Midshire:
widening participation and the Equality Challenge

Midshire University has had an equal opportunities policy since the early 1990s and a specific race equality policy since 1995. In terms of the indicators adopted by Carter *et al* (1999) to categorise policy development, Midshire University on the face of it fares well since its race equality policy exhibits six of nine policy items needed to qualify as having an advanced policy. In this sense it is in a comparable position to Midshire police which was judged by the HMIC as exemplifying good practice in its handling of racist incidents.

In contrast to Midshire police, however, the Macpherson report passed the institution by. The report was ignored by the Governing Council and did not further implementation of the race equality policy or generate any new initiatives. Far from it. In a context where the university was subject to increasing external demands and resource constraints, the race equality policy withered on the vine and became a dead document. The institution could not afford, however, to ignore the demands of its funding council and developed as required both a widening participation strategy and a human resources strategy.

The Midshire University widening participation strategy is colour and culture blind. Initiatives have been mounted to build compacts with schools and further education colleges in order to facilitate access but they show no serious reflection on the routine practices of the institution and focus primarily on measures to score better in terms of key performance indicators such as the proportion of students from state schools and low income backgrounds. While such initiatives may indirectly benefit young people from minority communities, no ethnic monitoring has been undertaken to ascertain for example whether there are any ethnic differentials in retention. What is more, an analysis of the departmental plans in this area reveals the total neglect of race or ethnicity. Despite the fact that the university has a lower proportion of students admitted through UCAS from minority ethnic communities than the national average, the implementation of the widening participation strategy continues to be colour and culture blind.

The most significant initiatives to promote equal opportunities in staffing have been a series of commissioned research projects. These reveal that staff from minority ethnic groups comprise a smaller proportion of the total staff than is to be expected from the population mix in Midshire, and that there is a significant mismatch between the staff and student profile. In addition, analysis of equal opportunities monitoring data for staff recruitment in the last four years points to applicants from minority ethnic groups being less likely to be appointed than those from the majority ethnic group. While this research has informed the target setting of the human resources strategy, only one initiative has specifically addressed the issue of minority ethnic staff, namely the use of adverts within the minority ethnic press, and the recruitment process has not been systematically reviewed. The few initiatives or consultations relating to race have been only as part of the development of a new equal opportunities policy statement.

So despite the Race Relations (Amendment) Act no coherent race equality strategy has been instituted, because responsibility for its the development was delegated to one department, Human Resources, whose concerns are tangential to the core activities of the institution. The Pro Vice Chancellor responsible for equal opportunities fell seriously ill and the department experienced staffing difficulties. But although this had little impact on the institution's management of priority areas such as quality assurance, it did affect the race equality strategy. This echoes the experience of the Special Crimes Unit in handling racist incidents. The earlier race equality policy was forgotten and the race equality strategy became effectively part of an equal opportunities strategy, itself only one component of the human resources strategy. Thus was race equality marginalised. The group responsible for advising the Vice Chancellor on issues relating to race – the equal opportunities committee – was still not part of the formal committee structure of Senate so its few recommendations were ignored. The committee made no contribution to the race equality strategy and interviews with its members indicated their ignorance of the institution's statutory obligation to produce such a strategy.

Unsurprisingly, the strategy submitted to HEFCE in November 2002 was judged inadequate by the independent consultants acting on behalf of the Equality Challenge Unit. Only then did the university seriously set out to develop its race equality strategy and action plan. Fearful of the consequences of non-compliance, the university set up a Race Equality Advisory Group, which in 2003 formulated a satisfactory strategy. There is little doubt that this is due to external pressure. Implementation of the strategy to bring about significant change may also depend on continuing external pressure. The requirement that HEIs now include in their annual operating statements to HEFCE an evaluation of progress made on their race equality plans may help to keep race equality on the agenda. Since, however, the HEFCE requirements have so far failed to ensure that issues relating to race are addressed, further measures, including inspections, are likely to be needed.

The persistence of a complacent culture in the academy?

As with the police, promoting race equality at Midshire University has been sidelined and there is little evidence of serious reflection on the institutional culture or changes in routine practices. Despite their statutory duties, the level of dissatisfaction of victims of racist incidents with the police and the persistence of a predominantly colour and culture blind approach to widening participation and equal opportunities at the university indicate that neither institution has really prioritised race equality. Both have dealt with the issues by delegating responsibility to a particular person or body and have then effectively ignored the issues.

Whether this means that both organisations can be said to similarly characterised by institutional racism is another matter. While there are manifest differences between the two organisations examined here, the questions posed by Parekh indicate some similarities between the police and the academy. For example, the senior staff in both organisations are disproportionately white; few members have experienced high quality training; very little positive action has been taken in involving members of minority ethnic communities in major decision making; and there is insufficient information on the organisation's impact on minority communities.

Asked to compare his experience as a policeman and later an academic, one respondent from a minority ethnic community commented:

> It's much more sweet sounding here in academia... but if we can talk of some bully boys in the police, I feel many in academia are smiling assassins. I really did trust those heads of department to do the right thing [in relation to a complaint of racial discrimination against a colleague] and on the surface what they had to say, everything was fine, but the consequences of their actions, it was business as usual... It's just the manner of expressions that are different. The outcomes are not dissimilar... Black and ethnic minority people have been around in the country for generations but we don't see them at the top of institutions and, once they get there, they are not exempt from experiencing racism. So there are those similarities but they're played out in different languages.

For academics who take pride in their liberal values, this judgement may seem harsh. But this study reveals the complacent culture of Midshire University. While there may be widespread agreement that race equality is desirable, there is little evidence of any active response to Macpherson's injunction to develop measures to promote race equality. The little that has been done has occurred belatedly and in response to external pressures. Such complacency is by no means restricted to Midshire University. The little debate about institutional racism in the academy rarely addresses the core business of universities. Even the race equality policies identified by the Equality Challenge Unit as exemplary disregard curricular issues and teaching and learning.

References

ACPO (2000) *A Guide to Identifying and Combating Hate Crime,* London: Home Office

Bett (1999) *Independent Review of Higher Education Pay and Conditions*, London: HMSO

Bucke, T. (1997) *Ethnicity and Contacts with the Police: Latest Findings from the British Crime Survey*, London: Home Office Research Findings 59

Carter, J., Fenton, J and Modood, T. (1999) *Ethnicity and Employment in Higher Education*, London: Policy Studies Institute

CUCO (1997) *A Report on Policies and Practices on Equal Opportunities in Employment in Universities and Colleges in Higher Education*, London: CUCO

Farish, M., McPake, J., Powney, J. and Weiner, G (1995) *Equal Opportunities in Colleges and Universities: Towards Better Practices*, Buckingham: SRHE/Open University Press

Fenton, S., Carter, J. and Modood, T. (2000) 'Ethnicity and Academia: Closure Models, Racism Models and Market Models', *Sociological Research Online*, 5 (2)

Gillborn, D and Mirza, H (2000) *Educational Inequality. Mapping Race, Class and Gender,* London: OFSTED

Green, D. (ed.) *Institutional Racism and the Police,* London:Civitas

Grosvenor, I. (1997) *Assimilating Identities,* London: Lawrence and Wishart

Gulam, W and Hapeshi, D (2000) 'Rediscovering the Lost Tribes in Higher Education', *Multicultural Teaching*, 18, (2)

HMIC (1997) *Winning the Race*, London: Home Office

HMIC (1999) *Winning the Race Revisited,* London:Home Office

HMIC (2001) *Winning the Race: Embracing Diversity,* London: Home Office

Holdaway, S. (1996) *The Racialisation of British Policing,* London: Macmillan

Home Office (2000) *Code of Practice on Reporting and Recording Racist Incidents*, London: Home Office

Jewson, N., Mason, D., Bowen, R., Mulvaney, K. and Parmar, S. (1991) 'Universities and Ethnic Minorities: The Public Face', *New Community,* 17,

Kirp, D. (1979) *Doing Good by Doing Little: Race and Schooling in Britain,* Los Angeles: University of California Press.

Macpherson, W (1999) *The Stephen Lawrence Inquiry,* London: The Stationary Office.

McManus, I., Esmail, A. and Demetriou, M. (1998) 'Factors Affecting Likelihood of Applicants Being Offered a Place in Medical Schools in the United Kingdom in 1996 and 1997: Retrospective Study', *British Medical Journal,* Oct. 24

Miles, R. (1989) *Racism*, London: Routledge

Modood, T. *et al* (1997) *Ethnic Minorities in Britain,* London: Policy Studies Institute

Modood, T. and Ackland, (1998) (eds) *Race and Higher Education,* London; Policy Studies Institute

Modood, T. and Shiner, M. (1994) *Ethnic Minorities and Higher Education*, London: Policy Studies Institute

Mortimore, P., Owen, C. and Phoenix, A. (1997) 'Higher Education Qualifications' in V. Karn (ed) *Ethnicity in the Census, Volume 4. Employment, Education and Housing among the Ethnic Minority Populations of Britain*, London: HMSO

NATFHE (2000) *Learning Through Diversity,* London, NATFHE

Neal, S (1998) *The Making of Equal Opportunity Policies in Universities,* Buckingham: SRHE/Open University Press

Parekh, B (2000) *The Future of Multi-Ethnic Britain*, London: Profile

Pilkington, A (1997) 'Ethnicity and Education' in M. Haralambos (ed) *Developments in Sociology*, Vol. 13, Ormskirk: Causeway Press

Pilkington, A. (1999) 'Racism in Schools and Ethnic Differentials in Educational Achievement', *British Journal of Sociology of Education*, 20 (3)

Pilkington, A. (2001) 'Institutional Racism and Social Exclusion: The Experience of Minority Ethnic Groups in the Labour Market' in M.Haralambos (ed) *Developments in Sociology*, Vol. 17, Ormskirk: Causeway Press

Pilkington, A. *et al* (2002) 'Macpherson and after: policing racist incidents in Midshire', *Police Science and Management,* 4 (3)

Pilkington, A (2003) *Racial Disadvantage and Ethnic Diversity in Britain,* Basingstoke: Palgrave

Scarman, Lord (1981) *The Brixton Disorders April 10th-12th 1981: a report of an inquiry,* London: Cmnd 8427 HMSO

Shiner, M and Modood, T (2002) 'Help or Hindrance? Higher Education and the Route to Ethnic Equality', *British Journal of Sociology of Education,* 23 (2)

Sims, L. and Myhill, A. (2001) *Policing and the Public: Findings from the 2000 British Crime Survey,* London: Home Office Research Findings 136

Swann, M. (1985) *Education for All*, London: HMSO

Troyna, B and Carrington, B. (1990) *Education, Racism and Reform*, London; Routledge

Troyna, B. and Williams, J. ((1986) *Racism, Education and the State*, London: Croom Helm

Wallace, J (1999) 'The Colour Blindspot', *Times Higher Education Supplement,* March 5

Turney, L., Law, I. and Phillips, D., (2002) *Building the AntiRacist HEI: A Toolkit*, http//www.leeds.ac.uk/cers/toolkit/toolkit.htm, Leeds: Centre for Ethnicity and Racism Studies, University of Leeds

CHAPTER FOUR

Understanding Institutional Racism: reflections from linguistic anthropology

Jacques Rangasamy

Institutional racism is rooted in cultural history. It is a symptom of fundamental maladjustments in the interactions of culturally and ethnically differentiated beings. This chapter is informed by research and reports in the field but also by a shared acquaintance of the problems that British non-white academics face today. In my view, the various theoretical positions and debates that discourse is producing deserve appropriate academic analysis. Only then can the wealth of good work and good intentions be founded on an understanding which effectively addresses the cultural problems that underlie institutional racism.

Quantitative data pertaining to career progression and promotion, curricula material, student performance and discipline provide indispensable indices of the magnitude and location of institutional racism within the educational sector. Facts and figures are useful guides for establishing realistic targets and pragmatic agendas for change. But quantitative data indicates the symptoms or outcomes of institutional racism; this must be cross-checked with qualitative material to produce the kind of diagnostic evaluations capable of identifying, and eventually neutralising, the hidden inequalities in patterns of structural racism. It is necessary to reveal the often disguised and therefore elusive obstacles to career progression and to the demoralisation and disincentive they secrete and feed upon. Indeed, discrimination on any ground is an assault on the integrity of one's professional being, and can have traumatic effects. It may induce a defensive, victim-like attitude that can undermine the optimistic expectations that fuel optimal performance within competitive contexts.

Theorising can construct patterns of meaningful connections between quantitative and qualitative data on institutional racism. It can thus produce critical analysis capable of ensuring fair and equitable judgement in the planning of human and professional relationships and their unfolding. But theorising that emerges from interpretative watchfulness is also a form of salutary vigilance, which the nature of racism in intellectual circles makes desirable, if not essential. Like a virus that nature has denied autonomous life, but which acquires a shared existence when hosted by a suitable living organism, intellectual racism can evolve from a relatively containable concept to become a determinant factor in the performance, identity and scope of action of institutions. Just as a virus can develop an immunological competence from and against the very remedy designed to neutralise its effects, institutional racism often survives and becomes wise to antiracist measures. It then manifests itself anew in subtler and more resilient forms in response to changing circumstances.

The preferred explanations for institutional racism are frequently isolated bureaucratic malpractice or perverted interpretations of institutional rules and regulations. But the extent of such 'innocent thoughtlessness' invites deeper reflection and analysis. The subtle biases operative in the distribution of opportunities and career rewards also configure the work force and its operational complexion for lesser performance. This inhibits the institution from expressing its true achievement capability. Tolerance of discrimination institutionalises a state of crisis and this alone warrants urgent action.

My own observation of the birth and evolution over several generations of embedded patterns of disparity suggests that institutional racism owes its endurance to the bigoted intent, overt or insidious, that underlines every act of discrimination. The intent, with its embedded stereotypes and biases, often surfaces in interactive situations such as job interviews, promotions and disciplinary hearings, when there is a measure of control over the destiny of non-white staff. Negative and disparaging assumptions, expressed or unexpressed, about the abilities of non-white staff are allowed to influence judgement and procedural outcomes. On their own, such assumptions are often too absurd to survive critical examination. But the protocols of collective decision-making provide effective camouflage for bigotry.

I share the view that the stereotypes and biases underlying institutional racism are historical and cultural constructs. Such stereotypes and biases contain residual attitudes formed during colonial history, so are rooted in the collective psyche. At the institutional level, they are likely to mould the energies and attitudes of successive generations and configure patterns of internal professional relationships. In some situations, people and institutional racism exert reciprocal formative influences. Institutional racism is not the proverbial grit in the machine that conventional programmes of race awareness training can remove. Rather, it is organic in nature and function and grows in cunning and resilience with each challenge it successfully overcomes. Perhaps the only effective way to remove or neutralise institutional racism is to transform the institutional culture. For this to happen, institutional racism must be located within its wider cultural and historical context. Remedial measures must likewise be calibrated to suit the breath of scope and attendant cultural complexity of the problem. They must also command commensurate energies and intellectual resources, otherwise they may contribute to the competence institutional racism has developed over decades to counteract change, and would therefore be counter productive.

An institution can be likened to a collective mind gathered around a range of professional concerns. Like the human mind, institutions exist, express their ethos and communicate their collective, and prescribed, thinking through language. They also use language to re-think policies and revise their thinking. But more importantly, just as language largely defines the possibilities of thought and action, so organisations use their institutional lan-guage to construct their structural identity and self-image, and they can adjust it periodi-cally to the calling of the times. So the institutional language can produce objective and subjective meaning capable of expressing and justifying the patterns of disparity in-grained in institutional life.

It was the work of Edward Sepir and Benjamin Lee Whorf that first inspired me to ex-plore the possible affinities that may exist between the vernacular and institutional lan-guage and to seek comparative premises for understanding the dynamics of institutional racism. In what came to be known as the Sepir Whorf hypothesis (see Koerner 1992 for a concise discussion. Also, see Duranti (2000), to which this chapter is indebted, for the broader context of linguistic anthropology), they explore the role of linguistic patterns on thinking and acting in and upon the world (Sapir, 1995). That aspect of language can easily be transposed onto an institutional context, for, like the vernacular, institutional language does indeed think and act upon the world. This hypothesis also established relations between language, culture and personality (Sapir, 1995). It endorsed an observation made over my eleven years as a part-time lecturer in as many institutions, namely that the leading personalities in an institution could potentially influence the emergent institutional language and culture. Institutional languages, like spoken lan-guages, operate a shared and pre-defined public code to express subjective experiences of its leadership framework. In other words, the institutional language can, and often is used to affirm, articulate and consolidate the status quo. This creates a predisposition to favouritism that can be based on cultural or gender affinities

Since the status quo and its key institutional functions are reliant on the exercise of power, institutional language offers interesting parallels with political language. And the body of rules and regulations by which institutions operate are inspired or influenced by political agendas. Maurice Bloch's work (Bloch, 1997) has special relevance here. He observed that political oratory, especially the institutionalised expression of reverence for tradition and leaders, constructs the moral and intellectual chassis for the receptive audience to accept authority and the status quo uncritically and often unconsciously. In Bloch's larger framework of analysis as well as within the confines of institutions, lan-guage enters the often private debate between individual questioning and collective com-pliance. Collective acceptance turns the institutional ways of thinking and doing into a powerful and often irresistible current that deters or makes professionally suicidal the critical resistance from isolated individuals. Bloch suggested that formalised speech restricts the range of possible questions and possible answers. The institutional language often structures its procedures in ways that limit freedom of expression and frustrate any real challenge to authority. The inflexible compliance with institutional rules can provide imaginative disguise for individual and collective aversions. This is illustrated in some cases where institutions follow the protocols that regulate recruitment and progression, but emphasise the weaknesses of non-white candidates and play down their strengths while doing the opposite for white candidates. Such procedures, which are unfortunately routine, caricature the abilities of both whites and non-whites, and undermine confidence and trust in the system.

However, as Bakhtin has observed, spoken language is not neutral; it lends itself to private use and serves the speaker's personal intention. Language is indeed saturated with the intentions of others (Bakhtin *et al*, 1983). The people behind institutional racism first secure ownership of the institutional language and of the corpus of rules and regulations through which it is expressed. Just as they would use spoken language, they take institutional language beyond its use for socialisation and employ it to articulate and celebrate their own experiences, but also and most importantly to deny the experiences of others. In institutions of education, prolonged and persistent denial undermines the self-esteem and professional stature of the excluded people and effectively creates trauma for them. The use of discriminatory institutional language to exalt and reward the experiences of some while devaluing and degrading that of others was a key colonialist strategy for subordinating colonised cultures. It is ironic that supremacist Eurocentric histories inform the curricula of the teaching establishments of former colonies still. But it is also evidenced in most universities' resistance to consulting black staff meaningfully as part of their obligations towards the Race Relations (Amendment) Act 2000.

Spoken as well as institutional languages are used for 'race making'. In spoken language it is overt, as used by some newspapers and screen and stage entertainers. But it is also used covertly, to keep alive, to live with and to justify the racial contradictions and paradoxes inherent in culture (Hymes, 1971: 51). The language of some institutions generates and supports systems of cultural behaviour proper to the organisation of diversity, but on the terms of the dominant sector, using its monocultural white, male and middle class notion of fairness to safeguard its interests. Therefore, communicative competence, which in terms of institutional language consists of a thorough grasp of institutional rules and regulations does not automatically qualify everyone for career progression – as non-white staff in British universities have long realised to their cost. The control over promotion and other rewards of progression is a function of ownership of the institutional language and of the status quo.

This language is an effective instrument of exclusion. Non-white staff have observed that the owners of the institutional language, at their own discretion and for their own subjective psychological comfort, place career-enhancing opportunities in the path of certain individuals and fine-tune their performance to the requirements for internal promotion and progression. Performance in institutional, as in spoken languages, determines not only what the speaker says but also the manner in which s/he says it. Just as there is an aesthetic dimension to speaking that could have social and political implications – Martin Luther King comes to mind – so too there is a way of articulating institutional language to enable precise things to happen in specific ways. It is not institutional rules and regulations that determine outcomes, but the individualities that interpret these rules and regulations.

The focus on performance highlights the role and participation of audience in the construction of messages and their meanings. The institutional language and the racism it may articulate is effectively the intersection of many mentalities, perceptions, modes of doing things, and particular brands of conservatism. Thus does the institutional language articulate the ethos of an organisation. Part of that ethos is a kind of knowingness, an unspoken entente that its time-honored and obvious ways of making decisions and carrying out procedures are essential for the health and well-being of the institution. The ethos also encodes the unwritten criteria and caveats that regulate entrance into the inner life of the institution, and access to the privileges of progression, that comes with a genuine sense of belonging. Institutional loyalty requires accepting this ethos and its implied knowingness uncritically. Challenging this is an intimidating prospect, even for victims of discrimination and bullying. Their involuntary compliance serves to endorse, albeit unwittingly, the institutional bigotry that victimised them in the first place.

The culture of a university is determined by the way it expresses and interprets its institutional rules and regulations, as much as by the quality of its teaching and research. Since the latter includes inspectors, funders, commissioning bodies for research, as well as students, the interpretation of rules and regulations necessarily touches several other operations, such as self-critique and evaluation, the contextualising of professional practices, auditing and accountability. The authority behind some interpretative procedures has been the subject of a number of studies. Charles Goodwin's (1994) contribution is of particular relevance. Goodwin analyses three practices that experts use in what he calls the construction of professional vision, and these practices lend themselves well to describing the processes that make institutional racism and other kinds of discriminatory practices possible.

Goodwin described the first practice as 'encoding', a process whereby all phenomena affecting the institution are encoded into objects of knowledge that animate the discourse of the profession. In the process, institutional racism and other forms of subjective aversion may also be encoded. This aberration in the interpretation of the rules relies on stereotypes for its legitimacy and critical parameters. Stereotypes are already encoded ideas and attitudes. They connect the institution to current or past narratives such as colonial history, nationalism and patriotism from which divisive interpretations can be evolved. The relationship between stereotypes and institutions is a subtle but interesting one. The institution refines and disguises the populist context of stereotypes to which it plays host, it legitimises its racist, xenophobic, sexist and other disturbing connotations. In return for this offer of a home, the stereotype lends to the institution its symbolic and critical dynamics. The conscious or unconscious use of stereotypes enables institutions to operate strategies of symbolic containment of people, ideas and processes that they consider threats or risks to the status quo. Stereotypes also help to identify and encode the target, as well as the processes involved in them-and-us situations.

The second process Goodwin identified was 'highlighting', which entails marking and emphasising specific phenomena and traits of character for the purpose of categorisation and pigeonholing. Institutions may choose to celebrate the achievements of certain individuals, for example, while ignoring or denying those of others. Making career-enhancing opportunities available to selected individuals is another strategy. Universities have evolved over several centuries on the basis of assumptions that heterosexual white men from the economically and socially privileged classes were naturally endowed for a university education. Consequently, the socio-economic and cultural values that govern the operational mode and management of universities, particularly the older ones, are derived from those social groupings. In the words of Anne Bishop (1997), university values form a 'complex set of interlocking systems, assumptions, principles and practices' that can be used effectively to thwart the progression of once-excluded people who had challenged the boundaries of the academy. They remain dormant caveats regulating the sense of institutional belonging beneath a crust of seemingly egalitarian protocols. But these caveats are reanimated to justify the exclusionary and punitive measures meted out to some of the once-excluded people who experience 'professional difficulties' in their struggles to acculturate themselves to what many of them perceive as a foreign and professionally alienating milieu.

Goodwin identified the third process as producing and articulating material representations of people and situations. This uses the negative stereotyping of undesirable groups, often 'from the motive to restore a threatened self-image' and accompanying self-esteem (Fien and Spencer, 1997). Non-white academics in British institutions are often erroneously accused of (stereotypic) aggressiveness and arrogance when they challenge discrimination and biased judgement in promotional and related matters. Notwithstanding the justified exasperation that such unfair rejections provoke, non-white academics feel they are expected be mindful of the fragile construction of the whiteness of some of their line managers. In procedures that address incidences of inequality, priority is often accorded to the management of white sensibilities. Some white managers use 'playing the race card' as a cover for professional incompetence and confirmation of their stereotypic evaluation.

The three processes operate interdependently to create the context for the material and spiritual existence and survival of the institution, which the institutional language would articulate. A brief examination of key elements of this context may suggest remedial measures against institutional discrimination:

- The processes help construct a particular image of the immediate physical environment of the institution, as well as at the wider social and intellectual worlds in which it is located and to which it has attuned its responsiveness. This self-perception, an integral part of an institutional identity nurtured and cherished over years, often serves as the first line of defence against changes imposed from outside. The self-assurance this generates can entrap the institution in its self-perception and knock it out of sync with evolving socio-economic and political currents.

- However, the fundamental purpose of the above self-perception is to maintain the conservatism that safeguard inner order and the attendant power structure while upholding specific sets of interests and the prevailing status quo in the process. But most importantly, it can help organise the internal dynamics of the institution to respond to perceived and real threats from within and without.

- The all-important need to survive often prevents flexible thinking and leads to policing opinions instead. It also legitimises the institution's monopoly over the apparatus for processing information and research. Some black academics have complained of exclusion from the Research Assessment Exercise schemes. Others have been overlooked for PhD supervision despite their competence and specialism.

- Necessarily, therefore, behind a façade of sameness and even-ness, institutions often hide active processes of judgement and discrimination that might be unlawful, but that justify their conduct towards specific categories of employees and students.

- British institutions, with their royal charters and long histories, subscribe to and maintain knowledge of the outside world patterned closely on the colonialist paradigm. So they present their institutional thinking and the racism that it articulates as a form of super-morality rather than a deficiency in knowledge.

My own observation over three decades suggests that the inflexibility that characterises institutional racism creates a comfort zone for those who practice it. It helps to preserve and safeguard the emotional, moral, political and other investments of the dominant sector for the dominant sector. Thus it is seen as ennobling, morally rewarding and gratifying. It reinforces the conviction that the existing relationships of power are fixed and necessary. More than that, it constructs an image of non-white staff as pathologically lacking in suitable professional responsibility and managerial competence. At best they are clever like apes.

At the convergence of the institutional currency of rules and regulations with individual perceptions and propensity for action there emerges institutional common sense. Institutional common sense nullifies the checks that verify stereotypical thinking and behaviour. It makes it unnecessary to debate or question the issues that challenge institutional interests (Pickering 2001). This process common to both language and institutional structures, has been allowed over many years to become routine and thus rooted in every day practices. Institutional racism has become enmeshed within the intellectual and moral standards of many universities and colleges of higher education I have worked in. However, the institutional language can even be applied to expressing and celebrating the experiences of non-white and foreign staff and students.

Cross referencing qualitative and quantitative data, as this chapter advocates, would help create the professional framework for processes of 'imaginative identification' that Chinua Achebe, in his essay 'The Truth of Fiction' (1978) describes as the opposite of indifference. Such identification is the ingredient in human relationships that facilitates self and mutual discovery, self and collective actualisation. Besides professional enrichment it would bring the democratisation of the institutional language would clear the path to natural justice. But first there will have to be an active, enlightened and compassionate leadership by institutional management in promoting, encouraging, managing and monitoring the changes so urgently needed in institutional culture and language.

References

Bakhtin, M.M. *et al* (1983) *The Dialogic Imagination, in Essays*, Texas: University of Texas Press

Bishop, Anne (1997) A Conceptual Framework for understanding the Institutional Dynamics involved in a University's Response to an Allegation of Racism, 27th Annual SCRUTREA Conference Proceedings, 1997, in *Crossing borders, breaking boundaries, Research in the Education of Adults*

Bloch, Maurice (1997) *Political Language and Oratory in Traditional Society*, Academic Press

Duranti, Allessandro (2000) *Linguistic Anthropology*, Oxford: Blackwell

Fien, Steven and Spencer, J. Steven (1997) Prejudice as self-image maintenance: affirming the self through negative evaluation of others, *Journal of Personality and Social Psychology*, 73, 31-44

Goodwin, Charles (1994) Professional Vision, *American Anthropologist*, 96 (3), 606-33

Hymes, D (1971) Sociolinguistics and the Ethnography of Speaking, in Edwin Ardener, (ed.), *Social Anthropology and Language*, Tavistock

Koerner, Konrad E.F (1992) The Sapir-Whorf Hypothesis: A preliminary History and a Bibliographical Essay, *Journal of Linguistic Anthropology*, 2 (2), 173-981

Pickering, Michael (2001) *Stereotyping: The Politics of Representation*, London: Palgrave

Sapir, Edward and Irvine, Judith (2002) *The Psychology of Culture: A Course of Lectures*, Mouthon de Gruyter

Sapir, Edward (1995) *Language: An Introduction to the Study of Speech*, Harvest Books

PART TWO
HIGHER EDUCATION EXPERIENCES

CHAPTER FIVE

The Others: extremism and intolerance on campus and the spectre of Islamic fundamentalism

David Tyrer

Introduction

Salman Sayyid has likened the contemporary resurgence of Islam to the super-natural, noting 'it is sometimes said that Muslims belong to cultures and societies that are moribund and have no vitality – no life of their own. Like ghosts they remain with us, haunting the present' (Sayyid, 1997: 1). I find Sayyid's observation pertinent in the light of my own research experiences while undertaking fieldwork for an ESRC-funded PhD on institutionalised Islamophobia in British universities from September 1998 to June 2000. My fieldwork was regularly punctuated and over-shadowed by warnings of Muslim ritual crime and an Islamic 'fundamentalist' threat to universities, spoken as melodramatically as if they were the terrified mother in the film *The Others*, desperately trying to keep her children safe from the threat of the super-natural.

So widespread were these warnings and so great the fears they aroused that they are worth closer examination. This is important for three reasons. First, discussions about 'Islamic fundamentalism' on campus have serious implications for equalities work, parti-cularly since they have been configured around the assumption of Muslims as perpetra-tors rather than victims of extremism and intolerance. Second, despite widespread cam-paigning against Islamic fundamentalism on campus over the past decade, each academic session is greeted by further warnings of Muslim extremism, suggesting that dominant attempts to understand and deal with this fear are having no effect. Third, des-pite Sophie Gilliat-Ray's (1999; 2000) contributions to our understanding of how univer-sities provide for religious diversity, there is no empirically reliable work on Islamic fundamentalism on campus.

Fundamentalism and higher education

Debates persist about the usefulness of Islamic fundamentalism as an analytical category and a descriptive term. Working vaguely within the limits of phenomenology, the appropriateness of the concept is of little consequence since however we frame and conceptualise Islamism, we are still referring to the same singular phenomenon (for example, Lawrence, 1995: xiii). To others, Islamic fundamentalism is of questionable use as a conceptual tool given the Christian origins and application of 'fundamentalism' (Shephard, 1987, 1988), or is tied to such stereotyping that it has almost become a shorthand for Muslims (Ahmed, 1992: 15). Yet the concept has been subject to widespread and uncritical usage in higher education settings, notably at the hands of the usually liberal National Union of Students (NUS). To explore the impact of this on Muslim students it is useful first to consider the emergence of debates about Islamic fundamentalism on campus. Note that like Sayyid (1997), I prefer to use the term Islamism rather than Islamic fundamentalism. But here use Islamic fundamentalism since I am referring to how notions of Islamic fundamentalism are constructed through the dominant logics of the National Union of Students and campaigning groups who have been circulating rumours of Muslim extremism on campus.

(i) Extremism and intolerance on campus: a problem emerges

The 1995 National Union of Students (NUS) annual conference marked a turning point for Muslims in Britain. Never before had the presence of Muslim students in the traditionally elite domain of British higher education been so openly debated. It was also significant because the ensuing discussions were predicated largely around the idea of an alleged threat to the academy and to non-Muslims posed by the spectre of Islamic fundamentalism. The outcome of this debate was motion 116 on Liberation Campaigns, which characterised the threat of Islamic fundamentalism on campus in stark terms:

> 4. Certain organisations in our society, which operate on college campuses, preach a hatred of different oppressed groups, such as Jews, Hindus, Lesbians, Gays and Bisexuals.
>
> 6. Hizb Ut-Tahrir preaches the death of Jews, Hindus, Lesbians, Gays and Bisexuals and has verbally and physically harassed Jewish students and has, on a number of occasions, affected the welfare of Jewish students.
>
> 7. This organisation has openly denied the Holocaust, referred to as a Jewish conspiracy in the media, financial institutions and the educational establishment.
>
> 8. This organisation is reported to have incited people to violence in the form of clashes between Moslems and Sikhs at a London college which resulted in the hospitalisation of several students and police officers.

In the wake of the conference, the Campuswatch telephone hotline for victims of hate crimes in universities was set up, and there followed organised campaigning against student 'Islamic fundamentalism' which was supplemented in 1998 by the publication of a report on *Extremism and Intolerance on Campus* by the Committee for Vice-Chancellors and Principals (CVCP).

However, it increasingly appeared as though neither organised campaigning against Islamic fundamentalism nor the CVCP's report were producing their intended results.

Warnings of militant Islamist activity on campus became increasingly melodramatic: no longer were the 'fundamentalists' merely threatening, harassing and assaulting other students but they were now actively recruiting for *jihad*[1], even when we had significant evidence of unreliable claims of fundamentalist university coups[2] and *mujahideen* recruitment[3].

(ii) Debating Islamic fundamentalism

Debates about Islamic fundamentalism among students were largely played out among political campaigners as diverse as the Union of Jewish Students, Hindu Vivek Kendra[4] and the British National Party[5], as well as in the pages of the printed media[6] and in the context of formal student politics. Despite the attention lavished on this assumed threat to campus harmony, no empirically reliable research into Islamism on campus was undertaken. In the light of this and wider dispute over the usefulness of the concept of Islamic fundamentalism the NUS-endorsed approach has been subjected to stinging, if under-reported, criticism.

The 1995 NUS annual conference had witnessed the curious spectacle of Socialist Workers' Party members distributing leaflets criticising the National Union of Students for using the Islamist group *Hizb ut-Tahrir* as a pretext for demonising Muslims. *Socialist Worker* (no. 1437, 8 April 1995) claimed that the NUS conference had seen the arbitrary branding of all Muslims as 'stupid, backward and ignorant' and indiscriminate allegations of Islamic fundamentalism levelled against visibly ethnicised delegates. In October 1995, the NUS President responded to a statistical breakdown of telephone calls to the Campuswatch hotline by declaring *Hizb ut-Tahrir* to be 'the biggest single extremist threat in the UK at the moment' (*The Guardian* 31 October 1995). *Q News* remained sceptical, questioning the reliability of the methods through which the NUS was gathering and analysing its data (27 October 1995).

Muslims greeted the publication of the CVCP report on *Extremism and Intolerance on Campus* with scepticism. As Gilliat-Ray notes, 'some Muslim critics of the report nevertheless regard the document to have been framed exclusively with the Muslim student community in mind' (Gilliat-Ray, 1999: 41). Q News implied that the report was tarnished by alleged vested political interests and Islamophobia on the part of one Vice-Chancellor involved in the report[7]. Under a *nom de plume* I also criticised the report in *Muslim News* (23 July 1999), drawing attention to the CVCP's failure to consult Muslim groups or individuals and highlighting the likelihood of institutionally racist mis-carriages of justice emerging from the report.

Sophie Gilliat-Ray acknowledges that the Federation of Student Islamic Societies (FOSIS) 'was sensitive to its...exclusion from the consultation process that preceded the CVCP report' (Gilliat-Ray, 2000: 133). More recently, Faisal Bodi voiced similar criticisms in *The Guardian* of 5 March 2002, prompting Lesley Perry, Director of Communications for Universities UK to respond that the CVCP's report was a defence of equalities principles (*The Guardian*, Education letters 12 March 2002). Perry's response is unconvincing: the report itself notes that the CVCP's aim was not to produce 'a different kind of study of, for example, how to promote multicultural, inter-racial and inter-religious harmony and mutual respect' (CVCP, 1998: 5). The potential for racism in allegations of extremism was indicated when one University Students' Union released a statement in October 2001 attacking the National Union of Students for 'scapegoating' Muslim students by issuing an unsubstantiated warning of Islamic fundamentalist recruitment in the university without having even contacted that Student's Union to verify the rumour. The President of Cambridge Union also spoke out against the NUS in October 2001, referring to its fundamentalist warnings as an 'alarmist faxing fetish', arguing that its campaigning against Islamic fundamentalists was pandering to white racism and demonising Muslims, and ruing the NUS' failure to provide any practical guidance on how to facilitate inter-group harmony on campus[8].

The emerging critique of the NUS-led campaigns against Islamic 'fundamentalism' on campus has focused largely on three main themes. First, that the campaigns against Islamic fundamentalism have marked the suspension of equalities principles on campus. Second, that many allegations of Islamic fundamentalism were empirically unreliable and often politically motivated. Third, campaigning against Islamic fundamentalism was conflated with increasing racism and Islamophobia. These criticisms of the campaigns against activities of *Hizb ut-Tahrir* and *al Muhajiroun* concur that the perpetuation of institutionalised racism and Islamophobia is a function of flawed definitions of Islamic fundamentalism and wider problems in accepting students who define themselves as Muslim. As a result, the attacks against Muslims became more general. So how was fundamentalism defined in university contexts and what does this tell us about Muslims?

(iii) Defining Islamic fundamentalism on campus
Campaigns against Islamic fundamentalism on campus have been justified by the claim that two Islamist groups known without reasonable doubt to be guilty of distributing hate literature – *al Muhajiroun* and *Hizb ut-Tahrir* – are particularly active amongst students. Since no empirically reliable research into their activities in universities has been carried out it is difficult to ascertain whether or not they are as active on campus as assumed. Despite this, allegations of widespread activity by the two groups abound.

(iiia) *Behaviouralism and fundamentalism*
It is striking that attempts to characterise Islamic fundamentalism in universities rely on general behavioural observations concerning the assumed essential characteristics of fundamentalists. For example, the NUS' 1995 motion 116 on Liberation Campaigns characterises Islamic fundamentalists primarily in behavioural terms, as preaching hatred of 'oppressed groups', preaching death to a range of other groups and individuals, holocaust denial and other forms of antisemitism, and incitement to racial violence against Sikhs. This echoed the NUS' 1995 LGB Campaign Briefing, which identified among the behavioural hallmarks of a fundamentalist member of *Hizb ut-Tahrir*: evangelism, oppression of women, belief in the pursuit of war to establish Islamic governance, practice of racial hatred against Jews and Hindus, homophobia, and activities against feminism and democracy.

The CVCP report on *Extremism and Intolerance on Campus* contrasts with the established – and mainly North American – literature on hate crimes on campus that emphasises the need for robust legalistic definitions (see, for example, Heumann and Church, 1997). The report makes no attempt to substantively define either extremism or intolerance, instead offering a number of exemplars to signify extremist political practices. These include coercion to religious conformity in dress and practice, such as praying, attempting to ban another group or society, intimidating or harassing other groups, or having a reputation for extremist activities. It is easy to understand how these exemplars of extremism were seen by many Muslims as a thinly-veiled Islamophobic attack. After all, claims of conformity to religious practice have been implicated in both Islamophobia in universities[9] and in unsubstantiated allegations of Muslim hate crimes I encountered during my fieldwork[10]. Attempts to ban groups and societies are associated with attacks – often by Muslims – against Jewish societies[11] but largely ignored when experienced by Muslim students[12]. Muslim students have gained a reputation for extremism because of racialised logic[13].

This proceduralist approach is thoroughly problematic. The idea that political motivations can be read from the actions they produce cannot convincingly account for any form of political mobilisation. For example, such a reading of political behaviour would leave us believing that the only possible motivation for organising a student protest against, say, tuition fees, would be the desire to protest. Once it is assumed that a particular group is discernible from other groups on account of its behaviour alone, it follows that behaviour is central to the constitution of that group and, further, that its behaviour constitutes its own motivation. Indicative of this logic was the assertion of the NUS' 1995 conference motion 116 that 'Hizb Ut-Tahrir, the Party of Liberation, stands not for the liberation of oppressed groups but instead, for their continued oppression'. The chief effect of this approach is to reaffirm decontextualised readings of political activities by Muslim students and represent Islamic fundamentalism, conveniently as a pathological condition. That is to say, the fundamentalist is driven by a compulsion to act in a particular way for no other reason than to behave unreasonably. Thus we are left with no substantive definition of Islamic fundamentalism but instead a vague conception of it as a sort of behavioural disorder.

(iiib) *Cultural and racial pathologies and definitions of fundamentalism*

The CVCP report offers us no indication of the underlying pathology but its advice on how to recognise extremists does direct us towards the logics of racialisation. According to the CVCP, all cases of extremism or intolerance should be 'judged at the time on the particular facts' (CVCP, 1998: 16), although it is not necessary to prove guilt beyond a reasonable doubt:

> clearly absolute certainty [that an extremist offence will occur] cannot be required... In our view, reasonable belief or suspicion will suffice. This... may arise through previous experience, whether at that institution or elsewhere. We do not think it is possible or indeed desirable to attempt to be more specific as to what is meant by reasonable belief or suspicion in this context. (CVCP, 1998: 16)

So it is not necessary to judge each case on its own merits since pre-emptive interventions may be made based on judgements emerging from cases of which university staff members may only have third-hand knowledge. Combined with its recommendation that judgements be based on 'common sense' (CVCP, 1998: 16) makes the report an extremely dangerous document. Given the circulation of media-fuelled moral panics about Islamic fundamentalism the dangers of combining reliance on reputation with the concentration of discretionary powers in the hands of staff members empowered to act on the basis of unspecified similarities among a particular 'type' of perpetrator are all too clear. The logics of the CVCP report are the logics of all racist miscarriages of justice, recommending that judgements do not even need to be based on fact but simply on patterns of crime assumed to be related to particular groups.

From the CVCP report we learn only that our ability to recognise the appearance of different forms of extremism and intolerance is contingent upon our ability to isolate particular offender types based on unspecified similarities. This is unconvincing. Rumours of Muslim student infractions are so contradictory that it is not possible to divine from them a singular pattern of extremist activity. For example, allegations of Islamic fundamentalism towards Hindu students emphasise the idea of forced mass conversions of young Hindu women. In contrast, warnings of fundamentalism towards Sikh women are often said to involve nightclubs, seduction, pornography, and Muslim men masquerading as Sikhs, whereas fundamentalist crimes against Jewish students are said to focus on violence.

Thus the pathology of extremism must somehow be related to the underlying conditions in each case. This logic is common to many discussions of Islamic fundamentalism on campus. Implicit is the idea that the behavioural disorder of Islamic fundamentalism is a symptom of some broader malaise affecting minority ethnic youth in Britain. As Talal Asad noted, this is the idea of religion as a curative pill taken by members of ethnicised minority groups in response to the challenges of life in modern racialised western societies (Asad, 1993: 280).

One of the most intriguing features of dominant readings of Muslim student fundamentalism is the idea that it is a response to the challenges and social exclusion facing South Asian youth in Britain today. This causal – even casual – assumption was regularly rehearsed throughout the 1990s. In *The Observer*, David Harrison (13 August 1995) argued that the space within which groups such as *Hizb ut-Tahrir* have become active is a 'vacuum' created as a

> result of the cultural chasm that has opened between young Muslims and their tradition-bound parents. Many eschew their parents' conservatism, and in the process largely eschew their religion too. But British society does not seem able to provide a palatable alternative. Unemployment in some Muslim communities is as high as 90 percent and drug-taking is rife. Housing is often poor, and racial discrimination a fact of life.

According to Madeleine Bunting (*The Guardian*, 20 November 1997),

> there is a strong sense of grievance that Muslims are suffering a high degree of economic discrimination which government has not addressed. Bangladeshis and Pakistanis combined

have a long-term unemployment rate which is nearly three times that of the next most disadvantaged ethnic minority, Caribbeans. In the inner cities, nearly half of Bangladeshi and Pakistani men and women are unemployed.

The appeal of this logic is manifested in the suggestion of the NUS' 1995 LGB Campaign Briefing that Islamic fundamentalists

> use the disillusionment of Asian youth. They identify the racism and poverty experienced by many and then take logic to absurd degrees... They exploit the ills of society to promote a far more dangerous and oppressive society, the dictatorial fundamentalist Islamic state.

The briefing further recommends:

> we must understand that many young Asian people may be attracted to Hizb ut Tahrir because of their experience of racism in this country. Fighting racism will also undermine and discredit Hizb ut Tahrir.

In a similar vein, the NUS' 1995 annual conference discussed the question of Islamist activity and resolved 'to campaign against the conditions of social deprivation that provides a breeding ground for racism – including unemployment, poor housing and cuts in services'.

There is nothing particularly new about this representation of minority youth as apparently incapable of operating successfully in post-industrial postmodern western societies, as riven by inter-generational conflict and consequently resorting to deviance and criminality. We can see this identified in almost any chapter in the Centre for Contemporary Cultural Studies' seminal *The Empire Strikes Back: Race and Racism in 70s Britain* (CCCS, 1982). As Husain and O'Brien note (2000: 1), 'while discrimination and resentment against Muslims are rooted in the fear of the 'other'...its modern representations have become fixed in family structure, international disputes and the rise of politico-religious Islamic groups'. The parallels with a 1972 *Sunday Times* quote noted by John Solomos in 1988 are clear: 'Young blacks could be forced to accept unemployment as a normal life-style and if there is a spark of conflict pent-up black anger could spill over into violence and be met with violence' (*Sunday Times* 23 July 1972, quoted in Solomos, 1988: 130). Furthermore, the juxtaposition of minority criminality and drug-taking, and social exclusion and the elite domain of higher education is, as Gilroy notes, significant because:

> where once it was the main streets of the decaying inner city which hosted the most fearsome encounter between Britons and their most improbable and intimidating other – black youth – now it is the classrooms and staffrooms of the inner-city school which frame the same conflict and provide the most potent terms with which to make sense of racial difference. (Gilroy, 1992: 55)

Defining Islamic fundamentalism thus is prey to the wider logics of racist pathology. First, it is neither helpful nor empirically correct to frame our understanding of Muslim students entirely within the context of second generation British South Asian male youth. No reliable empirical data on the demographics of Muslim student populations in Britain exists. However, the diversity of Muslim students was perhaps best reflected in one case study University where the Islamic Society President – an Indonesian woman – was supported by an Executive Committee which was truly international in every sense. A second complicating factor that it is disingenuous to suppose that Islamic fundamentalism emerges symptomatically to disrupt an essential order of secular South Asianness. The idea of South Asia as an essential unity interrupted by the scandalous articulation of Muslim identities in the Pakistan project is, as Sayyid and Tyrer (2002) note, a product of the orientalist discourse of Indology (Inden, 1992). Indeed, among those who have most forcefully lobbied the NUS for action against Islamic fundamentalists are Jewish and Hindu groups conflating religion and politics. Third, the argument that fundamentalism can only be understood through consideration of wider patterns of social exclusion contradicts the wider literature on Islamic fundamentalism which emphasises the middle class credentials of fundamentalists as generally upwardly mobile professionals educated in western-style technical institutions and working in areas such as engineering and medicine. It is significant that the fundamentalism we refer to is apparently not occurring on the streets of, say, Oldham – where the disturbances in response to racism had nothing at all to do with Islamism – but in the elite domain of the university.

Extremism and intolerance operationalised

To recap: three assumptions inform dominant definitions of on campus Islamic fundamentalism. First, is the idea that Muslim extremism occurs in response to the racism and social exclusion experienced by Muslims in wider society rather than on university campuses. Second, that Muslim students are essentially misguided South Asians who have turned to religion in a moment of pathological inauthenticity, and that campaigning against racism in wider society will rectify this condition. Third, that extremism is a largely compulsive condition, its motivation lies in its enaction. I explore these tensions through instances uncovered during my fieldwork that were characterised as Muslim extremism[14].

An early example of Islamic fundamentalism on campus demonstrates the invalidity of these assumptions. In April 1994 some unidentified Muslims in one case study University printed a spoof of the union newspaper, slipping copies into issues of the union organ as an 'erratum' notice. On the front cover of the leaflet was printed: 'MUSLIM CLEANSING TIME/SO IT'S.../UNION RACISM/APARTHEID IN ACTION/ETHNIC CLEANSING/AIN'T NO BLACK IN THE UNION... JACK!/YAKKETY YAK.../RACIST CRAP'. Elsewhere, a take-off of the union's mission statement said:

> Any Union member has the right to partake in the activities of the Union except if he or she is a Muslim, black or Asian... Minorities will not continue to be welcome and we will hinder their activities at every possible opportunity. The Union actively discourages minorities, especially Muslims, from getting involved in the Union.

The leaflet complained that Muslims were denied basic rights by a 'racist [Union] Executive [which] wasn't going to stand by and see a bunch of 'Pakis' and 'foreigners' dictate policies'. Clearly the leaflet was produced not by pathologically defective individuals affected by inter-generational conflict and drug use around them but by articulate, intelligent, motivated, and politically well-resourced individuals with a grand sense of irony. The leaflet can only be read within the context of Muslim students' political struggles to win equal rights in this University, where for example, notices advising Jewish students on how to obtain exemptions from examinations and assessments co-inciding with Jewish religious festivals were displayed across the campus in 1997. Although this was clearly good practice, Muslims felt aggrieved that there were no similar posters addressing their rights. As one respondent noted:

> Back in 1994 we campaigned to have rights for an exam exemption and we were told many, many times they [the university] were looking at it...They were looking at it and many of our Jewish colleagues were being exempted from their exams. So we demanded an exemption and weren't given one. This year [1998-1999], when a Muslim got elected on the [Union] Executive, [the request was made] via all channels within the University and after a short while they did exempt us but on certain conditions.

I also received reports of hate crimes against Muslim students. One notable case involved Aisha, who met me during the 1999-2000 academic session while moving from one hall of residence to another. Aisha reported having been subjected to Islamophobic harass-ment in a hall where no action was taken about it. So it boiled over into an assault involv-ing pieces of wood from broken furniture. The university finally acted. Instead of eject-ing the racists who had attacked Aisha, it just rehoused her in another hall. During 2001-2002 I caught up with Aisha again, when she reported having been racially abused as a 'fucking Muslim' by a student in her new hall.

Institutionalised Islamophobia was also on the mind of Mohammed, President of a case study University Islamic Society during 1994-1995. Mohammed reported repeated attempts by members of the Student's Union to ban the society despite there being no *al Muhajiroun* or *Hizb ut-Tahrir* presence on campus, and found that the most mundane of contacts with the union would be scrutinised by union staff convinced that the society was a haven for fundamentalists. Other respondents reported Islamophobic incidents during the early 1990s, including an assault by Students' Union security guards which hospitalised a Muslim student on a night out in 1995, threats against a Muslim woman student, and an assault in 1994 in which a Muslim student's *hijab* was torn off. Recalling one attempted banning of the society, Mohammed concluded that the only convincing explanation for the union's actions was racism and Islamophobia:

> It is really, really ironic that the National Union of Students, we had these issues about Anti-racism officer, Antiracism week when the majority of people who are actually in these positions are white from posh backgrounds.They may be from that background, totally naïve with no understanding of Antiracism issues, and even when there's a Black person in there it's a myth... it rates on the level of the Metropolitan Police in London... when [one student] did something [to challenge far right activity on campus] there was very, very few people who ever backed him up. A couple of the Asians and Black guys decided to back him up... but only when Black people do it themselves...Actually, it's not what you know, it's who you know... I interviewed [a university Dean] as part of my dissertation so immediately when I knew they [Finchton Union] were going to try to ban us I was afraid but I was one step ahead of them, and so then I went to see [the Dean]. He said 'listen, you've been truthful and honest, just go ahead and do your degree...

Mohammed's opinions resonated with the experiences of Latif, a former lecturer who recalled his first experience of being branded fundamentalist, during the early 1990s. Student demand in this case study university for provision of *halal* food prompted Latif to raise the matter with the Head of Catering Services, who in turn replied by railing against 'the bastardisation of our food'. Latif reported that a subsequent complaint of racism against the Head of Catering Services was waved away by the Vice-Chancellor on the grounds that he did not wish to be 'told what to do by a bunch of fundamentalists'.

Experiences such as this illuminate Mohammed's explanation for a brief tryst with *al Muhajiroun* under subsequent Islamic Society leadership during 1997-1998. Mohammed explained that in the context of wider Islamophobia on campus this had been a case of Muslim students effectively saying 'yah-boo' to a Students' Union which had so effectively demonised them that they had nothing left to lose by publicly asserting Muslim identities to bait the Union: 'the Islamic Society stuck its face out and waited for the union to kick it'. Interestingly, the university moved to prevent further Islamist activity by, among other things, significantly improving the facilities available to Muslims.[15]

It is interesting that even the only verifiable instance of *al Muhajiroun* or *Hizb ut-Tahrir* activity in any of the case study universities could be understood by Mohammed only in terms of the occurrence of institutionalised racism and Islamophobia. Khan notes that 'Muslim activism in Britain is influenced by the broad negative societal framework within which Muslims operate, and by their disillusionment with British state and society' (Khan, 2000: 40). On a macro level, disillusionment with specific institutional contexts also affects modes of Muslim political behaviour, and was a decisive feature in acts of Muslim resistance I found during my fieldwork.

Take an incident during union elections in 1999, in another case study University. Union activities were highly valued by Muslim students resisting institutionalised Islamophobia and they distributed a leaflet which claimed that 'Muslims in [this campus] have on a number of occasions been attacked and discriminated against' and exhorted them to vote. This is certainly not extremism. As Sarah Glynn (2002) showed, groups such as *al Muhajiroun* advocated Muslim non-participation in elections.

But these union elections were important to Muslim students resisting Islamophobia. So it was interesting to discover an allegation of Muslim hate crime during the 1999-2000 elections, which resulted in one student being denied his franchise. The chain of events leading up to it was alarming. When I met Amin he had cuts and bruising on his face and hands. That morning, like many other students Amin had rushed off to exercise his franchise in the union elections during a gap between lectures, holding a sheaf of papers. The papers did not worry the ballot officers who handed Amin his voting slips. But while trying to vote, Amin was approached by union security guards who demanded that he hand over his papers on the grounds that they constituted hate literature or an attempt to subvert the democratic process. When he protested his innocence, Amin was assaulted and thrown out of the union building. His complaint to the union left him afraid that the union's official line was that to persist with his complaint would brand him as a troublemaker and jeopardise his prospects of study in the institution. This was not the only allegation of Islamic fundamentalism in this University that year[16].

Muslim students in two other case study universities received far better provision than their peers in the institutions considered above, and found both unions and university authorities more willing to protect them against Islamophobia. Significantly, I found no evidence of Muslim students in either university being branded extremist, although with rising Islamophobia after 11 September 2001 fears were expressed and one of the Students Unions had to attack the National Union of Students for having issued an un-substantiable allegation of Islamic fundamentalist recruitment in one university. Signi-ficantly the groups *al Muhajiroun* and *Hizb ut-Tahrir* had no noteworthy support among students from any of the universities during my fieldwork[17].

Conclusion

Dominant debates about Islamic fundamentalism on campus are configured around racialised referents and the contingent nature of political behaviour. So any reference to Islamic fundamentalism directs us to an assumed essential hostility towards others as characterising Muslim political identities. Consequently they can provide no coherent means of explaining the political activities of Muslim students, Islamist or not, nor of the complex play of political and social identities on campus which occasionally spill over into conflict. This approach obscures the contingency of social and political identities and the possibility of harmonious relations between members of different ethnic groups. It effects a suspension of any meaningful consideration of equalities principles. For one reason the idea of Islamic fundamentalism as a shorthand for essential Muslim hostility to other assumed bounded ethnic or racial groups precludes the possibility of engender-ing harmonious relations on campus. For another, the pathology of minority youth that dominates discussions of Muslim students makes Islamic fundamentalism on campus as an analogue to wider racist notions of Black youth criminality. Thus, implicit notions of the inevitability of ritual crimes by Muslims against other student groups are paralleled by assumptions about the supposed challenge posed by Muslims to the elite domain of the university.

There is no doubt that *Hizb ut-Tahrir* and *al Muhajiroun* have distributed hate literature. What we hear far less of is the insignificance of these groups as a force in the vast majority of universities, or of the Islamophobic hate literature circulating in universities[18]. Our task in relation to inter-group conflict in British universities is not to seek further ways of valorising the idea of an assumed inherent extremism among Muslim students, but rather to explore why certain social and political identities and relationships should be so uncritically thought of as determined by phenotypal ethnic and racial characteristics. Polemical and ideologically invested discussions about an alleged Muslim threat to universities only succeed in playing to the racialisation of our campuses[19]. To challenge hate crimes, intolerance and extremism on campus is not done by valorising racialised logics but by abandoning the logics of cultural essentialism and racial pathology which presuppose an assumed essential propensity among Muslims to conflict with members of particular ethnic groups, and not suspending equalitiies initiatives.

I began this chapter by alluding to *The Others* which, like all good films contains a plot-twist at the end: the family, so terrified of ghosts, turn out to be ghosts themselves. Despite encountering endless warnings of the spectre of Islamic fundamentalism on campus, by far the most striking instances of extremism and intolerance found in my study were those in which Muslim students were victims, not perpetrators. This is not to deny that there are occasions when Muslim groups and individuals have committed hate crimes. But so long as we engage in racialised witch-hunts against extremists who are suspected on account of their similarity to other known or suspected perpetrators, our campuses will never be free of fear and loathing of the Other and the physical and epistemic violence that results.

Notes

1   See, for example, 'Call to arms', Abul Taher, *The Guardian* 16 May 2000.

2   See, for example, the case of Imran Chaudhry reported in *The Guardian*, 7 November 1995, who was wrongfully accused of leading a 'fundamentalist' union coup.

3   See, for example, Letter from Professor Hill to Lee Federman, General Secretary of LSE Students Union and LSE Islamic Society, sourced from LSE News and Views Volume 24 No. 9, 5 March 2001, written in response to unsubstantiable claims of Chechen separatist recruitment in London School of Economics.

4   Hindu Vivek Kendra, 'Secularism Extra-Ordinary' by Ramen Bando published London n.d.: Sahitya Porishad, also disseminated on HVK website (http://hvk.org/specialrepo/seo/index.html) (noted on web June 2002)

5   BNP leader Nick Griffin ('Behind the race riots', article found on the British National Party website, summer 2002, http://www.bnp.org.uk) refers to Muslim 'fundamentalism' and rumours of attempted conversion of Sikh women to Islam – rumours which have been widely circulated in the context of higher education.

6   See, as a typical example, Emily Sheffield, 'Higher Education: Middle East at the door', *The Guardian*, 5 November 1996.

7   *Q-News*, no. 300, January 1999: 9

8   News: get your Akhtar-gether', James Birchall, *Varsity*, 19 October 2001

9   For example, Latif, a former Finchton University Lecturer, reported to me that during the early 1990s Finchton colleagues had treated hijab wearing Muslim students as 'somehow less intelligent and less assertive' than their white and non-visibly Muslim peers because they assumed that they had been coerced to wear hijab.

10 For example, I received a number of warnings that Muslim students had either just held or were imminently planning a mass rally at which to hold forced mass conversions of Hindu women to Islam, the first taking the form of a telephone call from a respondent named Nina during May 1999. None of these warnings coincided with any large scale event involving Muslim students or groups, although I do note that one event at which Hindu women publicly converted to Islam does appear to have occurred during the mid-1990s.

11 For example, Gilliat-Ray (2000: 40) notes that during the 1970s 'the NUS came under considerable pressure to pass anti-Zionist resolutions, equating Zionism with racism, and to ban Jewish and Israeli societies from campuses'.

12 For example, during the 2001-2002 academic session, respondents from one case study University contacted me with the news that union staff had interrupted a jummuah prayer with the warning that any support for Palestinian self-determination resulting in any criticism of Israeli state policies would result in the Islamic Society being banned for infringing the right of the Jewish Society to support Israeli self-determination. Since Israeli state policy remains an obstacle to meaningful self-determination for Palestinians, it is extremely difficult to support Palestinian self-determination without criticising Israel in some way. It is only possible to deny the right to support Palestinian self-determination if one is locked into the logics of the zero-sum game of 'one state' solution.

13 For example, during the 1997-1998 academic session a memo was faxed to one case study University by one of its chaplains to request improved provision for Jewish students. The fax expressed concerns about the safety of Jewish students in halls of residence, complaining that the university had housed a Jewish student with 'Moslem' flatmates. The fax suggested that it was easy to see how such a practice could result in 'tragedy'. Although the groups *al Muhajiroun* and *Hizb ut-Tahrir* are known to have engaged in antisemitic activities, the fax did not refer to either group, instead referring broadly to 'Moslems' and being fundamentally concerned with the dangers of housing two inherently 'antagonistic' groups together. A number of Muslim respondents in this University were aware of the existence of this fax. It is easy to see how its line of reasoning could have been interpreted by them as implying that only by separating Muslim and Jewish students in halls of residence – in other words, racial segregation – could Jewish students be guaranteed safety. It is also easy to see how the fax's concern for improved provisions could be interpreted by others as vested political interest.

14   All names of institutions and individuals have been changed to protect their anonymity.

15   In particular, discussions with the Islamic Society on improved prayer room facilities were suddenly opened with great commitment by university management after a period of apparent indifference and a paid staff member was appointed to work with Muslim students.

16   For example, earlier in the 1999-2000 session the Islamic Society participated in the union's Antiracism Week, contributing a stand raising awareness about racism (including racism carried out by Muslims in the Nation of Islam). A leaflet highlighting racism experienced by Palestinians caused offence to some students and the rumour swiftly circulated across campus that the Islamic Society was distributing hate literature. The Islamic Society was found not guilty by the Union. However, this was not before national campaigners, barristers, and a member of university staff – none of whom had seen the offending leaflet – were reported to have called for serious sanction against the Islamic Society.

17   The only verifiable incident involving either group during the fieldwork period occurred during 1998-1999 when an individual unconnected to the university distributed leaflets and stickers attacking the NUS for partisanship. During the next year, I did see an al Muhajiroun leafleting stand in the vicinity of the university although the Islamic Society and the majority of Muslim students were hostile to the group.

18   For example, a variant of an offensive email I have received more than once from students can be found on the internet at: http://www.sikhnet.com/Sikhnet/discussion.nsf/78f5a2ff8906d1788725657c00732d6c/95EFDAEB3EF1CA 23872568A3000140E7?OpenDocument (url re-checked as correct October 2003)

19   Typifying the current hold of racialised logics is the idea, increasingly popular on campus, that any criticism of Zionism is by definition antisemitic. This argument is based on the racialised logic that Zionism is immutably tied to essential Jewishness.

References

Ahmed, A S (1992) *Postmodernism and Islam Predicament and Promise*. London: Routledge

Asad, T (1993) *Genealogies of Religion.* London: The John Hopkins University Press

Cambridge University Students Union (CUSU) (2001), *Varsity* 19th October 2001

Centre for Contemporary Cultural Studies (1982) *The Empire Strikes Back Race and Racism in 70s Britain.* London: Routledge

Committee for Vice-Chancellors and Principals (CVCP) (1998) *Extremism and Intolerance on Campus.* London: CVCP

Gilliat-Ray, S (1999) *Higher Education and Student Religious Identity.* Exeter: University of Exeter Dept. of Sociology and UK Inter-Faith Network

Gilliat-Ray, S (2000) *Religion in Higher Education: The politics of the multi-faith campus.* Aldershot: Ashgate

Gilroy, P (1992) 'The end of antiracism', in eds. Donald, J and Rattansi, A (1992) *'Race', Culture and Difference.* London: Sage, pp. 49-61

Glynn, Sarah (2002) 'Bengali Muslims: the new East End radicals?'. *Ethnic and Racial Studies,* 25, 6, November 2002, pp 969-988

The Guardian, 31 October 1995

The Guardian, 7 November 1995

The Guardian, 20 November 1997

The Guardian, 16 May 2000

The Guardian, 5 March 2002

The Guardian, 12 March 2002

Heumann, M and Church, TW eds. (1997) *Hate Speech on Campus: Cases, Case Studies, and Commentary.* Boston: Northeastern University Press

Husain, F and O'Brien, M (2000) 'Muslim Communities in Europe: Reconstruction and Transformation', *Current Sociology,* 48,4, pp. 1-14

Inden, R (1992) *Imagining India.* Oxford: Blackwell

Khan, Z (2000), 'Muslim Presence in Europe: The British Dimension – Identity, Integration and Community Activism', *Current Sociology,* 48,4, pp. 29-44

Lawrence, B B and Denny, F (eds.) (1995) *Defenders of God: The Fundamentalist Revolt against The Modern Age.* Columbia: University of South Carolina Press

LSE News and Views Volume 24 No. 9, 5th March 2001

Muslim News, 23 July 1999

National Union of Students (1995), *LGB Campaign Briefing*

The Observer, 13 August 1995

Q News, 27 October 1995

Sayyid, B S (1997) *A Fundamental Fear: Eurocentrism and the Emergence of Islamism.* London: Zed Books

Sayyid and Tyrer (2002) 'Ancestor worship and the irony of the 'Islamic Republic' of Pakistan', *Contemporary South Asia* (2002), 11, 1, pp. 57-75

Emily Sheffield, 'Higher Education: Middle East at the door', *The Guardian*, 5 November 1996

Shepard, W (1987), ' 'Fundamentalism' Christian and Islamic', *Religion,* 17, pp. 355-78

Shepard, W (1988) 'What is 'Islamic Fundamentalism'?', *Studies in Religion*, 17, pp. 5-26

Socialist Worker, no. 1437, 8 April 1995

Solomos, J (1991) *Black Youth, Racism and the State: The Politics of Ideology and Policy.* Cambridge: Cambridge University Press (first published in 1988 as hardcover)

CHAPTER SIX

Fish in and out of water: a theoretical framework for race and the space of academia

Nirmal Puwar

As a way of dealing with the death of her cat the owner painted numerous images of it. These paintings were then put on display in an art gallery. When people saw these images, even though they were strangers to both the woman and the cat, they could relate to the feelings of loss experienced by the painter. The feelings generated in the viewers by the paintings were universal; everybody felt them.

A lecturer at a famous cutting edge art college in London told this story to a South Asian student who had undertaken a project on dialogue. The project's subtle nuances could not be grasped by the lecturer because the work required familiarity with the indexicality of the language that informs Bollywood. The story of the cat was an attempt to encourage the student to produce art that could be understood universally rather than only by certain groups.

The universal (invisible) norm

We all know that cats and their loss do not carry the same meaning in all cultures. The sentiment is specific because this emotion is located within the power dynamics of whiteness. The lecturer has the educational authority to *claim* to speak for all humans (Dyer, 1997). Specific emotions, tastes and associations can be unthinking, placed as universal; while another set of sentiments and aesthetics is designated as particular and located in an ethnically marked position.

One of the core features of the power of whiteness is its positional privilege of being racially unmarked and invisible (hooks, 1992). It is borne in such a way that it is taken for granted and naturalised to the point of being invisible. Charles Mills states that:

> The fish do not see the water and whites do not see the racial nature of a white polity because it is natural to them, the element in which they move. (1997: 76)

In his work on class and habitus, Pierre Bourdieu says 'when habitus encounters a social world of which it is the product, it is like a fish in water: it does not feel the weight of the water, and it takes the world about itself for granted' (Bourdieu and Wacquant, 1992: 127). Simmonds states that, as a black[1] female sociologist, 'In this white world I am a fresh water fish that swims in sea water. I feel the weight of the water...on my body' (1997: 227),

When reflecting upon those who do and those who don't feel the weight or see the water it is useful to consider the work on whiteness and class together, via Bourdieu. This has been surprisingly under-explored. Thus far the analysis of whiteness has either been without reference to class or focused on white male and female upper and middle class locations (Frankenberg, 1997). Although fruitful for thinking through the contemporary context, it is itself of a predominantly historical nature (Hall, 1992; Ware, 1992).[2] Simmonds herself focuses on race and gender, at the expense of class, even though her discussion draws on a leading contemporary theorist of how class is lived in the everyday exercise of distinction and social exclusion.

A felicitous encounter: ontological complicity

Much of Bourdieu's theoretical and empirical work has been concerned with the positionality of bodies – as individuals as well as part of social groups – in social space. The world described by Bourdieu as objective structures and social fields lives in our habitus – or incorporated structures – not as a simple imprint that determines us, but rather as something we activate through our practices, however unconsciously and auto-matically. Bourdieu stresses that one's habitus is attained through an unconscious process; and not through rational choices. The schemas of the habitus operate 'beyond the reach of introspective scrutiny or control by the will', as they become embedded 'in the most automatic gestures or the apparently most insignificant techniques of the body-ways of walking or blowing one's nose, ways of eating or talking...' (1984:466).

Bourdieu notes that there is a felicitous encounter with the world when our habitus – de-fined as 'internalised embodied schemes' which are acquired 'in the course of individual history' (1984: 467) – matches the field of social space. Those who experience what Bourdieu calls 'ontological complicity', 'merely need to be what they are in order to be what they have to be...' (Bourdieu, 1990: 11). Being immersed in social worlds – espe-cially those of one's family and elite educational institutions – that exercise similar means of social measurement, specific agents have through 'practical mastery' acquired an automatic 'feel for the game'. Although 'familiarisation' does not mean that they lack inventiveness in their actions, or that these are simply determined. Nevertheless there is a remarkable regularity to the daily enactment of 'improvisations'. Their dispositions, comportment, gestures, speech and tastes place them ideally to meet the demands of the field in which they manoeuvre themselves – their work.

We all participate in the games of our field. Due to their social trajectory – most espe-cially their class background and scholastic training – however, some people are much more inclined to have a sense of the game, as well as the ability to play it in different pro-fessions. Within the professions, those with upper or middle class habituses are at an advantage because they have acquired the cultural capital to feel comfortable in these social spaces. Having moved through civilising social spaces, family or educational, they have almost unconsciously acquired the appropriate codes and conventions through the practical reasoning of their upper or middle class families or educational experiences, particularly public schooling and Oxbridge. Their dispositions have adjusted to Bourdieu's 'game'. There is a tacit normativity – of which the body is the prime site – that governs the social game on which the embodied subject acts. Each field[3] exercises its demands on the habitus. The position of a particular agent is the result of an interplay between one's habitus and one's place in a field of positions as defined by the distribution of the appropriate form of capital, be it social, cultural, economic or symbolic. Being perfectly adapted to the field, they take up the position of a 'virtuoso' whose 'habitus entertains with the social world which has produced it a real ontological complicity, the source of cognition without consciousness, intentionality without intention, and a practical mastery of the world's regularities which allow one to anticipate the future without even needing to posit it as such' (1990: 10-11).

Habitus mis-match

Those who don't experience immediate adaptation to the situation, feel conscious, acutely reflexive and ill at ease (Bourdieu, 1990: 13). It is these bodies who are more likely to become aware of the normative dispositions in any field precisely because there is discordance between what one's habitus is and what one is required to be, as, when for instance, there is 'a mismatch between scholastic mode of acquisition and 'high society' situation' (1984: 571). Bourdieu calls this the Don Quixote effect. Simmonds' experience can be located as one such encounter, although, significantly, the Don Quixote effect is solely through race and gender in her discussion: her black female body. She leaves class out of the conversation, even though it no doubt figures as a factor of discordance or adaptation. What she points out is how her black lecturing body is something that is out of place in academia; it is not the normative figure.

Bodies in space

If we accept that social space is a contested and dynamic entity (Massey, 1994)[4] and that the body bears and disrupts history (Foucault, 1970) then we are led to think about how the connection between bodies and space is built, repeated and contested over time. Social spaces are not blank and open for any body to occupy. Over time, through processes of historical sedimentation, certain types of bodies are designated as being the 'natural' occupants of specific spaces (Grosz, 1995). Some bodies have the right to belong in certain locations, while others are marked out as trespassers who are in accordance with how both spaces and bodies are imagined, politically, historically and conceptually circumscribed as being 'out of place' (Cresswell, 1996). As David Sibley states, 'Who is felt to belong and not to belong contributes in an important way to the shaping of social space' (1997:3). The coupling of particular spaces with specific types of bodies is no doubt subject to change. However, this is usually not without consequence, as it often breaks with how bodies have been placed before.

In a series of photographs titled 'Pastoral Interludes', artist Ingrid Pollard considers questions of 'place, space, and where we all fit in the world scheme' by placing black people, including herself, in the British countryside (Pollard, 1993; Kinsman, 1993;

Young and Pollard, 1995; Women and Geography Study Group, 1997: 184-185). Through these images she makes the point that black people are at odds in the rural idyll of the English landscape. The feeling of not belonging is underlined in the accompanying text: 'I thought I liked the Lake District, where I wondered lonely as a Black face in a sea of white. A visit to the countryside is always accompanied by a feeling of unease; dread' (www.autograph-abp.co.uk). A black body is conspicuous in rural areas of Britain, where their perceived alien presence can cause such great alarm that it can incite both verbal and physical violence (Malik, 1992).

Although the numbers of people of colour working in academia as staff has increased over recent years (Carter *et al*, 1999), they are still very much a minority, especially in senior positions. They are rather like Pollard's pictures of black people in the country-side: out of place. The whiteness of the normative figure of leadership within academia, and the fact that as, Theo Goldberg says, whites are the 'ghosts of modernity' (1997: 83) is made most apparent by the presence of staff of colour. They are not the somatic norm. The rest of this chapter examines why not.

Insiders/Outsiders

It is important to stress that we lecturers of colour in academia are not entirely fish out of water. The fact that we have managed to enter academia suggests that we are insiders and not marginal or total outsiders. Through our educational, and for some, class training in the family, we have, to various degrees, acquired the habitus and dispositions required in our academic locus. We have utilised resources of cultural, symbolic, social and economic capital (Bourdieu, 1990). So when we consider race, we should not deny that we can articulate, perform and assess the specialist language and analytical skills of our disciplines.

If we ask ourselves: what has enabled me to enter the staff ranks of academia? we are led to the various forms of patronage, social networking and social cloning that are part of becoming an academic. If we stretch Simmond's phrase and add class along with race and gender, we are not fish out of water but fresh water fish in sea water. But however much we may be steeped in the practical mastery of the airs, graces, and academic specialisms of our field, we do not represent the racial somatic norm in positions of authority in academia.

Disorientation

The double-take that so often accompanies the information that I am a lecturer can be explained by the fact I am fairly young. But I think there is something much more en-during here, because double takes do not disappear even in the case of mature black lecturers, especially women. The disorientation that hits students in that split second when a hall of 150 students suddenly see that the lecturer who will school them on Marx or Social Theory is not white applies to all ages.

Although avoiding an additive model of the race, gender, class mantra I would assert that authority is seen to be especially misplaced when it is clearly vested in a woman of colour.

Strait-jacketing

The academic subject one teaches can affect how one is received, so for instance it is probably much more accepted that the Race lecturer will not be white, and the Race and Gender lecturer will be non-white and female. Is this the ethnic niche available for black lecturers?

Rasheed Aareen (1984) pointed to 'ethnic pigeon holing' as common in the art world. Ethnically marked artists are expected to contribute international art in relation to specific ethnic groups, but not to mainstream subjects like, say, modernism. Artist Steve MCQueen (2001) said that one thing he hated when studying art at Goldsmiths College was that he was expected to produce African and carnival masks, but not to contribute to general questions on abstract art for instance. An academic version of this phenomenon is the strait-jacketing of non-white lecturers into 'race' issues. Here they are expected to carry authority, but struggle to be seen as experts on mainstream subjects.

And even though they are granted the space to speak on race, white students and academics wonder whether the lecturer is presenting a subjective, tainted version of race relations. White lecturers who teach race are likely to be seen as balanced and objective. The whole question of who is seen to be objective or subjective is entwined with the issue of positions of authority. It is black bodies who are marked and particularised as raced bodies, while, in the words of Patricia Williams (1997), 'race is ex-nominated' from white bodies. Whether non-white academics are allowed to be more than just some sort of representative of their racial positioning, is a sign of the silent processes of racialisation in the academy.

Now 'we' want to talk about race because it has been ignored for too long. And I think it important that we feel we can, but at the same time we should be able to be more than race or ethnicity specialists. What black academics do needs to be framed, especially if it is overtly engaging with specific questions of race.

Frantz Fanon's (1986) theorisation of the processes of racialisation (see Goldberg: 1997), identifies definite *infantalisation* that accompanies strait-jacketing: people are seen as less capable of certain skills or of being an authority in a particular field. In the academy this can mean that white colleagues and students assume non-white staff to be more junior than they are. Seniority is not easily imagined within specific racialised and gendered bodies. And there is a constant burden of doubt. This clearly influences career progression.

Hyper-surveillance

Because they are not the 'natural' bodies for academia, black academics have to endure a burden of doubt from those around them. And it comes with a high level of hyper-surveillance, giving a feeling that colleagues and students are more likely to pick up on any mistakes and see them as signs of misplaced authority. This can become apparent in student feedback forms and also in the way senior staff respond to complaints or abuse written by students. Are flaws less likely to be tolerated if the member of staff is a person of colour? Some departmental heads and managers may use such criticisms to justify closer and longer periods of surveillance. So for instance probation periods could be extended and teaching observations stepped up.

There are instances where lecturers of colour are received with great fanfare for bringing diversity to a predominantly white faculty. But the slightest glitch in their work performance turns the awe and fascination about their appointment to disappointment that warrants special surveillance and disciplinary measures.

As a practising psychiatrist who moved from the French colony Martinique to France, Fanon made an observation which has parallels in the ways in which institutional racism becomes manifested across different fields of work. Fanon offers an intense observation of the surveillance monitoring the authority of black bodies in professional posts. He shows how the burden of doubt and the tendency towards infantalisation operates along with hyper-surveillance:

> We had physicians, professors, statesmen. Yes, but something out of the ordinary still clung to such cases. 'We have a Senegalese history teacher. He is quite bright... Our doctor is colored. He is very gentle.' It was always the Negro teacher, the Negro doctor; brittle as I was becoming, I shivered at the slightest pretext. I knew, for instance, that if the physician made a mistake it would be the end of him and all of those who came after him. What could one expect, after all, from a Negro physician? As long as everything went well, he was praised to the skies, but look out, no nonsense, under any conditions! The black physician can never be sure how close he is to disgrace. I tell you, I was walled in: No exception was made for my refined manners, or my knowledge of literature, or my understanding of the quantum theory'. (Fanon, 1986:117)

The tenuous position of black professionals means there is a very thin line between being praised and being displaced of authority. The margins for making mistakes are extremely small. The tiniest error in a performance can be picked up as proof that the person is not quite up to the job. This can be utilised to justify greater surveillance, with observations becoming closer and closer. Such microscopic inspection not only leaves little leeway for inaccuracies but is likely to find what it is desperately searching for. Undue pressure can itself provoke mistakes because of the person's consequent anxiety and nervousness rather than ability.

Natives in the academy

In an essay about the dynamics involved in the recruitment of a Chinese scholar from mainland China in her faculty in a Northern American University, Rey Chow sharply analyses how academics respond to the presence of racialised ethnic minorities, who have for centuries been objects of study within the academy as academics. She notes that having invested whole lifetimes in constructing ideal types of these 'others' and their communities, their presence in the academy can be disturbing. Scholars may find that the frameworks they developed to make sense of these people no longer seem to fit. Thus as 'ethnics' enter the academy as something other than pure specimens, what 'confronts the Western scholar is the discomforting fact that the natives are no longer staying in their frames' (Chow, 1993:28).

For instance at present the entry of South Asian women, whether from the West or the Indian sub-continent, into different locales in Western academia has resulted in some disorientation among those who have studied them in factories, picket lines, youth clubs, women's refuges or in development projects. They find that these women are not quite as they had imagined. In lecture halls, canteens and staff meetings scholars, find that while these specimens can incite an unhealthy level of intrigue in times of global multiculturalism, they can also disappoint those who thought they knew them from textbooks and fieldwork even before they met them. There exists a fetish for difference or what Spivak (1988) called a 'multicultural hunger' in the academy, especially in the humanities and social sciences. Aiwa Ong (2001) observed that black women have become 'hot property' as text for research projects, publications and teaching materials. The enthusiasm for black women to join the academic ranks is accompanied by a guarded tolerance, an assimilative pressure to speak the accepted and legitimate language in both a theoretical and embodied sense. Those who fail to conform and defer to the authorities are considered too stubborn and radical because they refuse to play the game of trying to be 'one of us' through the silent manoeuvres of social cloning.

Social cloning

Spivak (1988) noted that there exists a kind of 'benevolent imperialism' which enables her to speak as an Indian woman today. She observed that 'A hundred years ago it was impossible for me to speak, for the precise reason that makes it only too possible for me to speak in certain circles now'. As mentioned earlier, the restrictions on women of colour within the academy speaking are most apparent when they go outside the remit of benevolent multiculturalism and write about mainstream subjects that occupy a central place in the academic canon. This becomes particularly problematic if they use unconventional idioms. Those who engage in the legitimate idioms of various disciplines are more likely to be embraced as 'one of us', as those 'who can speak our language" (Chambers, 1999: 26) – not just the dialects but also the theoretical paradigms. Spivak situates Terry Eagleton's much publicised critique of her book *Post-Colonial Reason* (1999) in his discomfort with the fact that the texts she engages with 'are not confined to Third World women and yet I don't write like Habermas in drag' (Spivak, 2001:21). She notes that her presence in the academy is troubling because:

> I am a woman and as it happens a woman of colour who does not remain confined to the modes of discourse that she is allowed to engage in – speaking about women and speaking about Third World women and speaking about our victimage. That's fine. If a person such as me de-anthropologises herself and reads the great texts of European tradition in a way that does not resemble the general rational expectations way of reading then she is punished. (*ibid*: 22)

The effort firstly to be more than an anthropological specimen of South Asian womanhood and secondly to open up existing rather unwieldy modes of engagement, highlights the guarded and even repressive tolerance in the desire for difference. It carries in the small print of assimilation a 'drive for sameness' (Maharaj, 1999: 6), especially on mainstream issues. Through these processes the kind of questions asked and the voices amenable to being heard within the regular channels of academia can become inhibited and stunted.

Patronage

The final process discussed concerns terms of inclusion in academia. Although academia takes pride in being an open space, patronage is implicit in how careers are made. To slightly extend Gramsci's commentary on the state and civil society, universities are supported by 'a powerful system of fortresses and earthworks'. The avenues to visibility and recognition within academia, like other professions, are underlined by networks, mentoring and small recommendations. Academia is not sustained by a neutral mechanical machinery of measurement. Rather networks, chains and cliques of human beings sustain the machinations. And while there are competing elements seeking to redefine the academic field, these struggles are conducted via networks and connections. Opportunities are made or broken within this context.

In practical terms, this means that publications, refereeing and perhaps most of all, given the current HE climate, research funding, are not made solely on the basis of individual talent. Collegiate support is intrinsic to the making of careers. So people who don't quite know how to play the game or obtain the endorsement of significant peers will fall by the wayside. Furthermore, those who don't share the language of the trauma of the death of a cat – of the normative style and perception – will be forever rambling in the landscape of academia, where the maps are so subtle that no course in orienteering will do away with latent racism. Why else is Du Bois, as noted by David Sibley in *Geographies of Exclusion* (1997), a marginal if not altogether ignored figure in urban geography? Robert Parks' powerful position in the making of urban geography and sociology in Chicago University enabled him to define the methodological and political terms of research on the black population and race relations. Du Bois study of race and the city, most famously published in *The Philadelphia Negro* was not granted the endorsement and patronage given by Park to other black academics. Both DuBois's methods, which were too interpretative and hermeneutic for a Chicago school eager to establish itself as a serious discipline by mimicking the natural sciences, conflicted with the assimilationist and apolitical slant preferred by Burgess and Park, 'who had the power to marginalise or block alternative perspectives' (1997:154). Thus when we think about how race impacts upon race relations in the academy, likeness or social cloning in comportment, manner, social connections, theoretical persuasions and politics is still important.

Collegiate support and patronage within departments and disciplines is vital for all academics – white, black, female, male, young and old – if they are to rise in the hierarchy. At the same time there is an institutional narrative, tied strongly to an identity of professionalism in which talent and jobs are rewarded according to meritocracy. More academics now study race as a subject, but naming race and racism as issues within their own ranks is not dealt with. Despite the recent legislation it remains taboo. In this context of denial, there is an aversion firstly in seeing racism and secondly in confronting colleagues and superiors. This means that one has to be prepared to interrogate and perhaps even break links with those one has formed working and 'chummy' relations. Those brave enough to speak of racism among their colleagues risk being labelled as un-professional, uncollegiate whistle blowers.

Acknowledgements

The ideas in this chapter are a development of Puwar and Raghuram (2003). They are given fuller attention in *Space Invaders: race, gender and bodies out of place* (2004).

Notes

1   There has been a productive and contentious discussion of the use of the category 'black'. I use the term to refer to people associated with the African and South Asian Diaspora (Hall, 1992; Brah, 1992; Mercer, 1994). I also use the term people of colour. These terms have a similar, socially constructed, instability and ambiguity attached to their usage, although they relate to different aspects of history (Butler, 1989, 1993).

2   Bourdieu's work easily lends itself to a nuanced appreciation of class and race together as they are manifested in institutions as well as daily encounters. In fact, elsewhere I have specifically sought a working relationship between Frantz Fanon and Bourdieu in order to comprehend the weight of the imperial/legitimate language, the former deriving from Fanon and the latter from Bourdieu (Puwar, 2003b).

3   Each field is *semi-autonomous*, characterised by its own agents, its accumulation of history, its own logic of action, and its own forms of *capital*. Fields are not fully autonomous. Capital is transferable. Each field is immersed in an *institutional field of power*. Each field is the site of struggle. There are struggles within given fields, and there are struggles over the *power to define a field*. Hence there is a struggle to define the criteria of measurement. There is a 'diversity of hierarchies' that struggle over the terms of classification (2003: 18).

4   Massey emphasises that space, like time, is never constant or static. Space is not dead but a living entity. Space and bodies work together to produce the social, rather than bodies simply acting in space.

References

Araeen, R. (1994), *Making Myself Visible*, London: Kala Press

Bourdieu, P. (1984) *Distinction: a social critique of the judgement of taste*, London: Routledge and Kegan Paul

Bourdieu, P. (1990) *In Other Words*, Oxford: Polity Press

Bourdieu, P. (2003 [first published 1988]) *Homo Academicus*, Oxford: Polity Press

Bourdieu, P and Wacquant, L (1992) *An Invitation to Reflexive Sociology*, Cambridge and Oxford: Polity Press/Blackwell Publishers

Brah, A. (1992) 'Difference, diversity and differentiation' in J. Donald and A. Rattansi (eds.) *'Race', Culture and Difference*, London: Open University/ Sage

Butler, J. (1989) *Gender Trouble: feminism and the subversion of identity*, London: Routledge

Butler, J. (1993) *Bodies that Matter: on the discursive limits of 'sex'*, London: Routledge

Carter, J, Fenton, S. and Modood, T. (1999), *Ethnicity and Employment in Higher Education*, London: Policy Studies Institute

Chambers, E. (1999), 'Eddie Chambers: Interview with Petrine Archer-Straw' in E. Chambers (ed) *Annotations* 5, London: International Institute of Visual Arts (INIVA)

Chow, R. (1993) *Writing Diaspora*, Bloomington and Indianapolis: Indiana University Press

Cresswell, T. (1996) *In Place/out of Place: Geography, Ideology, and Transgression*, Minnesota: University of Minnesota Press

Du Bois, W.E.B., (1967) *The Philadelphia Negro*, New York: Benjamin Bloom (first published 1899)

Dyer, R. (1997) *Whiteness*, London: Routledge

Fanon, F. (1986) *Black Skin, White Masks*, London: Pluto

Foucault, M. (1970) *Discipline and Punish: the Birth of the Prison*, London: Allen Lane

Frankenberg, R. (1997) *Displacing Whiteness: essays in social and cultural criticism*, Durham, NC: Duke University Press

Goldberg, D. (1997) *Racial Subjects: writing on race in America*, New York: Routledge

Grosz, E. (1995) *Space, Time and Perversion: Essays on the Politics of Bodies*, London: Routledge

Hall, S. (1992) 'New ethnicities' in J. Donald and A. Rattansi (eds.) *'Race,' Culture and Difference,* London: Open University/Sage

Hall, C. (1992) *White, Male and Middle-Class: explorations in feminism and history,* Oxford: Polity Press

hooks, b. (1992) *'Representations of Whiteness' Black Looks: Race and Representation,* Boston: South End Press

Kinsman, P. 1993 'Landscape, race and national non-identity: the photography of Ingrid Pollard. *Area,* 27, 300-10

Maharaj, S. (1999), 'Black Art's Autrebiography', in E. Chambers (ed.), *Annotations* 5, London: International Institute of Visual Arts (INIVA)

Malik, S. 1992 'Colours of the countryside – a whiter shade of pale' *Ecos,* 13, 33-9

Massey, D. (1994) *Space, Place and Gender,* Cambridge: Polity

Mercer, K. (1994) *Welcome to the Jungle: new positions in black cultural studies,* London: Routledge

McQueen, S. (2001), in conversation Kobena Mercer at the Institute of Contemporary Arts (ICA), London

Mills, C. (1997) *The Racial Contract,* Ithaca: Cornell University Press

Ong, A. (2001) 'Colonialism and Modernity: Feminist Re-Presentations of Women in Non-Western Societies', in Bhavnani (ed.), *Feminism and Race,* Oxford: Oxford University Press

Pollard, I. (1993) Another View *Feminist Review,* 45, pp. 46-50

Puwar, N. and Raghuram, (2003) (eds.) *South Asian Women in the Diaspora,* Oxford: Berg

Puwar, N. (2004) *Space Invaders: race, gender and bodies out of place,* Oxford: Berg

Sibley, D. (1997) *Geographies of Exclusion,* London: Routledge (first published 1995)

Simmonds, F. (1997) 'My body, myself: How does a Black woman do sociology?' in H. Mirza *Black British Feminism,* London: Routledge

Spivak, G. S. (1988) *In Other Words: Essays in Cultural Politics,* London: Routledge

Spivak, G. S. (1999) *A Critique of Postcolonial Reason,* Cambridge MA: Harvard University Press

Spivak, G. S. (2001) 'Mapping the Present: Interview with Gayatri Spivak', by M. Yegenoglu and M. Mutman, *New Formations,* 45: 9-23

Ware, V. (1992) *Beyond the Pale,* London: Verso

Williams, P. (1997) Reith Lecture. BBC Radio 4

Women and Geography Study Group (1997) *Feminist Geographies: explorations in diversity and difference,* Harlow: Longman

Young, L. and Pollard, I. (1995) 'Environmental Images and Imaginary Landscapes', *Soundings,* Issue 1, London: Lawrence and Wishart

CHAPTER SEVEN

Unveiling South Asian Female Identities post September 11
Asian female students' sense of identity and experiences of higher education

Shirin Housee

Introduction

Shifting identities are a response to external political, social and global changes, but also responses to the internal dynamics of the self that are in constant play. This chapter raises these pertinent issues of student positionalities at university, exploring particularly students' racialised and gendered identities. It illustrates how South Asian female students are continually negotiating and renegotiating their identities. The key objective is to assess whether the *space* and *place* at university allows for the articulation and free expression of differences and identities. South Asian female students' experiences and perceptions at the University of Wolverhampton are used to explore:

- cultural and religious specific experiences and expressions of identity articulated in the University of Wolverhampton

- the impact of September 11 on the experience of cultural and religious identities

I began this research in the summer of 2001, just before the end of the academic year, having interviewed only two students. I returned in September to this research but found that September 11 had taken over in many ways, and my questions and answers to them became far sharper than I had expected. The visibility of Muslims as a group has increased since the recent Gulf War, 9/11 and the War on Terror. Bin Laden and Saddam Hussain have become the favourite bogey men of the media and such negative media coverage can precipitate Islamic reassertion of identity (Modood, 1997). I wanted to explore whether the events of 9/11 had affected students' identities. September 11 seemed to have a range of significance among the Muslim students.

Discussions around identity have become critical for many of them. Those who chose to practise their faith were confident of doing so, and 9/11 had made them more assertive. Those who were not practising Muslims were defensive about Islam and weary of the racist backlash. It was evident that Islam was a source of strength, the driving force for their academic assertiveness and feminism. Non-Muslim Asian female students read 9/11 as a 'Muslim thing'. It was recognised that the racists were wrong to be Islamophobic, but there was also concern that Muslims were letting the Asian side down, suggesting that they should keep a low profile until the racism subsided.

This chapter offers personal accounts in the form of reflective narratives from South Asian female students at Wolverhampton. Notions of agency expressed are characteristic of the ongoing complex assessments made by these women in relation to perceived familial restrictions, religious obligations and their own aspirations. This research indicates that the students interviewed continually negotiated and renegotiated their cultural, religious and personal identities and that these processes operate in complex and sometimes contradictory ways. It was clear that gender, race, ethnicity, sexuality, class and religion do intersect and interact with internal dimensions of the self. And my presence as an Asian lecturer also has an impact on the students.[1]

Background

The University of Wolverhampton is one of the highest recruiters of people from disadvantaged backgrounds and has a strong record in recruiting women and ethnic minority students. Ethnic minority students make up almost 30% of the undergraduate population (see www.wlv.ac.uk/insight/committee – 2002). Most of our ethnic minority students are from modest working class backgrounds in the West Midlands. In my fourteen years of teaching here I have witnessed a shift in the students' representations of their cultural and religious identities. For example, when I first began teaching, I remember being comfortable with Black being used as an inclusive term for all non-whites, but later it became inappropriate. Students from both African Caribbean and Asian backgrounds wanted me to be more specific and separate Asian from Black. Asian was preferred to describe those from the Asian subcontinent and Black the reference for Caribbean and African origin students (see Housee, 2001).

Particularly since 9/11 I have noticed a further fragmentation of student identity: Asian students prefer to describe themselves by their religious background rather than as Asian. Practising Muslim women students wear the hijab and not just salwar khameez and chuni[2]. These shifts in identity representations are interesting and inform the theoretical thinking underpinning this research.

Theorising Asianness – Asian women's experiences

Asian women's experiences are barely mentioned in early British sociology literature. They were invisible or marginalised within the race, gender and class framework. The first discussion, appeared in the 1970s ethnicity school literature, presenting these experiences in exclusively ethnic and cultural terms and often through a cultural pathological framework (Khan, 1979, Watson, 1976). According to this perspective, problems faced by young Asian women stem from their familial and cultural backgrounds, and the assumption is that their background was somehow inferior and backward compared to modern western or British culture. Asian women were stereotyped as shy, passive and victims of their overly strict patriarchal families (Parmar, 1988).

In much of this literature, young Asian women's experiences were presented without reference to social or historical frameworks. Instead these essentialist accounts of Asian cultures supported static representations of homogeneous Asian communities incapable of change.

In the 1980s Asian feminist sociologists and others began to critique some of this work. They challenged the negative imagery of young Asian women by situating their accounts within a wider social and historical framework (Parmar, 1988; Brah and Minhas, 1985). This work challenged the ahistorical and essentialist accounts of the ethnicity school but its focus on positive Asian identity meant that divisions and internal struggles were over-looked and not explored. In the 1990s literature in the field focused mainly on subgroups exploring the specificity of experience, for example, Sikhs (Bhachu, 1991 and Dury, 1991) and Muslims (Basit, 1997a, 1997b). Because of the focus on specific subgroups the analysis did not explore the commonalities and divisions existing within and across Asian women.

What is needed is research that examines commonalities and differences between Asian women's experiences. There has been little research on diversity between and within ethnic groups. Qualitative research that explores the actual experience of higher educa-tion are rare. This chapter is written in the spirit of broader research that accommodates the shifting cultural terrain in British universities where social localities of race, gender, ethnicity, age and sexual orientation are of growing importance in a student's experience.

My study on black women's experience in higher education (Housee, 2001) showed clearly that student perceptions of their identities were articulated in complex, not linear, ways and were always in a state of flux. In looking for commonalities I discovered the extent to which students were experiencing and articulating specific cultural, religious and national differences. It was apparent that black and Asian women's experiences at Wolverhampton University were diverse and in some cases contradictory and warranted further research. This chapter addresses these issues by interviewing Asian women more systematically.

Retheorising Asian women's experiences

Identities within universities are constructed in conditions where white, middle class cul-tures are represented as universal and the norm. Working class experience is margina-lised and particular masculinities have cultural weight. In this context, our identities as Asian and Black female lecturers and students are racialised and gendered in a way that sometimes presents us as passive and powerless while at other times our differences are privileged (Rassool, 1999). By showing how students perceive their identities from inside I begin to interrogate those sometimes inaccurate assumptions. This chapter tells *their* stories of these Asian women's experience at the University.

I have tried to develop an analytical framework that captures the complex reality of the lived experiences of young Asian women with reference to the intersections of their experience in educational institutions and constructions of this. Race, gender, religious, class and age divisions cannot be mechanically added or reduced to one category or another – they must be seen as interrelated in a complex fashion, that analyses the 'structure, culture and agency' (Brah, 1996). Only by taking into account these interconnecting structures can we properly analyse Asian women's experiences in education. Identities are not fixed or static but relational, complex, differentiated and constantly repositioned. Our definitions or representations of our identities are always specific to a time, place and context that we speak from (Hall, 1992).

Identities are also historically specific: social relations in capitalist patriarchal societies such as Britain are set against the background of colonialism and imperialism (Brah and Minhas, 1985). The class locations of the families of Asian women cannot be understood without reference to this global, social, economic and historical context. Thus Asian women, like other people, are located in economic contexts that are historically shaped. Their experiences are always in-between or connected to the 'over here' and 'over there.'

In the cultural sphere too there are complexities. The racialisation of religion has been prominent, particularly since the demise of Communism and its replacement by Islam as the new threat to the Western world order. In Britain this threat has been symbolised by the Rushdie affair, the War on Terror (ists), and the recent second Gulf War (2003), which has contributed to the contradictory images of Muslim peoples. Thus Asians are seen as traditionally religious and respectable folks on the one hand, and on the other as posing a terrorist threat to civil society.

Only against this social, global and historical background can the responses of South Asian women to education and other social institutions be analysed. Assumptions that Asian women are constrained by cultural requirements do not take into account that many are active in resisting and crossing cultural boundaries or in accommodating or embracing different cultural experiences. Some Asian women are constrained by their specific gender relations within their families but others are not. Gendered relations within Asian families are as diverse and complex as in white English families. Other axes of difference, for example class position, religion, language, caste, ethnicity, and so on also affect their gendered experiences. Asian women students, like other categories of students, may define their experience of university in very different ways. Most importantly Asian women, like others, are active agents who act out and respond to the context that they find themselves in and are not simply recipients of those cultural definitions.

As Shain puts it:

> I want to argue that people are not determined by the social conditions they find themselves in. Instead there is space to resist and challenge dominant cultural definitions within the sphere of civil society. The cultural spaces inhabited by Asian young women are not static but are historically variable, and Asian women can play an active part in either confirming or transforming them... Asian young women are able to confirm or transform the cultural spaces they inhabit, including those of education. (Shain, 2000:161)

The study

The Asian female students chosen for the study were drawn from my second and third level race modules. These modules recruit almost 50% ethnic minorities so are multicultural. Student evaluation has been positive and suggests that the modules provide an environment that gives many students the confidence to speak out in class. Students were generally very assertive in class and contribute to seminar discussion.

My findings are drawn from one to one interviews conducted with seven South Asian women: three Muslim, three Sikh and one Hindu, all aged 20-30 and all from modest working class families. Four were born in Britain of parents who migrated here in the 1960s and three had one or both parents who were born here. Two of the students lived away from home and the rest with their families. All were full-time students, although all had some jobs during their degree, at weekends and in vacation periods.

The semi-structured interviews lasted approximately one hour. I was keen to explore family issues, educational aspirations, personal development, and religious/cultural differences and identities. The accounts here do not reflect or represent a wider Asian community but express the diversity of experiences only amongst South Asian female students from the University of Wolverhampton. Students have a voice – so let's listen. Feminist theory was among the first to suggest the metaphor of 'voice' as a means of promoting the female perspective. Having a voice means students being allowed to speak for themselves to locate their often marginal culture in relation to core experiences. The study presents a way of bringing the margins to the centre of sociological analysis in the form of South Asian women's experiences.

Identities as they see it

Although I did not probe the question of religion and identity too closely at first, it was evident from the outset that students were marking religion as an important signifier of their identity. One told me

> My most dominant identity is Muslim, Islam comes first and Asian second. I choose to wear a *hijab*, living away from home led to many questions being asked by my community. e.g. is she abusing her freedoms? (at university) is she becoming a bad girl? In response to this I began to reassure my parents and myself by choosing to read the Quran and dress more obviously Muslim. (Muslim student A)

Religion also plays a part in the way this Sikh student expresses her identity:

> Religion is important to me hence choosing a husband from Sikh background means a lot to me.
>
> Why?
>
> Because when I have kids I want to give them a religious identity, my roots/my history is important to me (Sikh student A)

Religion gave some students personal strength:

> Islam is my source of strength. When I first started covering up I was scared to go out. I would never go into McDonalds on my own, I would send a friend that did not wear a *hijab*, my sister said to me, you have chosen to wear a *hijab*; you have to be proud and fearless.

> One day she forced me to go into a McDonalds and yes people did stare. Now, I go in myself and the staring does not bother me. (Muslim student A)

Religion is important also to the following students, but more interesting is the way in which other signifiers such as class, nationality and traditional practices also play a role in their identity formation.

> I come from a typically traditional working class Asian family. I am the only one to have gone to uni. As a child I was defiant, determined, and spoke my mind. I have been very assertive about not wanting an arrange marriage, this is nothing to do with rejecting my community or my religion, I am proud of being Muslim and Pakistani. I simply want to branch away and do things for myself (Muslim student B)

> Knowing about my religion has informed my identity, I now know, that being a Muslim adds to the differences articulated by race, nationality, class and other social differences.... I would (also) say that I am British – this is home. (Muslim student A)

> I define myself as British Asian, whilst I know that my parents see me as just Asian..

> I feel that I have similar experiences to a lot of English, and I could define myself as a western girl. I dress mainly western clothes, and only for weddings will I dress in Asian suits. I am Sikh and proud of it, but I am also British Asian... I like to fit in with the wider (British) community, but, I also like to feel part of my culture, know my roots.... (Sikh student A)

> My identity is informed by my religion, and my national (Indian) background... I still remember who I am, where I am from, (but) I still got my own British identity. (Hindu student A)

I was interested to hear that September 11 had led some students to reflect on their identity. One student said

> Sept 11 has really opened my eyes. As a child I thought I was British... Recently, I overheard a conversation about the recent attacks on the twin towers, and how the Quran encourages such violence. I was furious and stood up and challenged their ignorance, ...This incident made me feel that I am different and a target for racists. (Muslim student B)

Shifting and changing identities

Most of the seven students interviewed made reference to the way their identities had shifted while they were at university. Interestingly, these shifts were not in a single direction. For some students the university experience was about embracing diversity and difference from other cultures, in other words articulating a cultural experience that is more hybrid.

> Before uni I identified more readily with my Pakistani origin, my Muslim religion, I was attached to my culture, I had a very Pakistani way of thinking. Before uni I only had Pakistani friends. Since, university I have had the opportunity to meet people from the different communities, and cultures, and my thinking has changed. (Muslim student B)

One student reported that university has made her question her Sikh identity.

> Uni has made me more open minded, as an Asian kid you're brought up quite prejudiced, racist, into your own community. My parents were into caste, and against mixed relationships of any type, white, blacks and other religious groups. I no longer have a strong Asian Sikh identity. (Sikh student B)

For others, however, cultural and religious identities had to be held on to tightly for fear of loosing one's roots.

> As I get older my identity becomes more important to me. I do want to marry from my own background... It is about not loosing ones roots, I use to think that when I get older I want to marry anyone, but the opposite has happened, I have become more traditional, I want to choose someone from my own background. (Sikh student A)

One student in the sample was concerned about the segregation on campus. She believed that when expressed in communal ways, religion and cultural differences could at best lead to separatism and at worst to conflict and racism. For her, sticking to one's religious identity was seen as rejecting cultural diversity:

> I don't like the cultural divide that exists on campus, we hear students say,' Sikhs are like this, they go off with Muslim girls, and Muslim boys use Sikh girl, and whites are like this and that. I hate this divisiveness. (Sikh student B)

She saw integration as assimilation and breaking from one's own cultural and religious roots.

> I want to see more integration. I am not like a lot of the other Asian girls, I don't believe in traditional practices such as arranged marriages. I would marry anyone I fell in love with no matter what the community says. (Sikh student B)

Family issues and going to university

Modood (1998) suggested that 'high ethnic participation rates in HE are a reflection of the value ethnic minorities place in academic qualifications and their high aspirations'. It has been assumed that Asian students' participation at University is due to family support and self-motivation. I was interested to examine whether this was the case and whether students from the three differing religions shared this experience. One student said

> I have had a lot of support from my parents, they're safe, and they have encouraged me and want me to do well. (Hindu Student)

Another said

> My mum supported me going to uni ...A degree was about giving me confidence. I want to be a teacher when I graduate, because it is important that children see me as a role model for Muslim children, I want to send out the message that Muslim women can be assertive, confident professionals. (Muslim Student A)

Intriguingly, aside from these two, most of the students across the three religions had to struggle with their parents to be allowed to study at university. For two of the Muslim students, Islam was not only a spiritual expression, but became a source of strength that gave them courage to struggle for their educational rights.

> It was Islam that brought me here, I struggled at home to come to uni, my parents argued against it. I began to read the English translation of the Quran. I soon realised that education was a god given right, and encouraged in Islam. I argued with my parents and defiantly left to go to university. Religion gave me the courage to fight for my educational rights. (Muslim student B)

For this student and another Muslim student, Islam had provided legitimacy to study at university.

> The Quran made me realise that as a Muslim I have rights, ...indeed, Islam encourages education. (Muslim student A)

The lack of support from home for another Muslim student was largely about the fear lest their daughter become anglicised or westernised and like the white students.

> My family was unhappy about me going to uni. The fear of clubbing, drinking, boyfriends etc. I was a disappointment to them, as the others (in my family) had arranged marriages, they basically followed mum and dad's plan. (Muslim student C)

The students I interviewed had not all received support from their parents; most of the women indicated that going to university entailed a struggle within the family. Some of this struggle was on religious and cultural lines, but one student spoke about her family's thoughts about the irrelevance of HE, much like the educating Rita scenario. Her working class background was the obstacle – her parents did not value education and thought that it was a waste of time.

> There's been a shift at home. Five years ago my parents did not want me to go on to university, and I left school and got a job, they wanted me to get married. But I fought back and returned as a mature student, and now my mum and dad have said that I don't have to get married and they now support the idea of me going on to do a masters and sort out my career. (Sikh student A)

What has changed?

> My dad has said to me, you have what we never had, an education, it all boils down to education. They can see that those with education can have an easier life. My mum has worked in textile factories all her life, and my dad in factories, they know that with an education I can live more comfortably. They want this for me. (Sikh student A)

However, she had to accept certain compromises and follow some family traditions.

> Education is important, but my freedom and choices are not unlimited. I have to marry one day, and I have to marry a Sikh from my own caste. (Sikh student A)

Personal development

For all the students I interviewed education was about more than achieving qualifications. It was about their personal development, about becoming independent, assertive, confident, learning about different cultures, mixing with different communities, and about being a more worldly person.

> Uni has made me more confident, and more independent. I am no longer bothered by the smears and comments made against my dress wear [hijab]. I feel a cut above these people now; I would simply smile at them. (Muslim student A)

> Uni life is so different, it is a learning experience in itself that should come to all of us. Uni has matured me, it has made me independent, I can support myself financially economically and emotionally. I have become a survivor. (Muslim student C)

> I came here to get a degree and I think I have gained a lot more than education. I have become more confident, being able to speak out, I have gained personal and social confidence, which has allowed me to mix with people from different communities.

> Education is very important for Asians and blacks, because we want to make something of ourselves. (Hindu student)

University education was more than classroom teaching and discussions:

> University has informed my thinking. I have learnt lots in terms of knowledge and social development, but for me the informal structures, where the real conversations between students take place, have also been very important for me. (Sikh student C)

Student voices – the case on Islamophobia

Where the personal and the political are inseparable, how should debates concerning the nature of racism be incorporated into academic study? It is important to provide a space for black students' own views. As lecturers, black and white, we enter the student arena knowing that any discussion around race and racism can be at great personal and emotional cost.

Teaching about racism is often about managing the tension between students. Like a referee, I sometimes mediate between students. This is not always easy, and I am aware that it is often not what is being said that needs to be checked but the silences. There follow examples from a seminar discussion on Islamophobia in the media. The students were asked whether there had been a rise in anti-Muslim sentiments and attacks following 9/11.

One Muslim student shared the fact that racist attacks against Muslims were on the rise, but that she felt that non-Muslims did not believe this to be the case,

> Recently I was in conversation with a Sikh friend of mine and he was saying that racism is not as bad as before. I could not believe this and said that since 9/11 there has been an unprecedented rise in attacks on Muslims... (recently) these white guys came towards my friend and asked if he was Muslim... and beat him to a pulp... Muslims are being blamed for what a few people have done. Racism and racists will attack anyone that is the flavour of the month; at present Muslims are the scapegoats.

Another Muslim student reported on her experience of racism:

> I was on a train on the way to university, this journey I have been doing for three years now. There was a little girl who kept smiling at me. I returned the smile, the girl then began to approach me to sit next to me. Her mother (white) pulled her away. At first, I gave her the benefit of doubt and I thought well she is obviously wary of strangers. I then heard her say to her daughter 'you don't sit next to people like that'. 'Like that' meant for me – Muslim people [she wears a hijab] did she think I was carrying a gun or something.

This example was shared in class and the class were outraged. The Muslim students thought that there was a rise in racism against Muslims. Interestingly, the reactions of some of the non-Muslims varied. One African Caribbean student seemed annoyed by the Muslim student's reaction to the debate, commenting that it was not only Muslims that were suffering from racism. She asserted that other minorities also suffer from racism, and that anti-Muslim racism should not be made a special case. A Hindu student said angrily 'but what do you expect being dressed like that and singling yourself out from other Asians?', I intervened and asked the student to explain herself. She replied, ' Given that we are living in dangerous times should she not blend in and be more discreet?' One Muslim student told the group that racism is not her problem and that she should have the right to dress as she pleased. She assured us that her fear of reprisal was not going to deter her. 'I have been in fear in the past – I am not going to hide my identity now' [she is the student that was afraid to wear the hijab in public]. The white students refrained from comments during this debate, but one said to me in the corridor, 'I could not believe that third year students could come out with such reactionary politics, I expected more from students on this module.'

It is interesting that she was unable to say this in class. Some students believe that the subject of race and racism can be too sensitive to discuss in an open forum such as the classroom. So discussions about racism may begin in the classroom but continue outside in the corridors, bars and canteens.

Commonalities and divisions – which way forward?

This experience made me think about issues of commonality and divisions. Given the tensions over the differences between Muslims and other religions, can we still talk about a commonality? Clearly the students showed loyalty to their own communities but I wanted to explore whether such differences allowed for alliances and unity that spoke against racism. One Muslim student indicated that the tensions across the different religious groups have led to divisions:

> I've noticed that since September 11 many of my Asian friends who are not Muslim have begun to disassociate themselves with the inclusive term Asian. They now define themselves as Hindu, and Sikh. I think the conflict and the disunity between Asians is a direct result of 9/11. (Muslim student B)

She went on

> The fragmentation of identities has made the targeting of minorities easier once nonwhites united against one banner – black. At least we looked united and we saw ourselves as Asian. Now our enemies are not only the anti-Muslim racists but also those [Asians/blacks] who wish to disassociate from us, making Muslims a more vulnerable group. (Muslim student B)

One student strongly blamed the racism on the moral panic encouraged by the media

> I blame the media, the news never portrays us in a positive light, the Muslim world and people. (Muslim student A)

Muslim students certainly felt under threat, alienated and rejected, but it was reassuring to hear that Asian commonalities did continue on other levels:

> I am glad that there are lots of Asians here. Although I have some white and black friends, my friends are mainly Asian. I believe we do have an affinity with Asians, we have common values within our cultures, we share similar languages, follow certain cultural practices etc. (Hindu student)

> Before Uni I did not have any Muslim friends. I realise how similar they are to Sikhs. Our family values are similar, e.g. support education, arrange marriages, succeed economically etc. (Sikh student A)

Another student said

> I have a wide range of friends – blacks, Sikhs, Muslims and whites. As Asians most of our references are the same e.g. family expectation. We integrate and relate to each other very easily. (Hindu student)

Feminism and resistance politics

Finally, one of the aims of this research was to question the stereotype of South Asian women as victims and recipients of oppressive patriarchal cultures. To assume that all Asian women are passive, as some of the literature suggests, overlooks the complexities discussed in this chapter. Asian women, like other women, come from varied class, cultural and religious backgrounds, all of which inform identity. Their feminism will be informed by their experiences. What was telling was the resistance of the women I interviewed. All were from working class backgrounds, and all seemed to have assertive, independent and confident personas. This I believe is much to do with their fighting back. The students I interviewed were not going to accept racism, sexism or any other -ism, as the way they argue shows:

> I certainly dispel the stereotype of passive Asian women, but I think Asian women have to be selfish about their needs and desires and fight for them. Changes will occur but they have to come from within. If we are unhappy about our lot we have to do something about it, otherwise we only have ourselves to blame. (Muslim student B)

Another student confirmed this:

> I think that Asian women are not passive, they are taking a stand... education and knowledge is very important and has given us the confidence to speak out, Asian girls are not under the thumb, they are given opportunities. They do not simply and passively accept arranged marriages and stay at home – we are a living example of this. (Hindu student)

The research demonstrates that Asian female students play an active role in the construction and reconstruction of their social and personal identities, within and despite patriarchal structures both in public – university – and private – home – domains. Their experience of higher education was not about a rejection of their religion and culture – in some cases, university made them more religiously inclined. Their agency in this is notable: Islam or Hinduism or Sikhism were not forced onto these students. They freely chose to become more or less religious. Some even needed religion as the vehicle in which to fight for education and personal rights. So agency was a process of negotiation and re-negotiation, through which social, cultural and religious identification were expressed and freedoms won. Their drive for education and qualifications is a testament to their determination and resilience.

Acknowledgements

I would like to thank the student participants in this research, without whom this chapter could not have been written.

Notes

1   The term Asian is applied to people who have, or whose parents or grandparents have, migrated from the Indian subcontinent to Britain. The term black is used in its political sense and therefore includes those of both African Caribbean and South Asian origin.

2   Shalwar khameez – loose trousers and tunic worn throughout the Punjab area in India and Pakistan. Chuni – long scarf draped over the head and shoulders worn with the shalwar khameez. Hijab refers to the veil, which prevents men from gazing at women. The respondents who favoured this form of head covering, did so, because they had adopted a more self-conscious Islamic identity.

References

Ahmad, F (2001) Modern Traditions? British Muslim Women and Academic Achievement in *Gender and Education*, 13, 2, pp137-152

Basit T (1997a) *Eastern Values, Western Milieu: Identities and aspirations of adolescent British Muslim girls*, Aldershot Ashgate

Basit T (1997b) I want more freedom but not too much, *Gender and Education*, 9,4, pp425-439

Bhachu, P (1991) Culture and ethnicity among Punjabi Sikh women in 1990s Britain, *New Community* 17, 3, pp401-412

Brah, A (1996) *Cartographies of Diaspora: Contesting identities*, London: Routledge

Brah, A and Minhas, R (1985) Structural racism or cultural difference in G Weiner (ed) *Just a bunch of girls,* Milton Keynes: Open University Press

Drury, R. M. (1991) Sikh girls and the maintenance of an ethnic culture, *New Community*, 17,3, pp387-399

Dyer C (1998) Contested Identities. Challenging dominant representations of young British Muslim Women in T. Shelton and G. Valentine (eds.) *Cool Places: Geographies of Youth Cultures* London: Routledge.

Hall S (1992) New Ethnicities in J Donald and A Rattansi (eds) *'Race', Culture and Difference*, London: Sage

Haw, H (1994) Muslim girls school: a conflict of interest? *Gender and Education*, 6,1, pp63-76

Housee, S (1990) Black Students in Higher Education, a survey of their experiences and expectations, *Journal of Access Studies*, Autumn

Housee, S (2001) Insiders or Outsiders? Black female voices in the academy; in J. Wlliams and P. Anderson (eds.) *Difference and Identity in Higher Education: Outsiders Within*, Aldershot: Ashgate

Khan, V S (1979) *Minority Families in Britain*, London: Macmillan

Parmar, P and Amos V (1981) Resistance and responses to the experience of black girls in Britain in A McRobbie and T McCabe (eds) *Feminism for Girls an Adventure Story* London. Routledge Kegan Paul

Modood T, *et al* (1997) *Debating Cultural Hybridity,* London: Zed Books.

Modood, T and Acland, T (eds.) (1998) *Race and Higher Education*, London: Policy Studies

Parmar, P (1988) Gender, race, and power, the challenge to youth work practise in P Cohen and H Bains (eds) *Multiracist Britain*, London: Macmillan

Parmar, P (1990) Black Feminism and the politics of articulations in J Rutherford (ed.) *Identity, Community, Culture, Difference*, London: Lawrence and Wishart

Rutherford J (ed) 1990) *Identity, Community, Culture, Difference.* London: Lawrence and Wishart

Rassool, N (1999) Flexible Identities: exploring race and gender issues among a group of immigrant pupils in an inner-city comprehensive school, *British Journal of Education*, 20, 1, pp23-36

Shain, F (2000) Cultural, Survival and Resistance: theorizing young Asian women's experiences and strategies in contemporary British schooling and society, *Discourse studies in the cultural politics of education*, 21, pp155-175

Watson J (ed) (1976) *Between Two Cultures: migrants and minorities in Britain,* Oxford, Blackwell

CHAPTER EIGHT

'It is possible to have an education and be a Traveller': Education, Higher Education and Gypsy/Travellers in Britain

Colin Clark

Introduction: setting the agenda

I believe that Gypsies reject education not because they are constantly moving around but because they are constantly faced with attitudes which deny them their culture whilst in the education system. (Lee, 2000: 23-25)

Education has not cancelled out my Traveller identity. It gives you more of a chance to be independent in life. Whatever happens in the future, you know you can survive. It is possible to have an education and be a Traveller. (Hedges, 1999: 15)

Ideas such as cultural diversity and celebrating difference are being heard on an increasingly regular basis across many forms of popular culture and media in Britain today. In a liberal country like Britain such positive expressions should not just be voiced and tolerated but also respected and celebrated. However, for many minority ethnic children in Britain there is little to celebrate when it comes to accessing an education that seems relevant to their needs and free of racism. Indeed, even in a pluralistic and multicultural environment, the very right to an education can be an issue, and this can apply to the group of ethnic minorities who tend to be collectively known as Gypsies and/or Travellers. Whether through blatant examples of individual racism or more subtle exclusionary forms of institutional racism, schools, colleges and universities are too often failing to help Gypsy and Traveller children learn new skills and acquire different bodies of knowledge that will allow them to prepare for the challenges of the 21st Century. Whilst it is true that the family and extended family has, and will always be, the primary learning environment for Gypsy and Traveller children, schools, colleges and universities have a part to play in nurturing talent and helping them fulfil their potential. The two quotes that began this chapter, both from female Gypsy students who are in higher education, alert us to the fact that much is at stake here. Factors such as nomadism, attitudes, culture, identity and independence all need to be addressed if Gypsies and Travellers are to participate in further and higher education in Britain, both as students and as teachers.

The limited empirical evidence available on issues of access, pupil/student experiences and achievement rates within HE are stark. The work in which I have been involved with Save the Children revealed that less than 20% of Gypsy and Traveller children of secondary school age in Scotland attend with any degree of regularity (Clark, 2001). This applies across Britain and is usually explained in terms of Gypsy/Traveller cultural difference and their family occupations and mobility. Other nomadic minority groups in Scotland such as Travelling Showpeople have similar experiences of secondary schooling (Jordan, 2000).

Much of the debate on the education of Gypsy and Traveller children is heavily contested and can be deeply divisive. Some educationalists insist on the centrality of formal education – at least until secondary age – within a school environment, whereas Gypsy and Traveller families offer several culturally coherent reasons for not entering children into the settled or *gaujo* (non-Gypsy) education system. Bullying and other social or moral concerns, such as boys and girls mixing freely, concerns regarding drugs and also sex education classes, are cited and the usefulness of what is taught in schools may be questioned. There is tension because the arguments generally rely on anecdotal evidence and uninformed impressions. For example, there is no substantial empirical research or evidence on how young Gypsy and Traveller adults experience the college or university environment in Britain. But low attendance at primary school and lower attendance still at secondary level restricts routes into further and higher education for an ethnic minority group that is almost universally feared and loathed. They are largely invisible in the sense of their exclusion from academic debates on ethnicity and racial studies and among government policy-makers (Morris, 1999). Though accurate numbers are a problem because there was no box for them to tick in the 2001 census, Gypsies and Travellers are roughly as numerous as the Chinese community in Britain – approximately 200,000-250,000 according to most informed estimates, or 0.4% of the total UK population (Kenrick and Clark, 1999; Morris and Clements, 2002). And unlike the gaujo community, it is a young and growing population – so these issues are pressing. Interestingly, whereas in the central and eastern parts of Europe the high birth-rates of the Romani population are seen as a social, economic and political threat to society (see Kohn, 1995) in Britain, perhaps due to Western concerns over the forthcoming demographic time-bomb and the looming pensions crisis, high rates of reproduction may be welcomed. Couples are seldom childless and it is not unusual for families to have five, six or more children (Hawes, 1997; Smart, Titterton and Clark, 2003).

In this chapter I draw upon some of the key findings of the Save the Children study and demonstrate that there is an urgent need for extending the boundaries of what we mean by cultural diversity to include the needs and experiences of Gypsy and Traveller children. If questions about access and academic attainment levels are to be adequately addressed, the experiences of racism and discrimination Gypsy and Traveller children face in every sector of the British education system need to be acknowledged and then tackled and monitored.

Gypsy/Travellers in Britain and Europe: a snapshot of a culture

The Gypsy and Traveller population of Britain clearly has much diversity within it; it is not a homogenous grouping although tthere are many commonalities. The main groups are, in their own languages, *Romanichals* (English Gypsies), *Kale* (Welsh Gypsies), *Minceir* (Irish Travellers), *Nachins* (Scottish Travellers), New Travellers, and Romanies who have come from various parts of Central and Eastern Europe and groups such as Travelling Showpeople and Circus people. Within that 200,000-250,000 population figure it would be a conservative assumption that around 60,000-70,000 are under the age of 18. In Ireland, where there was an appropriate category in the recent Census, nearly 24,000 Travellers were enumerated (Central Statistics Agency, 2003).

Other reports and sources that might be expected to mention the Gypsy and Traveller population's experiences have generally failed to do so – such as the influential Policy Studies Institute's research on Britain's ethnic minority populations. Even in the 1997 study (Modood *et al*), Gypsies and other Travellers are not mentioned. Without accurate quantitative and qualitative information, it will be a struggle to implement innovative policy.

The legal situation also has implications for access to education. In the eyes of the law, English Gypsies (as of 1989, *CRE vs Dutton*) and Irish Travellers living in England (as of 2000, *O'Leary and others vs Punch Retail and others*) are protected under the Race Relations Act 1976 from racial discrimination. These are significant legal rulings and should offer the communities concerned some protection, but this is not always the case and examples still abound of anti-Gypsy prejudice and discrimination, whether in the education system or in other public services (Discrimination Law Association, 2002). In Scotland the status of Gypsy-Traveller ethnicity is still undecided in a court of law although the Scottish Executive have stated that until such a case comes forward the community should be regarded as a minority ethnic group under the terms of the Race Relations Act, 1976 as amended in 2000 (McKinney, 2003).

If a family wants their children to attend school and perhaps go on to college or University, one important thing they need is secure accommodation, at least during term-time. As of January 2002 there were 325 local authority Gypsy sites in England providing pitches for some 5,005 caravans. But, even according to the government's own figures, this local authority network provides accommodation for fewer than 50% of the total number of Gypsy caravans in England (ODPM, 2003). The situation in Wales, and particularly Scotland and Northern Ireland, is quite different (see Kenrick and Clark, 1999 for more detail). However, across the UK the shortfall in local authority site provision and pitches has meant that private site developments that are on the increase – if families have the money to buy land and the time and money to obtain planning permission. This can be costly and problematic as suitable land is often in the green belt. One common statistic quoted illustrates the scenario vividly – the success rate for planning applications overall, including those made by Gypsies and Travellers, is around 80% whereas for Gypsy and Traveller site plans alone it is a mere 10% (Morris, 1998: 3). As a result of local authority shortages and private site planning difficulties, roadside sites such as lay-bys, quarries, industrial estates and the like are still used today by at least 3,000 – 3,500 people at any time who have no legal place to stop (Kenrick and Clark, 1999: 183).

Government legislation and tougher policies on the policing and eviction of unauthorised sites have made things much harder. In particular, the Criminal Justice and Public Order Act 1994 (CJPOA) was very damaging and continues to cause many Gypsy and Traveller families severe accommodation problems (Bucke and James, 1998). Not only did this Act tear up the hard won Caravan Sites Act of 1968, which placed a legal duty on local authorities to provide sites, it also transformed trespass from a civil into a criminal act carrying severe penalties (Card and Ward, 1994). The Act effectively criminalised a nomadic way of life, regardless of whether it had an 'economic purpose' as one case suggested (*R vs South Hams DC ex p Gibb [1993] 26 HLR*). The CJPOA did not affect only Gypsy and Traveller accommodation options and patterns of travel, it had a number of unintended consequences in different areas. As Police officers became more familiar with the CJPOA, the police, local authorities and other agencies would be trying to get the family moved on, if they were illegally camped, while the Traveller Education Services were trying to get Gypsy children into schools. Thus the children's education was disrupted. In the words of Cathy Kiddle:

> The CJA [Criminal Justice and Public Order Act, 1994] demonstrated a clear will to force people off the road into settled accommodation denying the right to a nomadic habit of life... For the families with no legal place to be the options are few and bleak. Trying to get a school based education with any kind of continuity for children in these circumstances is difficult indeed. For some, who experience a series of swift evictions right across the country there is scant chance for school access at all. (Kiddle, 1999: 59-60)

A recent study by a team of researchers at Cardiff Law School noted the disruption and financial consequences of repeat evictions and the impact this has on learning and employment opportunities:

> Travelling people have told the TLRU [Traveller Law Research Unit] about having to drop out of evening classes or college courses, and being forced to relinquish good jobs; being unable to reach them any longer following an eviction cycle which forced them to ever greater distances. (Morris and Clements, 2002: 53-54)

They point to the 1999 European Commission report on the case of *Sally Chapman v UK*. To avoid facing court action over alleged planning irregularities with respect to land they owned and lived on, the family had to return to a nomadic way of life that led to a cycle of evictions from one local authority to another:

> The applicant's eldest daughter had started a hairdressing course at a College of Further Education and the second daughter was about to start studying at college for a Diploma in Forestry. Both of these courses had to be abandoned and the two younger children could no longer attend school. (European Commission, 25-10-99, quoted in Morris and Clements, 2002: 54)

A brief overview of history and trends in Gypsy education in Britain

The last two decades have seen some efforts to improve experience of formal educational provision for Gypsies and Travellers. On a practical level, England and Wales, have specialist teams called Traveller Education Services (TES) whose remit it is to offer support to pupils from Gypsy and Traveller families. At formal policy level the Office for Standards in Education (Ofsted), the HM Inspectorate of schools and LEAs in England and Wales, identified 'Gypsy/Traveller pupils as the group most at risk in the education system today' (Ofsted, 1999: para.8). Likewise, the Parekh Report on *The Future of Multi-Ethnic Britain* (2000: 146) noted the 'generally low [educational] attainment' of Gypsy and Traveller children as being 'a matter of serious concern'. Such concerns are not new. As far back as 1967, for example, the Plowden Report stated that Gypsies and Travellers are 'probably the most deprived group in the country' due to cultural restraints within Traveller communities as well as bullying and 'negative attitudes' towards children when in school. At the time of the report it estimated less than 10% of school-age children were attending regularly. The Swann report went even further:

> The situation of Travellers' children in Britain today throws into stark relief many of the factors which influence the education of children from other ethnic minority groups – racism and discrimination, myths, stereotyping and misinformation, the inappropriateness and inflexibility of the education system and the need for better links between homes and schools and teachers and parents. (Department of Education and Science, 1985: para. 26)

By the mid-1990s, Ofsted was reporting that attendance levels at primary school age were up to 80%, that old attitudes were starting to shift and relationships between homes and schools were beginning to improve (Ofsted, 1996). But certain factors needed attention, such as school exclusions, high levels of non-registration at secondary level and, consequently the low number of those going on to further and higher education. Seven years on these are still the main issues on the agenda.

The few words we have on record from Gypsy and Traveller pupils who have gone through the system best explain why so few choose to attend school past 12 or 13 years of age and why parents may be reluctant to send their children to secondary school:

> The secondary school I went to was a nightmare, and our education was just about survival. We did not have the time to read and write because we were being spat upon, bullied and generally abused by the pupils and the majority of teachers. (MK, Adult Male Gypsy, Scottish Gypsy-Traveller Association, Equality Opportunities Committee hearings: Oral evidence given to the Scottish Parliament in May 2000)

> You leave school at the age of 11 or 12 or at the time of your first confirmation, whichever comes first. Then you are expected to act like a man.... You would be mocked by the others [young Travellers] for wearing a school bag after the age of 14. It makes it very hard to go on at the schooling. It is very discouraging. (Irish Traveller, boy, quoted in Donahue and McVeigh, 2001: 4)

In 2000 a DfEE funded study in London examined good practice entailed when working with Gypsy and Traveller pupils (Bhopal *et al*, 2000). It described how six schools in England and had taken successful steps to improve attendance and achievement rates of Gypsy and Traveller pupils. Certain factors were found to be crucial: the role of Traveller

Education Services, strong leadership and effective school policies on race equality and bullying, good working relationships between schools and parents and the need for flexibility and a culturally relevant curriculum. The recommendations are a model for schools with Gypsy and Traveller pupils. The research was important in recognising the need for resources and investment to fund inclusionary practices and support head-teachers who promote good practice for pupils from Gypsy and Traveller background. The case studies demonstrated that with hard work, leadership, dialogue and money, educational provision for Gypsy and Traveller children could improve.

There has also been progress on counting numbers. In 2003 the DfES statement(2003a, Table 3) on pupil characteristics and class sizes reported that, as of January 2003, there were some 7,000 pupils from Gypsy and Traveller backgrounds in primary schools in England and 2,800 in secondary schools. However, as the DfES acknowledges, there are around 42,000 school-age Gypsy and Traveller children in England (DfES, 2003b). With regard to achievement, Ofsted (1999) has shown that Gypsy and Traveller children have the lowest results overall of any minority ethnic group and are at risk in the education system. A recent document from the DfES (2003c) has promised that data on Gypsy and Traveller achievement will be collected as part of the 2003 Pupil Level Annual Schools Census so that their needs can be considered alongside those of other minority ethnic pupils. But the main issue for Ofsted today is the refusal of some schools still to even admit Gypsy and Traveller children, or imposing discriminatory conditions on admission or delaying the registration procedure. Bhopal (2000) identifies this as a major hurdle: an admissions policy that is open and accessible to Gypsies and Travellers is essential to good attendance and working relationships between parents and teachers. Little will change until this fundamental equality issue is addressed.

Denied a future? the Save the Children report and European perspectives

Interviewer: If you were Minister of Education for a day what changes [to the education system] would you make to promote education for Roma?

Roma student: I would prefer to be Minister of Finance and allocate money to implement it effectively.

This insightful answer from one of the tiny minority of Romani University students in central Europe illustrates one dimension of the key findings from the Save the Children report *Denied a future?* Changes in educational systems are ruled by their budgets (SCF, 2001). The report examines the current situation of Roma/Gypsy and Traveller education across a range of European countries including the UK. The findings from fourteen countries make grim reading. Amongst the repeated reports of poor access and provision, exclusion, lack of legal redress, poverty and racial discrimination were the voices of children who were trying to learn. 'School is good for the future, we can achieve something', said one 12 year old Romani girl. A 16 year old Romani boy expressess the difficulty of trying to take up education in a society in the grips of economic transition: 'I would like to continue, but my parents don't have enough money for the books and everything else I need' (Andruszkiewicz, 2001).

The principle aim of the Save the Children report is to make available a text which for the first time critically questions the legislation, policy and practice of the type of education being offered to Romani children – one of Europe's largest, most impoverished and discriminated against ethnic minority groups. The continental population of Roma/Gypsy and Travellers is estimated at some 7 to 9 million people with more than half thought to be under the age of 18 (Barany, 2002). It is a young and growing population that will not just go away. The report is based on a rights model: one that fuses minority, human and child rights to create a holistic approach to investigating issues relating to education. Although not entirely unproblematic, this model can deal with the wider social and political context of the democratisation and economic restructuring process across Europe and how it impacts on specific issues for specific groups – principally Roma/Gypsy and Travellers' right to education.

The problems with this framework are that it allows for contradictions and tensions. For example, Brian Barry has argued in the *New Left Review* that the law on attendance for nomadic Gypsy/Traveller children (50% the attendance of settled children in a school year) is 'an ill-conceived example of deference to minority cultures'. He acknowledges that 'children belonging to cultural minorities should be able to enjoy their own culture' but asks 'but must this culture be frozen in time forever? That convention [the Convention on the Rights of the Child] and other UN documents also contain 'the unequivocally expressed right of all children to education', and I would argue that parents should not be able to deny them such a right' (Barry, 2001: 71). Jane G. Lee, a Gypsy woman currently studying for a Ph.D. at the University of Durham, goes some way to explaining the situation for many Gypsy and Traveller students and pupils:

> So we may well ask why offer education to Gypsies at all? It might be 'equal' to do so, but are there any benefits to the education of Gypsies? After all, education prepares an individual for their life as an employee, *but what is the use of teaching children the skills they will never use as adults?* Although the majority of Gypsies would agree with the education authorities that it is beneficial for a basic level of education to be acquired, I believe they consider that there is a price to be paid (assimilation) and so opt out [at secondary level]. (my emphasis). (Lee, 2000: 23)

Thus the rights of Gypsy/Traveller parents to operate as commercial nomads are presented as conflicting with the rights of the child to a stable and full-time education. But need they be mutually exclusive? This is where the Traveller Education Services (TES) comes in with distance learning packages and other education provision outside the school gates. It is evident that minority, human, and child rights are becoming problematic when fused together like this. Scottish Gypsy-Traveller families may refuse to be labelled ethnic minorities, attributing the label to visible minorities. At one Save the Children seminar in Dundee in 1999, I saw one Gypsy-Traveller woman take issue on this matter with the leader of the workshop session on equality issues and the law. She demanded: 'Do I look Black to you, son?' (Clark, forthcoming).

Essentially, the SCF work is asking whether the money currently spent by governments, intergovernmental agencies and international NGOs on educational reform across Europe for Roma/Gypsy and Traveller groups is actually paying dividends. Certainly the

World Bank, European Union and many national and local governments and other agencies are interested to find out if their investment is worthwhile (see, for example, Ringold *et al*, 2003). But equally crucially, what noticeable impacts are these investments having? How are they being monitored and measured? Are innovative and temporary pilot initiatives leading to secure and robust long-term projects? Is systemic change a future possibility or current reality? Or are Roma/Gypsy and Traveller children continuing to lose out? Much is still to be done. The answers are far from simple but the report is at least asking these difficult questions and indicating that putting them on the European political agenda might be a way forward.

The current European context demands that safeguarding the right to education of Roma/Gypsy and Traveller minorities should be of primary concern to politicians and policymakers. From debates about European Union enlargement, migration and asylum policies to questions of democratisation and human rights, there is usually some mention of Roma/Gypsy and Traveller groups in the European corridors of power. The UK situation also deserves attention at this level – in particular why so few Gypsy and Traveller students make it to college and University.

Gypsies and Travellers in further education and higher education

> There are still many secondary aged [Gypsy] children who are not receiving adequate secondary education, or even in many cases registered with a secondary school... *There is likely to be less than twelve Gypsy students in further or higher education in Britain at any one time.* (Morris, undated: 2 – my emphasis)

> I've never heard of a Gypsy girl going to college... no Gypsy goes to school after the age of thirteen or fourteen. Perhaps one in ten might. (Anonymous Gypsy, Heath Common Site, Wakefield, quoted in Daley and Henderson (eds.) 1998: 70)

Empirical research on how Gypsy and Traveller children experience further and higher education in Britain is urgently needed. All we have are scraps of anecdotal evidence and personal testimony from families whose children have tried to get a place at college or University and the few who have made it. There is, however, some literature and research on secondary schooling (Kenny, 1997; Derrington and Kendall, 2004). One survey from 2001 found that in the entire south of Ireland there were only 38 6th form pupils in secondary schools and just one Traveller enrolled in further education (Birkett, 2002). Similarly in Central and Eastern Europe, few Roma progress to secondary level or attend college or University. It is estimated that in Hungary for example – which has managed relatively well since the post-1989 changes – only 1.5% of Roma graduate annually from High School and 0.001% from University (United States Embassy, 2003). Despite the funding efforts of financier George Soros to create Roma-focused specialist primary and secondary educational opportunities, and thus help establish a new Roma intellegentsia in Hungary, success is still some way off (Open Society Institute 2003).

In Britain the situation is grim but appears to be improving. Some local colleges, when approached directly or via third parties (e.g. Gypsy civil rights groups or voluntary agencies that work with Travellers) are providing specific courses to meet the needs of the community in their local areas. This has been evident in central Scotland, the north east of England and Cambridgeshire. The courses tend to be vocational in nature (such as welding, building and construction work, car mechanics, nursery nursing, landscape gardening, childcare) or in the arts and humanities with a view to university access. Young Gypsies and Travellers are breaking through into certain professional areas such as the law, journalism, academia, the voluntary sector and town planning. With regards to legal and public administration training, the respected European Roma Rights Centre (ERRC) offers scholarships to students from a Roma/Gypsy or Traveller background to take up degree courses in such subjects at local universities in their own countries (see: http://errc.org/capacitation/index.shtml). There is some media exposure about those who enter such occupations but some individuals understandably do not want publicity or to be identified as someone from a Gypsy or Traveller background. It is evident that pre-judice and discrimination can operate even in the most liberal of institutions. Beyond undergraduate studies at university, an increasing number of postgraduates are doing critical work on their own culture and on different topics – such as at Greenwich, Leicester and Durham Universities.

Interestingly and perhaps surprisingly, most students are female, which challenges the assumption of feminist commentators who view Gypsy society as overtly patriarchal (see Okely, 1983). Gypsy men, like many of their working class peers in the wider settled society, are still concerned to have 'real jobs' and carry on family businesses working with uncles, brothers and cousins. The family name, whether associated with being a general dealer, landscape gardener or scrapping, is important to pass on – although with room to adapt to new business opportunities when they arise.

Ethnic invisibility is an issue. Unlike many ethnic minority groups in Britain, Gypsies and Travellers can opt whether to disclose their ethnicity. There are certain identifiers such as an address on a caravan site, or a surname and style of appearance, but in terms of physiology and skin colour then there is room for manoeuvre. Witness what one female Traveller has said regarding her identity and how it is both presented and received by others within a higher education setting:

> There are only a few teachers at college who know I'm a Traveller... it's a hard thing to come out with. If I were to tell other students, some wouldn't speak to me again and some would say 'So?' You just can't tell what their reaction will be, even though, being a Traveller, you come to be a good judge of character. (Hester Hedges, Traveller, female student, quoted in Klein, 1997: 4)

Institutionally, current admissions process and the basis of how decisions are made needs examining – just when the government is also interested in this. This applies for all ethnic minority communities. Funding mechanisms also need to be examined. How are the government-backed Partners/widening participation programmes working for Gypsy and Traveller populations? Are such initiatives extending to Traveller sites and sixth form colleges that may have Traveller students? More pro-active careers advice is needed at the secondary school level, that respects the opinions and wishes of both pupils and parents, whilst also pushing the boundaries of what may be considered do-able. Stereo-typed ideas of Gypsies and Travellers looking after their own is no reason for witholding advice that could make the difference in students considering applying for further or higher education.

Conclusion

Many teenage children still take time off school to learn their parents' trades. But secondary school attendance is better from Thistlebrook [Gypsy caravan site, Greenwich] than from most Gypsy sites, because the site is so well established. *The schools have taken steps to respect the Gypsy way of life and make sure they meet Gypsy pupils' needs'* (my emphasis). (Acton and Gallant, 1997: 8)

This chapter has shown that a holistic approach to issues affecting how Gypsy and Traveller children experience educational institutions is essential. Matters such as accommodation and family work schedules will often have a direct bearing on how educational opportunities are regarded and whether they are taken up. As the Thistlebrook example shows, with some work and understanding on all sides positive results can be achieved.

What hopes are there for Gypsies and Travellers in Britain in the future? In January 2001 the Traveller Law Reform Unit at Cardiff Law School published the Traveller Reform Bill. This working document, drafted as a Bill and now going through Parliament under the direction of the multi-ethnic Traveller Law Reform Coalition (http://www.travellers law.org.uk/) – outlines a clear agenda for change across many areas of public life that currently affect Gypsies and other Travellers adversely. The Bill addresses concerns about sites and other forms of accommodation, health care, criminal justice, social security and education. Clauses 10-12 of the Bill directly address problematic issues in the funding mechanisms for Traveller Education Services. But it is uncertain whether this Bill will have the support it needs in the House to lead to significant legislative changes, especially as the current government is pre-occupied with other competing social and political issues.

How high up the political agenda can issues affecting Gypsies rise (Turner, 2002)? Much attention is given in the press and in parliament to evictions and other law and order issues involving Gypsies and Travellers, but pro-Gypsy policies are rarely heard and will rarely win votes. Instead in many countries including the UK, the issues are seldom addressed directly but are spoken of in terms of the problem with Gypsies and Travellers and what the cure or solution might be. Such an approach can lead potentially useful discussions back into the racist and assimilationist problematic that generated them.

This chapter and the SCF work on which it draws suggest that what we should be examining are the problems faced by Roma/Gypsy and Traveller communities in accessing the right to an education that is inclusive, relevant, participatory, appropriate and responsive to the needs of those engaging with it. The many recommendations outlined in the SCF report, from the use of stronger affirmative action programmes to wider access to pre-school provision, suggest that much can be done in both the long and short term that will not be too costly to the countries and education systems involved. It is hoped that the SCF work will create an established European educational benchmark and a new beginning for the many Roma/Gypsy and Traveller children and their families who continue to face major barriers in taking up their right to education. Commitment to multiculturalism and antiracism will hopefully inform education systems and Gypsy and Traveller children will look forward to the challenges and indeed the frustrations of further and higher education.

References

Acton, T. and Gallant, D. (1997) *Romanichal Gypsies,* Hove: Wayland Press

Andruszkiewicz, A. (2001) *Denied a future? The right to education of Roma/Gypsy and Traveller children in Europe – summary,* London: Save the Children

Barany, Z. (2002) *The East European Gypsies: regime change, marginality and ethnopolitics,* Cambridge: Cambridge University Press

Barry, B. (2001) 'The muddles of multiculturalism', *New Left Review,* 8 March/Apri.

Bhopal, K. with Gundara, J, Jones, C. and Owen, C. (2000) *Working towards inclusive education: aspects of good practice for Gypsy Traveller pupils,* London: DfEE

Birkett, D. (2002) 'School for scandal', *The Guardian,* January 15

Bucke, T. and James, Z. (1998) *Trespass and protest: policing under the Criminal Justice and Public Order Act,* Home Office research Study 190, London: Home Office

Card, R and Ward, R. (1994) *Criminal Justice and Public Order Act: a practitioner's guide,* Bristol: Jordan Publishing

Central Statistics Agency. (2003) Press statement: *Central Statistics Office: 2002 census of population – principal demographic results,* 19 June 2003, Dublin: CSO

Clark, C. (2001) 'The United Kingdom: England, Northern Ireland, Scotland and Wales', in K. Pinnock (ed.) *Denied a Future? The right to education of Roma/Gypsy and Traveller children in Europe,* London: Save the Children

Clark, C. (Forthcoming) 'Ethnicity, the law and Gypsy-Travellers in Scotland: which way now?', in C. Pronai (ed.) *Papers from the Annual Gypsy Lore Society Meeting,* Budapest, Hungary, 2002, Washington D.C.: GLS Publications

Daley, I. and Henderson, J. (1998) *Static: life on the site,* Castleford: Yorkshire Art Circus

Department of Education and Science (1985) *Education for all: the report of the committee of enquiry into the education of children from ethnic minority groups (Swann Report),* London: HMSO

Department for Education and Skills (DfES). (2003a) *Pupil Characteristics and class sizes in maintained schools in England, January 2003 (provisional),* London: DfES/National Statistics

Department for Education and Skills (DfES). (2003b) Press Release: '*We must give Gypsy Traveller children more support at school – Stephen Twigg*', 1 July 2003, London: DfES

Department for Education and Skills (DfES). (2003c) *Aiming High: raising the achievement of minority ethnic pupils,* London: DfES

Derrington, C. and Kendall, S. (2004) *Gypsy Traveller Students in Secondary Schools – culture, identity and achievement,* Stoke on Trent: Trentham Books

Discrimination Law Association (2002) *Gypsies, Travellers and discrimination law,* Briefing Paper number 230. February. pp. 9-12

Donahue, M. and McVeigh, R. (2001) The real deal for Travellers: what young Travellers really think about government, politics and social exclusion, unpublished report; Belfast: SC-UK

Hawes, D. (1997) *Gypsies, Travellers and the Health Service: a study in inequality,* Bristol: The Policy Press

Hedges, H. (1999) As quoted in an article from *The Cambridge Evening News,* 8 April 1999

Jordan, E. (2000) 'The exclusionary comprehensive school system: the experience of Showground families in Scotland', *International Journal of Educational Research,* 33: 253-263

Kenny, M. (1997) *The routes of resistance: Travellers and second-level schooling,* Aldershot: Ashgate Press

Kenrick, D. and Clark, C. (1999) *Moving On: the Gypsies and Travellers of Britain*, Hatfield: University of Hertfordshire Press

Kiddle, C. (1999) *Traveller children: A voice for themselves,* London: Jessica Kingsley

Klein, R. (1997) 'Upwardly mobile', *Times Educational Supplement,* May 23 1997: 4-5.

Kohn, M. (1995) *The race gallery: the return of racial science,* London: Jonathan Cape

Lee, J. G. (2000) The Traveller Gypsies reconsidered, BSc Degree Dissertation, University of Durham Stockton Campus, Durham

McKinney, R. (2003) 'Views from the margins: Gypsy/Travellers and the ethnicity debate in the new Scotland', *Scottish Affairs*, 42: 13-31

Modood, T. *et al* (1997) *Ethnic minorities in Britain: diversity and disadvantage,* London: Policy Studies Institute

Morris, R. (undated) *Factsheet: Travelling People in the United Kingdom* http://www.cf.ac.uk/claws/tlru/Factsheet.pdf (accessed October 2003)

Morris, R. (1998) 'Gypsies and the planning system', *Journal of Planning and Environment Law,* July, Pp: 635-643

Morris, R. (1999) 'The invisibility of Gypsies and other Travellers', *Journal of Social Welfare and Family Law*, 21(4): 397-404

Morris, R. and Clements, L. (2002) *At what cost? The economics of Gypsy and Traveller encampments*, Bristol: Policy Press

Office of the Deputy Prime Minister (2003) *Local Authority Gypsy/Traveller sites in England,* London: ODPM

Ofsted (1996) *The Education of Travelling Children*, Office for Standards in Education, Ref. no. HMR/12/96/NS

Ofsted (1999) *Raising the attainment of minority ethnic pupils*, London: HMSO

Okely, J. (1983) *The Traveller-Gypsies*, Cambridge: Cambridge University Press

Parekh, B. (2000) *The Future of Multi-ethnic Britain (Parekh Report),* London: The Runnymede Trust/Profile Books

Ringold, D., Orenstein, M. A. and Wilkens, E. (2003) *Roma in an expanding Europe: breaking the poverty cycle*, Washington: The World Bank

Smart, H, Titterton, M. and Clark, C. (2003) 'A literature review of the health of Gypsy/Traveller families in Scotland: the challenges for health promotion', *Health Education*, 103(3): 156-165

The Open Society Institute (2003) *School Success for Roma Children: step by step special schools initiative interim report* http://www.osi.hu/exhibition/hungary.html (accessed November 2003)

The Scottish Parliament (2000) *Equality opportunities committee hearings*: oral evidence given to the Scottish Parliament, May 2000, Edinburgh: HMSO

Turner, R. (2002) 'Gypsies and British Parliamentary language: an analysis', *Romani Studies,* 12(1): 1-34

United States Embassy (2003) *The Roma of Hungary,* http://www.usis.hu/ (accessed November 2003)

CHAPTER NINE

Disability and Racial Discrimination in Employment in Higher Education

Ozcan Konur

Introduction

Disabled people and people from the ethic minorities have been under-repre-sented in higher education employment (Konur, 2000b; Fenton, Carter, Modood, 2000). Of the 136,000 academic staff in higher education in the year 1999/2000 only 1% and 4% were disabled or from ethnic minorities respectively (HESA, 2001). Moreover, detailed statistical information is sparse. The Sex Discrimination Act (SDA) (1975) and the Race Relations Act (RRA) (1976) sought to increase access for minority groups and outlaw discrimination on grounds of gender and race. Employment, services, and education including higher education are covered by these laws.

After several private bills to outlaw discrimination on the grounds of disability, the Disability Discrimination Act (DDA) (1995) came into force in December 1996. Part IV of the DDA was amended by the Special Educational Needs and Disability Act (2001) to outlaw discrimination against disabled pupils and students in all sectors of education (see Konur, 2002i for an annotated copy of this Act as relating to higher education). A private bill to amend the DDA, the Disability Discrimination (Amendment) Bill (2002), introduced in the House of Lords in January 2002, revealed the relative deficiencies of the DDA (see Konur, 2002g for the report on the Report Stage of this Bill). The DDA followed similar Acts in the US in 1990 and Australia in 1992. The Americans with Dis-abilities Act (1990) and the Disability Discrimination Act (1992) were used by disability right campaigners to apply pressure to the Government of the day. The deficiencies of the DDA (1995) become more apparent when the respective provisions regarding access to employment, education and services in these disability laws are compared.

The law has moved on since 2002. The enactment of two European Directives in 2000 was the starting point (Council Directive 2000/43 and Council Directive 2000/78). The Race Relations Act 1976 (Amendment) Regulations (2003) and Disability Discrimina-tion Act 1995 (Amendment) Regulations (2003) were enacted in 2003 in the light of these Directives (see for example Rubenstein, 2003 for a brief discussion of these and other regulations made under these Directives). The Race Relations (Amendment) Act (2000) also changed the scene. So it is timely to consider the application of legislation in higher education employment before the implementation of new disability and race regulations by October 2004 and other regulations by October 2006.

A short version of this chapter was presented at the Institutional Racism in Higher Education Conference held in Leeds on 3 July 2002 (Konur, 2002h). The experiences of disabled people and people from ethnic minorities in gaining employment in higher education were mapped using the appellate case transcripts available from 1998 to June 2002. This chapter updates the conference paper and has the same aim and methodology. But, due to constraints of space, a sample of appellate cases considered was restricted to 2002 with some selected cases from 2001. The scope of the cases considered by appellate courts in 2001 and 2002 were enough to cover a number of legal issues encountered from 1998 to 2002.

I developed a four-prong framework to analyse the application of the rules of the DDA (1995) in relation to jurisdiction and procedure, disability, discrimination and enforcement (Konur (2002a, pp. 252). Disabled applicants first have to comply with certain rules restricting access to justice. For example, they have to file their claims within three months of the alleged act of discrimination, such as dismissal or refusal of employment. Assuming the first hurdle is passed, disabled applicants next have to prove that they are disabled within the meaning of section 1 of the Act. Contrary to lay knowledge, disabled applicants have to prove that they have an impairment which has a substantial adverse effect on their normal day-to-day activities and which is long term, lasting over one year. Next, disabled applicants have to prove that they were discriminated against in relation to relevant comparators. The Act defines discrimination in two ways: as less favourable treatment and the failure of the employer to make reasonable adjustments under sections 5(1) and 5(2) of the Act. However this is not the end of the road, since employers have extensive rights to justify their discriminating behaviour on a number of grounds such as health and safety or academic and professional standards. Finally, disabled applicants have to go through a remedy trial for the calculation of compensatory awards. They may have to file claims before a county court to enforce the compensatory awards made by the employment tribunal. The case history of the DDA (1995) has proved that application of rules in these four areas has substantially limited access to justice by disabled people (Konur, 2002a-f).

The same conceptual framework can be extended to racial discrimination and the rules of the game can be grouped under the same four tests: jurisdiction and procedure, race, discrimination and enforcement. Within this framework, an applicant has to first comply with a number of rules restricting access to justice. For example, they have to file their claims within three months of the discriminatory act. Next, the applicants have to show that they are from one of the the racial groups within the meaning of the Act. However, these tests have proved to be less problematic than the proof requirement of the DDA. Then the applicants have to prove that they were discriminated against in relation to their comparators. Discrimination is defined in two ways under the Act: as less favourable treatment and indirect discrimination. Again, the employer has extensive rights to justify their discriminatory behaviour on a number of grounds such as health and safety and academic and professional standards. The final hurdle is the enforcement test. The applicants have to go through a remedy trial for the calculation of compensatory awards. Finally they may have to file claims before a county court to enforce the compensatory awards made by the employment tribunal. The case history of the RRA (1976) has proved that all four tests have substantially limited access to justice from ethnic minority people.

The Experiences of Ethnic Minority Staff who go to Tribunal
(i) The jurisdiction and procedural tests of the RRA
Costs

One of the stated benefits of the employment tribunals has been the relatively low risk of cost orders made against the ethnic minority applicants. The *Kovacs* case has changed this and increased the risk for ethnic minority as well as disabled applicants having to pay the university's legal costs. Ethnic minority applicants often lose their case because universities fail to comply with the orders of the tribunals for the disclosure of relevant documentation. One such case was *Deman v. London Business School and Bains* (2002).

In *Kovacs v. Queen Mary and Westfield College; Royal Hospital NHS Trust* (2000 and 2002), Kovacs was ordered to pay for the full costs of the Royal Hospital NHS Trust (£62,000) regarding her sex and racial discrimination claims following her 'unfair dismissal' by Queen Mary and Westfield College by the Employment Tribunal on 30 July 1999. This was because, under Rule 12, she was seen as acting 'frivolously, vexatiously, abusively, disruptively, or otherwise unreasonably' in bringing her case. Kovacs appealed to the Employment Appeal Tribunal (EAT) and then to Court of Appeal (CA), where it was dismissed. The Court noted that the Tribunal found that Kovacs vexatiously conducted her case against the Hospital since 'there was not and has never been a genuine claim of race and sex discrimination against' the Hospital (para. 13). It also made clear that 'ability to pay is not a factor' in this decision and that the County Court has statutory powers to deal with the enforcement of costs ordered by employment tribunals.

Time limits
Rules on time limits have proved an insurmountable barrier for some ethnic minority staff in trying to access justice, as in the *Leander* case. In *Leander v. Goldsmiths College* (2001) CA, Leander, a contract-based lecturer at Goldsmith's College, London filed a claim for wrongful and constructive dismissal as well as racial discrimination. The tribunal dismissed her case due to time limits, but continued to hear it and decided that her claim would have been unsuccessful (para. 2). She brought bias claims against the tribunal before the EAT and her appeal was dismissed on 11 May 2001. She further made an application to appeal against the EAT's decision before the Court of Appeal. She contended that the tribunal's extended reasons caused her victimisation by the College (para. 4), and she also contended that the tribunal was biased and that she was denied justice under the Article 6 of the *Human Rights Convention* (para. 6, 7). Lord Justice Laws

refused her application for leave to appeal and noted that there was no evidence to show any causal link between victimisation and the tribunal's decision (para. 8). Furthermore, it is often amendments made by applicants which are refused as out of time as in the case of *Moore v. University of Greenwich* (2000) EAT.

Disclosure

The disclosure of documents regarding their case by universities has been a serious problem for ethnic minority staff. The *Jindal v. University of Glasgow* (2001) EAT case underlined the importance of such disclosure as recognised by the courts.

Adjournment

The adjournment of the tribunal hearings has been another difficulty, as in the *Deman v City University* (2002) EAT case. Inappropriate requests for adjournment often result in cost orders against the applicants and the dismissal of their cases for the 'want of prosecution' as in the case of *Zalzala v. University of Sheffield* (2002) EAT. In *Kumar v. University of Strathclyde* (2002) EAT, Kumar brought a race discrimination claim. The tribunal chairman scheduled the hearings for eight days, spread over a five-month period, originally due to start in April 2002 and conclude in August to minimise clashing with the professional commitments of the employer's witnesses. Kumar asked for the Chairman to reschedule the hearings for a speedy and fair trial, but the Chairman refused. Kumar appealed. A panel of the EAT in Scotland chaired by Lord Johnston allowed the appeal and remitted the case back to the tribunal on 26 June 2002. Lord Johnston gave the EAT's judgement as:

> In the first place, we consider that deliberate scheduling of a case whereby there are gaps between every day of a proposed hearing is unsatisfactory and to be avoided unless it is absolutely necessary. This is because it lends itself to the risk of there being a division between examination and cross-examination of a witness, which is unsatisfactory and not conducive to good case management. If the gap in time terms is substantial furthermore, it would appear to make it more difficult for the Tribunal to ompare examination in chief to cross-examination by way of recollection.

Res judicata

Discrimination claims are often entangled with other claims, resulting in the risk of them being dismissed on grounds that these issues were dealt with in other courts or tribunals. The term *res judicata* is used in law to refer to claims previously dealt with and which therefore can not be litigated again. In *Anyanwu and Ebuzoeme v. South Bank Students' Union and South Bank University* (1998, 1999, and 2001), students Anyanwu and Ebuzoeme were elected to serve as union officers for the year starting 1 August 1995. They were disciplined by the university, suspended and expelled as students on 29 March 1996 and their employment contracts were terminated by the Students' Union on 2 April 1996. They were refused permission to apply for judicial review regarding their expulsion as students (see for example, *R v. South Bank University and South Bank University Students' Union, ex parte Anyanwu, Gillespie and Williams* (1996) CA). They also brought complaints of racial discrimination against both the union and university in connection with their expulsion and their dismissal. The tribunal refused their claims on the grounds of *res judicata* on the application of the university. The Employment Appeal Tribunal reversed the tribunal's decision. The Court of Appeal raised the issue of section 33(1) of the Race Relations Act (1976) regarding their expulsion by the university. The majority of the Court of Appeal held that the university was a 'prime mover' and therefore did not aid the students' union to dismiss the applicants. The House of Lords reversed the Court of Appeal's decision on 22 March 2001 and remitted the case to an employment tribunal for hearing on its merits.

(ii) The discrimination tests of the RRA

The *Anya and Deman v Association of University Teachers* (2002) EAT, CA cases were rare examples of race discrimination cases. In *Anya v. University of Oxford* (1999) EAT, (2001) CA, Anya filed a racial discrimination claim before a tribunal against the University and a member of the selection panel with whom he had previously worked. The tribunal dismissed his claim on 26 March 1998 and the Employment Appeal Tribunal chaired by Justice Holland refused his appeal on 17 December 1999. He filed a further appeal before the Court of Appeal which was upheld. Anya had a doctoral degree in Metallurgy from Strathclyde University and had post-doctoral research experience in Materials Science. From 1994 he worked as a post-doctoral researcher under the direction of Dr. Roberts at the University of Oxford for two years. He was shortlisted for a new post in a relevant research project together with a white researcher. The key figure in the selection panel was Dr. Roberts 'who had already formed an adverse view of (Anya's) suitability for the post' as alleged. The tribunal found out that there was no 'person specification' for the post and that none was used in short-listing the applicants. Complex information about the research project was delivered hours before the interview. Furthermore, no references were taken up. Anya's application was rejected by all the members of the panel. The Grievance panel upheld the selection panel's decision but noted the lack of compliance with university policies. The Court of Appeal remitted the case back to a new employment tribunal and asked the tribunal not to consider the EAT's notes on the case. It also referred to Justice Mummery's remarks in *Qureshi v. Victoria University of Manchester* (1996) as an example of the current law on the determination of discrimination claims. The CA noted that this was a:

> Textbook example of a race discrimination claim. It makes it possible to see with some clarity how the principles established by the authority ought to work out in practice ... good administration requires that he be chosen fairly ... and law has now added for a quarter of a century that the choice must not be affected in any way by his race. If it is, the unsuccessful candidate will have been treated less favourably on racial grounds and the university will be liable for direct racial discrimination. This was true for Dr. White as it was for Dr. Anya: both were entitled to the protection of the Race Relations Act 1976. Very little direct discrimination is today overt or even deliberate. What *King* and *Qureshi* tell tribunals and courts to look for, in order to give effect to legislation, are indicators from a time before or after the particular decision which may demonstrate that an ostensibly fair-minded decision was, or equally was not, affected by racial bias.

The strong criticism of the Tribunal's decision was also applied to the reasoning of the EAT. However, the final Employment Tribunal held that the university did not racially discriminate against Anya because he performed less well in technical assessments and at interview (*Anya v. University of Oxford* (2002) ET).

The Experiences of Disabled Staff at Tribunal

(i) The jurisdiction and procedural tests of the DDA: costs

In *Rudzki v. University of Sunderland* (2002) EAT, Rudzki appealed against the tribunal's decision for him to pay the university's legal costs. But, this was subsequently withdrawn and the case was dismissed by the mutual agreement of the parties.

(ii) Disability tests of the DDA

The *Hobbs* case considered by the EAT illustrates how disability tests as devised by the DDA (1995) have been an insurmountable barrier for disabled people, as do *Mowat-Brown v. University of Surrey* (2001) EAT and *Morgan v. Staffordshire University* (2001) EAT. In *Hobbs v. College of Ripon and York St. John* (2001) EAT, Hobbs was employed as a lecturer at the College from September 1995 and was on sick leave for 13 months from March 1997. She returned to work in 1998 but was signed off work again from summer 1999. She filed a disability claim on 18 August 1999 before the employment tribunal and contended that the College failed to make reasonable adjustments for her within the meaning of the Act since she had experienced slow, progressive muscle weakness and wasting. The College contested that Hobbs was a disabled person within the meaning of the Act. On the tribunal's instructions, Dr Bates reported on 15 January 2000 that 'there were symptoms of muscle fisculation consisting of muscle twitching and muscle weakness which created difficulty in mobility. There were also muscle cramps leading to muscle spasms'. However, he also reported that there was 'no evidence to indicate the presence of a disease affecting the central or peripheral nervous system to account for her described disability. There is no organic disease process causing the symptoms described ... and that her disability is not therefore organic'. The tribunal found that Hobbs was a disabled person within the meaning of the Act and upheld her disability claim against the College on 22 March 2000. It interpreted the term 'physical impairment' as meaning 'there is something wrong with the body as opposed to the mind' and that the twitching of the muscles was 'a product of a physical impairment' since she suffered pain and comfort caused by attacks of muscle cramps. Therefore her muscle dysfunction is 'sufficient to bring her case within the expression of physical impairment' and 'it was not necessary for the tribunal to know precisely what underlying disease or trauma has caused the physical impairment'.

The EAT chaired by its President Judge Lindsay, considered in the appeal by the College filed on 3 May 2000 that the tribunal erred in law in finding that Hobbs had a physical impairment, although it conceded that this impairment affected her normal day-to-day activities adversely within the meaning of the Act. The appeal was dismissed since the tribunal did not err in law in finding that Hobbs has a muscle weakness as a physical impairment and there was no contrary evidence. He also noted that there was no statutory definition of 'impairment' in the Act and that its accompanying guidance does not require the drawing of:

> any rigid distinctions between an underlying fault, shortcoming or defect of or in the body on the one hand and evidence of the manifestations or effects thereof on the other. The act contemplates that an impairment can be something that results from an in illness as opposed to itself being the illness. It can thus be cause or effect'. The Tribunal therefore rightly held 'directly or by ordinary reasonable inference, that there was something wrong with (Hobbs) physically, something wrong with her body.

(iii) Discrimination tests of the DDA

The question as to whether discrimination had taken place was a key consideration in a number of case including *Hanlon v University of Huddersfield* (1998) EAT, (1999) EAT, *Rudzki v Manchester Metropolitan University* (2000) EAT and in *Murphy v. Sheffield Hallam University* (2000) EAT. In the last case, Murphy applied for a post of learner support co-ordinator in November 1997 and disclosed his hearing disability, which required sign language interpreting support. He was short-listed for an interview in December 1997 but this had to be postponed for two days as no adjustments were made for sign language interpreting. Murphy was assisted by a friend as his interpreter during the interview. He was not selected for the post and he filed a discrimination claim before the employment tribunal. The tribunal held that he was less favourably treated regarding the lack of reasonable adjustments for interpreting his sign language. He was awarded £2500 compensation. However, it further held that he was not less favourably treated and therefore not discriminated against by the outcome of the interview process. It held that because, on the facts of the case based mainly on evidence from the chair of the selection panel, his non-selection was related not to his disability but to lack of qualifications for the post. However, the tribunal rejected Murphy's claim of discrimination and accepted the chair's contention that 'disability was not a related factor in the decision to appoint (someone else)'. Murphy appealed against this decision, but this was dismissed, confirming the tribunal's view that there was no causal relationship between Murphy's disability and his non-selection for the job in question.

Conclusions

This chapter has sought to map some of the experiences of disabled or ethnic minority staff in accessing employment in higher education, using selected case transcripts from 2001 and 2002. These highlight key hurdles with which claimants have had to contend in pursuing cases of discrimination. The context of higher education policy and law is of importance here as the professional judgement of selection or dismissal panels in universities has been considered with respect by the courts, for example, the *Murphy* or *Anya* cases where the courts showed deference to the professional judgement of these panels. There are serious problems here, including lack of timely access to legal advice and adequate representation in filing complaints against universities. Most applicants find themselves unable to file their complaints within the three-month time limit without such advice and representation. As the *Kovacs* case showed, disabled and ethnic minority staff often found themselves at a substantial disadvantage in developing and defending their case in comparison to the distinguished lawyers defending their universities' cases. The high risk of costs awards being made against disabled and ethnic minority staff and the long time spent resolving jurisdiction and disability tests, as in *Hobbs* (3 years) or *Anyanwu* (5 years), suggests that these rules may have not been not designed to achieve the aim of eliminating discrimination set out in the DDA (1995) and RRA (1976).

Close reading of these cases and the *Disability Discrimination Act* (1995) and the *Race Relations Act* (1976) suggest that individual complaints are the main mechanism through which enforcement takes place. However, the rules of the game have been set out so as to disadvantage ethnic minority and disabled staff. Bearing in mind that the RRA has been in force for over a quarter of century, the experiences of ethnic minority people in accessing employment and justice generally, and particularly higher education, suggest that it has achieved little in improving greater equality of opportunity. There is a crucial need to develop evidence-based research, practice, law, policies and dissemination regarding access to higher education employment by people from minority groups. For the stated aims of the discrimination legislation to be realised, the rules of the game regulating access to higher education employment need to be wholly changed. This is particularly urgent as new rules on both disability and race discrimination come into operation by October 2004 under European Directives (see Thusing, 2003 and Hannett, 2003 who highlight the impact of European and international laws on the development of the anti-discrimination legislation in the UK).

The author thanks Ian Law and Debbie Phillips for their scholarly and editorial support for this paper. He also thanks the participants at this conference presentation on 3 July 2002.

References

Americans with Disabilities Act (1990) Public Law 101-336, US Code 42 Ss. 12101

Anya v University of Oxford (1999) Employment Appeal Tribunal, EEAT/739/98, 17 December 1999

Anya v University of Oxford (2001) Court of Appeal, [2001] IRLR, pp. 377

Anya v University of Oxford (2002) Employment Tribunal, 20 January 2002

Anyanwu and Ebuzoeme v South Bank Students' Union and South Bank University (2001) House of Lords, All ER, 2, pp. 353

Anyanwu and Ebuzoeme v South Bank Students' Union and South Bank University (1999) Court of Appeal, All ER, 1, pp. 1

Council Directive 2000/43 implementing the principle of equal treatment between persons irrespective of racial or ethnic origin

Council Directive 2000/78 establishing a general framework for equal treatment in employment and occupation

Deman v Association of University Teachers (2002) Court of Appeal, [2002] EWCA Civ 1732, 1 November 2002

Deman v Association of University Teachers (2002) Employment Appeal Tribunal, EAT/746/99, 22 April 2002

Deman v City University (2002) Employment Appeal Tribunal, EAT/1065/02, 18 October 2002

Deman v. London Business School and Bains (2002) Employment Appeal Tribunal, EAT/0357/99, 7 August 2002

Disability Discrimination (Amendment) Bill [HL] (2002) House of Lords, First Reading, HL Bill 40, 8 January 2002. (London, House of Lords)

Disability Discrimination Act (1992) (Canberra, Government Printing Office)

Disability Discrimination Act (1995) Chapter 50, 8 November 1995, (London, Stationery Office)

Disability Discrimination Act 1995 (Amendment) Regulations (2003) SI 2003/1673, (London, Stationery Office)

Employment Tribunals (Constitution and Rules of the Procedure) Regulations (2001) SI 2001/1171, (London, Stationery Office)

Fenton, S.; Carter, J and Modood, T. (2000) Ethnicity and academia: Closure models, racism models and market models, *Sociological Research Online*, 5(2), pp. U59-U83

Hanlon v University of Huddersfield (1998) Employment Appeal Tribunal, Disc. LR, pp. 82

Hanlon v University of Huddersfield (1999) Employment Appeal Tribunal, EAT/1235/99, 22 November 1999

Hannett, S. (2003) Equality at the intersections: The legislative and judicial failure to tackle multiple discrimination, *Oxford Journal of Legal Studies,* 23(1), pp. 65-86

Higher Education Statistical Agency (2001) *Resources of Higher Education Institutions,* 1999/2000, (Cheltenham, HESA)

Hobbs v College of Ripon and York St. John (2001) Employment Appeal Tribunal, [2002] IRLR, pp. 185

Jindal v University of Glasgow (2001) Employment Appeal Tribunal, EAT/74/01, 31 May 2001

Konur, O. (2000a) Creating enforceable civil rights for disabled students in higher education: An institutional theory perspective, *Disability and Society*, 15(7), pp. 1041-1063

Konur, O. (2000b) *Response Paper: Improving Equal Opportunities for Higher Education Staff,* HEFCE Consultation 00/21, 26 June 2000, (London, the Author)

Konur, O. (2002a) Access to employment by disabled people in the UK: Is the Disability Discrimination Act working? *International Journal of Discrimination and the Law*, 5(4), pp. 247-279

Konur, O. (2002b) Access to nursing education by disabled students: Rights and duties of nursing programs, *Nurse Education Today,* 22(5), pp. 364-374

Konur, O. (2002c) Assessment of disabled students in higher education: Current public policy issues, Assessment and Evaluation in *Higher Education,* 27(2), pp. 131-152

Konur, O. (2002d) *Current Public Policy Issues regarding Access to Justice by Disabled People,* (London, the Author)

Konur, O. (2002e) *Current Public Policy Issues regarding the Disability Tests of the Disability Discrimination Act* (1995) (London, the Author)

Konur, O. (2002f) *Current Public Policy Issues regarding the Jurisdiction Tests of the Disability Discrimination Act* (1995) (London, the Author)

Konur, O. (2002g) *Disability Discrimination (Amendment) Bill [HL] Annotated*, House of Lords Report Stage, HL Bill 62, 6 March 2002, House of Lords, (London, The Author)

Konur, O. (2002h) Emerging public policy issues from a quarter century of the Race Relations Act's application to staff in higher education for access to higher education employment by disabled people, *Institutional Racism in Higher Education Conference*, 3 July 2002, University of Leeds, Leeds, (London, the Author)

Konur, O. (2002i) *Special Educational Needs and Disability Act (2001) Annotated*, Part 2. Discrimination in Education, (London, the Author)

Kovacs v Queen Mary and Westfield College and Royal Hospital NHS Trust (2002) Court of Appeal, EWCA Civ 352, 22 March 2002

Kovacs v Queen Mary and Westfield College and Royal Hospital NHS Trust (2000) Employment Appeal Tribunal, EAT/1157/99, 1 December 2000

Kumar v University of Strathclyde (2002) Employment Appeal Tribunal, EATS/0003/02, 26 June 2002, Independent 19 July 2002

Leander v Goldsmiths College (2001) Court of Appeal, EWCA Civ 1709, 23 October 2001.

Moore v University of Greenwich (2000) Employment Appeal Tribunal, EAT/745/00, 4 July 2000, 23 June 2000

Morgan v Staffordshire University (2001) Employment Appeal Tribunal, [2002] IRLR, pp. 190

Mowat-Brown v University of Surrey (2001) Employment Appeal Tribunal, EAT [2002] IRLR, pp. 235

Murphy v Sheffield Hallam University (2000) Employment Appeal Tribunal, EAT/6/99, 11 January 2000

Qureshi v Victoria University of Manchester (1996) Employment Appeal Tribunal, 21 June 1996

R v South Bank University and South Bank University Students' Union, ex parte Anyanwu, Gillespie and Williams (1996) Court of Appeal, 9 July 1996

Race Relations (Amendment) Act (2000) Chapter 34, 30 November 2000

Race Relations Act (1976) Chapter 74, 22 November 1976, (London, Stationery Office)

Race Relations Act 1976 (Amendment) Regulations (2003) SI 2003/1626, (London, Stationery Office)

Rubenstein, M. (2003) New discrimination regulations: an EOR guide: Part 2: Race, religion and sexual orientation, *Equal Opportunities Review*, 119, pp. 20-28

Rudzki v Manchester Metropolitan University (2000) Employment Appeal Tribunal, EAT/640/99, 27 June 2000

Rudzki v University of Sunderland (2002) Employment Appeal Tribunal, EAT/1341/01, 19 July 2002

Sex Discrimination Act (1975) Chapter 65, 12 November 1975 (London, Stationery Office)

Special Educational Needs and Disability Act (2001) Chapter 10, 11 May 2001 (London, Stationery Office Limited)

Thusing, G. (2003) Following the U.S. example: European employment discrimination law and the impact of Council Directives 2000/43/EC and 2000/78/EC, *International Journal of Comparative Labour Law and Industrial Relations,* 19(2), pp. 187-218

Zalzala v. University of Sheffield (2002) Employment Appeal Tribunal, EAT/0201/01 MA, 29 November 2002

PART THREE
AGENDAS FOR CHANGE

CHAPTER TEN

Tackling Institutional Racism in Higher Education: An Antiracist Toolkit

Ian Law, Deborah Phillips and Laura Turney

Introduction

Higher education has, until recently, remained relatively insulated from the kinds of policies that have developed in local authorities, schools, the health service and the police to challenge racism and promote ethnic and cultural diversity. Higher education institutions generally operate in a 'colour-blind' manner and seldom admit that all might not be well in the liberal academy. Recent research has, however, indicated that we have no right to be complacent. For example, Sarah Neal's (1998) exploration of equal opportunities policies in universities, John Bird's (1996) study of the experiences of Black students in higher education and Carter, Fenton and Modood's (1999) analysis of ethnicity and employment in higher education all highlight areas of concern. What emerges from these and other studies is a picture of ethnic inequalities in student access, racial discrimination by admissions tutors, the racist experiences of Black and Asian students on entering higher education institutions, disillusionment with the lack of diversity in the teaching and learning environment, racist discrimination in marking and assessment, racism in work placements and race discrimination in graduate access to employment. A major survey by the Association of University Teachers (AUT), which considered race issues and attitudes among academics and support staff in the old universities, also revealed that racialised tensions are common in higher education institutions, where Black and minority ethnic staff may well experience racist harassment, feel unfairly treated in job applications, and believe institutional racism exists in the academic workplace (Major, 2002).

In 1999, Carter, Fenton and Modood identified a need for what they called an 'institutional antiracism'. Their study suggested a number of approaches to challenging institutional racism, including the idea that institutions need to recognise that racism is an issue for the entire institution and not simply Black and minority ethnic staff and students. The message was that effective race equality strategies would require much more than just tinkering with admissions procedures or employment practices. However, at the time it was evident that many higher education institutions lacked the conceptual and methodological tools to put in place a strategy for tackling racism across their organisations, and were ill-equipped to fulfil their new race equality obligations under the law (following the enactment of the Race Relations (Amendment) Act 2000).The need for guidance on how to work towards an antiracist college/university was clear. To this end, the Centre for Ethnicity and Racism Studies at the University of Leeds set out, as part of a wider project examining institutional racism in higher education, to develop a set of conceptual and methodological resources on which practitioners (academic, administrative and human resource professionals) could draw. A programme of research, which examined race equality issues across all areas of institutional activity at the University of Leeds, informed the development process. This case-study involved an analysis of documents relating to race equality planning at the University of Leeds, email questionnaires (which targeted students and staff in twenty sample departments), semi-structured interviews with key staff in the sample departments and focus groups with students. The project resulted in the development of an antiracist toolkit, which was launched at a national conference on Institutional Racism in Higher Education in July 2002 at the University of Leeds.

The toolkit

The toolkit is a web-based resource (http://www.leeds.ac.uk/cers/toolkit/toolkit.htm), which aims to provide a holist view of the workings of a higher education institution (HEI). It acknowledges that all aspects of an organisation's operations would, at some level, impact upon Black and minority ethnic staff and students' experiences. The core functions of the HEI are teaching and research. The practices and operations of the HEI go well beyond these core activities. It has myriad relationships with local and national communities. As an employer, the HEI draws from a broad pool of workers, such as administrative and ancillary staff from the local population or academic staff drawn from a more international pool. The HEI also has a great deal of spending power in terms of the products and services it requires to keep the institution functioning: new building works, services and so on. The HEI also has an impact on the development of the local communities of which it is a part, through its investment strategies and as a knowledge producer. Consequently HEIs have a responsibility to ensure that they are using their powerful position as an agent of change and fulfilling their obligations to promote race equality within the educational community and beyond.

The toolkit is structured around the processes involved in the construction of an antiracist action plan for an institution or organisation. It operates at two levels: either it can be viewed as an integrated plan for the whole institution, or it can be regarded as a set of resources to be accessed selectively as required. The toolkit begins by providing some background to the sector and goes on to summarise some of the conceptual tools and debates that structured our understanding of institutional racism, antiracism, whiteness and eurocentrism. The chapter outlines the legal requirements placed upon institutions of higher education with respect to equal opportunities and race equality, and defines terms such as 'positive action', 'targeting' and 'ethnic monitoring'. The toolkit goes on to address race equality issues in a wide range of organisational spheres, including student recruitment and support, employment, contracts and purchasing, research, teaching and learning, external affairs, and equal opportunities action planning.

The toolkit is not a list of do's and don'ts that HEIs should follow in order to be a successful antiracist institution. Failing to engage with the wider issues would ignore fundamental questions about attitudes and assumptions that structure relationships among staff, between staff and students, and between the institution and local communities. Instead, the toolkit invites institutions to reflect and act upon a number of critical areas where there is potential for discrimination. In order to effect change, however, it is important to understand how race inequalities have become embedded within an organisation like a university in the first place. So the toolkit provides conceptual tools with which to work.

The conceptual tools

(i) Institutional racism

Central to the development of this toolkit project is the concept of institutional racism and debates relevant to this area. A critical reading of the Macpherson Report (1999) raises a number of considerations for research into institutional racism in HEIs. That races, ethnicities and cultures are socially constructed seems to be commonly accepted in current debates. It is no longer acceptable to argue that race is a biological, natural construct with intrinsic and essential properties (this is not to say, however, that this kind of thinking no longer exists). A contradiction arises as those opposed to racism (anti-racists) must deny that races exist whilst simultaneously invoking racialised categories. Race does not exist in a scientifically meaningful sense. This, however, does not mean that people have ceased to relate to these categories as if they were fixed and natural – it is still reflected in popular and political discourse. Although social scientists now tend to talk more about ethnicity and culture than race, assumptions that once related to concepts of race often continue to proliferate and structure understandings of self and other (Bonnett, 2000; Modood, 1992; 1997).

Recognising that race is a social construction, modified and transformed through human interaction, does not deal with the problem of the continued use of racialised terminology within sociological inquiry. Neither does it deal with the problem of the continued use of this terminology in everyday speech or in the language of ethnic monitoring. As Gillborn (1995) and Law (1996) have pointed out, however, abandoning these categories would frustrate sociological analysis and policy formulation. So, in spite of reinforcing terms that we might wish to see discarded, the language and terminology of racialised discourse has to be used if inquiries are able to be pursued and 'where it is treated by social actors as a real basis for social differentiation' (Law, 1996: 3-6).

Essed's (1991) concept of everyday racism has been integrated into the toolkit. This idea counters the view that racism is an individual problem – a notion that one is or is not 'racist'. 'Everyday racism' refers to forms of discrimination that manifest themselves in 'systematic, recurrent, familiar practices'. Everyday racism 'is infused into familiar practices, it involves socialised attitudes and behaviour' (Essed, 1991: 3). Essed usefully describes racism as both structure and process. It is structure because dominance and discrimination exists and is reproduced through the formulation and application of rules, laws, and regulations and through access to and allocation of resources. As a process, it does not exist outside everyday practice where it is reproduced and reinforced, adapting continually to the ever-changing social, political and economic societal conditions (1991: 44).

That an HEI could be described as a site of institutional racism, however, frequently excites denials. Interview and survey data from research at the University of Leeds indicated that large numbers of key staff were opposed to understanding an HEI as an institution in which racial discrimination is embedded across policy, practice and organisational culture. As Ross (2000) has observed, an institutional culture of denial can foster apathy and resistance to the introduction of equal opportunities/antiracist training programmes. Even so-called antiracist institutions, however, can find themselves reproducing discriminatory practice. For example, when the Commission for Racial Equality investigated a case of alleged racial discrimination in staff appointments at Hinckley College of FE, they found that discrimination had occurred in 'the most unexpected places', in this case, in a College controlled by a local authority 'with a long standing equal opportunities policy' (Commission for Racial Equality, 1991: 9).

The dangers of 'uncritical self-understanding' highlighted in the Macpherson Report (1999) are clear. It calls for a critical evaluation of institutional values, ethos and driving forces. This may be especially important in an organisation such as an HEI, which perceives itself to be liberal and simply assumes that all is well. So we have to question what 'excellence in education' means and whether institutional performance can be measured by more than income to the HEI, low dropout rates, degree results, graduate access to job market and research ratings.

Staff working in HEIs often fail to recognise their position in the wider context. For example, a common belief among staff at the University of Leeds was that they were powerless to effect change if applications from Black and minority ethnic groups were low. The potentially active role of the HEI in the wider educational system and the acknowledgement of responsibility for tackling some of the barriers that bias the selection process prior to HEI entry are rare. As Ross concludes from her research with quality assurance managers in HEIs, 'that factors other than academic ability are at play in the selection process is simply denied, or possibly not understood, by most staff working in higher education' (Ross, 2000: 67).

Racism takes different forms in different settings. We would not therefore expect the experience of institutional racism in HEIs to mirror that in the police force, although there will be broad structural similarities. Furthermore, we would not expect institutional racism within HEIs to always express itself in the same form. Rather, it will reflect historical policies, practices and processes, and the contingencies that arise from particular geographical contexts and institutional settings. There are likely to be significant differences, for example, between community based HEIs and those who seek to recruit students in the national and international arena.

(ii) Eurocentrism

The toolkit also provided a short introduction to the concept of eurocentrism and its impact on the structures and processes of an institution. According to the Oxford English Dictionary, the term 'eurocentrism' has its roots in the term 'Europcentrism', the idea or the practice of placing Europe at the centre of one's world view and an assumption of the supremacy of Europe and Europeans in world cultures. The term emerged relatively recently and has been used to describe the relationship between Western Europe and the 'rest' of Europe as well as the relationship between the 'West and the rest' (Hall, 1992). Eurocentrism should not be perceived as simply a form of racism but, rather, as a discourse that is often manifested in ways that can be described as racist. Intersecting with eurocentrism is the question of whiteness. Although eurocentrism should not be reduced to the centring of whiteness, whiteness, as a racialised identity or identification, is crucial to its operations. Furthermore, although racism can be critiqued as a eurocentric device, racisms also operate in many societies outside the West.

(iii) Unpicking whiteness

The toolkit explores the idea of whiteness, which is intrinsically interlinked to the concepts of racism and eurocentrism. For many HEIs, the whiteness of the institution goes unnoticed and is rationalised into a day-to-day perception of normality. The research at the University of Leeds indicated, however, that when forced to identify the face of the institution, many people working there described it (with reference to staff) as not only predominantly white, but also predominantly male. For the most part, however, people rarely notice the whiteness of an institution and are unaware of the implications that this normative whiteness has for staff and students there. What is more, people tend to overestimate the numbers of Black and minority ethnic people working and studying in an institution. They also often assume that equality policies of any kind will work primarily in favour of Black and minority ethnic people, women and disabled candidates (both staff and students). The advantages accruing to white people in an institution are unrecognised or downplayed.

(iv) Critical boundaries

Although the toolkit prioritises race and racism, we were sensitive to the interconnections and intersections between issues around gender, disability, class, sexuality, religion and age. Experiences of racism and discrimination are not uniform; they are experienced in different ways by different people in different times and places. The toolkit thus alerts users to the need to be mindful of the intersection of racism with the other types of discrimination.

The legal and organisational framework

A number of the legislative requirements in place provide a framework for action. These include the Race Relations (Amendment) Act 2000 and the 1998 Human Rights Act. The Race Relations Act 1976, as amended by the Race Relations (Amendment) Act 2000, makes it unlawful to discriminate against anyone on grounds of race, colour, nationality (including citizenship), or ethnic or national origin. The Race Relations (Amendment)

Act 2000 places a positive General Duty on all HEIs to promote race equality. This means that HEIs, in all their identified relevant functions, must have due regard to the need to eliminate unlawful racial discrimination, promote equality of opportunity and to promote good race relations between people of different racial groups. All HEIs in England and Wales were required to have an Action Plan in place by May 2002. In Scotland the date for compliance was November 2002.

In accordance with the legislative framework in mind, the toolkit provides a guide to concepts such as direct/indirect discrimination and victimisation; harassment; positive action; targets; ethnic monitoring; and dealing with/deconstructing stereotypes. It also provides examples of positive action strategies, targets and benchmarking, and explores the value and necessity for monitoring. We also introduce HEIs to ideas of accountability, responsibilities and liabilities with reference to race equality and antiracist practice. We explore the indicators of good and bad practice and consider the training needs an HEI may have to address. The toolkit is careful to discuss training issues in a constructive and proactive way. There is no 'one size fits all'. When we talk about the kinds of training available in an institution, we should not only be considering equal opportunities training, cultural and religious diversity training and antiracist training, but also positive strategies to encourage Black and minority ethnic staff and students to train for career progression.

Training, however, is simply the beginning. To affect practice it has to be effective, useful and constructive. Reena Bhavnani (2001) argues against specific training days. Citing the Stephen Lawrence Inquiry, she maintains that the antiracist training for the police was a disaster, as many police officers could barely remember the training process or failed to understand why it was necessary. Antiracist and diversity training should not be seen as something extra to the policy and practice of an institution, but as integral to its operations.

Operating antiracist strategies in different areas of the HEI

The toolkit aims to provide the tools to assist an organisation in developing antiracist strategy across a wide range of organisational areas. It begins with the basics, such as deciding a general statement of aims, before moving on to look more specifically at equal opportunities and race equality policies and practices in HE. The extent to which equal opportunities in general, and race equality issues in particular, have been considered in an individual institution will depend on how the planning and organisation of equal opportunities issues has been pursued. An examination of equal opportunities at the University of Leeds found that implementation was haphazard and that there were examples of both good practice and bad across different departments and units. There was also a broad range of attitudes towards equal opportunities policies and their effectiveness. Some staff members were positive and enthusiastic about the potential for change through equal opportunities policies, whilst others were sceptical, indifferent or even hostile to the idea of promoting opportunities for particular groups of people.

For the most part, equal opportunities were not necessarily perceived as unimportant by the staff we surveyed at the University of Leeds, but many saw them as irrelevant or peripheral to the day-to-day running of their department and/or institution. Some staff argued that there were too few Black and minority ethnic staff or students in the University to place priority on such issues, whilst others believed that fairness and equity were endemic to liberal institutions such as HEIs, so no special policy initiatives were required. Staff reactions to the University's declaration of an equal opportunities policy were varied and ambivalent. The feelings expressed included: first, the view that policy was not being put into practice; second, that there was a lack of explicit prioritisation of equal opportunities issues; and third, worries about how equal opportunities initiatives would affect staff workloads. Many staff also conflated questions of race equality with those of equal opportunities as a whole. Thus, in keeping with previous studies such as Neal (1998) and Bird (1995), we found that race issues had low priority. At best they are mentioned tokenistically, at worst not considered at all.

The toolkit recommends that to be effective race equality needs to be addressed across all organisational areas in an HEI. The particular areas explored within the toolkit are as follows:

(i) Employment
Concerns about race equality and employment in higher education often focus solely on recruitment and appointments. It is one thing to address the appointments procedure for an institution but another to ensure that the principles enshrined and promoted in the recruitment and appointments process are carried through to staff career progression and staff support. Carter, Fenton and Modood (1999) found that even institutions with a race equality policy have often failed to address key areas relating to employment. This study found that approximately 25 per cent of Black and minority ethnic academics believed they had personally experienced discrimination in the process of applying for a job; this figure rose to 30 per cent amongst Black and minority ethnic *non-British* minorities. Fifteen per cent felt the same about promotion and almost 20 per cent had experienced some form of racial harassment from staff and/or students – with Black and minority ethnic women being more likely to experience racial harassment. The study also found that Black and minority ethnic staff were significantly less likely to be in senior positions, particularly professorial, and more likely to be on fixed-term contracts.

The toolkit explores the areas of appointments, recruitment, career progression, promotions and harassment, bullying and dignity at work. Examples of positive action strategies (as well as bad practice) are presented alongside targets for redressing any identified inequities.

(ii) Student recruitment, support and transition to employment
The toolkit addresses issues relevant to student recruitment, support and the transition into employment and provides ideas and strategies for incorporating and promoting anti-racist and race equality measures into student admissions (via a review and evaluation of publicity literature, open days, widening participation strategies and the interview process). We suggest that institutions consider ways for Black and minority ethnic students to be supported through their studies by provision of appropriate and sensitive coun-

selling, careers services, and safe and secure accommodation. We also encourage HEIs to think about ways of addressing the inequalities faced by Black and minority ethnic graduates when they enter the world of employment.

(iii) Teaching and learning

The toolkit provides some tools to help institutions address issues relevant to teaching and learning. These issues are integral to the question of student support and perceptions of the institution from the outside. We ask institutions to reflect upon assessment procedures and the curriculum in order to consider the various ways in which current content and practice may discriminate against Black and minority ethnic students because of inappropriate resources and a eurocentric perspective.

The kinds of courses taught in HEIs are central to students' experiences. The toolkit enables departments to think about the inclusion and integration of voices, perspectives, works and ideas that come from beyond a white, eurocentric core. Questions about teaching methods also include considerations of delivery as well as course content and resources. To address potential inequity within the curriculum, a consideration of race, racism and race equality can be incorporated into the process of module review (the review of individual course modules) and periodic review (the strategic overview of an entire department's teaching and learning activities). The toolkit suggests that race equality measures be incorporated into the normal process of course and programme design and institutional monitoring. The toolkit recommends that race equality and racism issues be incorporated into the review and planning process of institutional boards and committees. The goal is to mainstream or routinise the consideration of race equality issues into organisational practice and to challenge organisational cultures that accept and reinforce discriminatory attitudes and practice.

(iv) Learning issues

The toolkit identified what teaching staff need to be mindful of when considering the learning environment and the needs of students. The process of learning should be inclusive and take into account the needs of all learners in terms of ethnicity, gender, disability, religion and so on. Lecturers and tutors should be aware that their own expectations of students may be based on stereotypes and assumptions about particular ethnic groups and their potential for achievement. International students are particularly vulnerable, as assumptions of academic inferiority often circulate about students from non-Western countries.

Other issues to be taken into consideration are that, firstly, assessment of a student's language abilities should not influence the assessment of other skills; secondly, that assessment is monitored by ethnicity, gender and so on, so that, if appropriate, positive action can be taken to redress inequalities; and thirdly, that examinations and assessment procedures should be sensitive and culturally inclusive.

(v) Research

We argue in the toolkit that research on race, ethnicity and racism can positively affect the working and teaching environment of an institution. We briefly indicate how research in these areas can be reviewed, promoted and organised by institutions and also raise questions about ethical research practices when embarking on research projects. A consideration of the types of research that take place in the HEI is important because it has implications in terms of staffing and recruitment, the image of the HEI and its position in terms of contributing to a particular field of research activity. This has implications for the public face of the institution as well as, though not necessarily, the recruitment of staff from a diversity of backgrounds. The question of research also has implications for the recruitment of students and strong connections with teaching, learning and the curriculum. Some HEIs have been sites from which dubious theories of race and ethnicity have emerged. Scientific and social theories about the inferiority of particular races and ideas about distinct biological races have had far-reaching and damaging effects. In the present context, the HE sector has the power and the resources to counter these ideas.

Thinking about research is also important in relation to the question of employment. Carter, Fenton and Modood's (1999) study found that Black and minority ethnic staff were much more likely to be working in fixed-term contract research. For non-British nationals, this concentration is even more marked. Research is one of the pivotal and central activities of a HEI. However, an institution may want to consider how its research practice and employment policies intersect to produce an environment where Black and minority ethnic academics are disproportionately represented on short-term research contracts.

(vi) Contracts and purchasing

In reviewing issues related to contracts and purchasing by the HEI, we draw upon the work of the Commission for Racial Equality to demonstrate the potential impact of antiracist and race equality practices on outside agencies. Its purchasing potential gives the HEI a great deal of power and it can thus constitute a significant force for positive change. This can be done by setting a good example and sending out positive messages to local and regional organisations on the importance of antiracist practices. Under the Race Relations Act (2000), it is unlawful for public bodies to discriminate whilst carrying out any of their functions. By including conditions relating to race equality in their contracts, the HEI could play an important role in encouraging private sector employers to tackle the issue of race equality and address discrimination at all levels.

(vii) External affairs

A further area for antiracist action relates to the various facets of the public face of the HEI. The toolkit explores the various ways in which the HEI could, by incorporating antiracism into its own practice, help to address racism and discrimination inside and outside the sector. The kind of relationship that an HEI is able to establish with communities, organisations and institutions outside is a crucial aspect of its presentation of itself, both externally and internally. In the case of the University of Leeds, we referred its Alumni Relations Office, the City and Regional and Widening Participation Office, the European Office, the International and Schools Liaison Office, the Press Office, the Public Relations Office, the Publications Office. We explored the opportunities available to an HEI for representing the organisation through, for example, its prospectuses, departmental flyers, web materials, leaflets and its in-house newspapers and newsletters. An institution can draw on its considerable publicity resources to promote race equality and antiracist issues. HEIs can also review the representation of diversity in departmental flyers, brochures and prospectuses and include clear statements on equality within these public documents.

Reviewing an institution of higher education

Finally, the toolkit provides readers with the methodological tools to enable a review of equality and diversity among the staff and student body. To obtain information about both good and bad practice, what is working and what is not, HEIs need to listen to both staff and students. We suggest an 'attitudes' or 'perceptions' audit. Obtaining the views of all academic staff (support, research and academic-related) as well as students and listening to their experiences, opinions and ideas will provide a base from which action can be taken. The paper policies and committees may be in place, but, as we found at the University of Leeds, staff may not be fully committed to implementing those policies, or even know how to go about it. To borrow terminology used in the housing sector, the keys to understanding what needs to be done are: communication, consultation, participation and knowledge. Knowledge and understanding of the issues and strategies employed by an institution are integral to their success and continuation.

Conclusion

The toolkit aims to provide the HEI with a set of tools, both conceptual and methodological, to enable it to address racism and race equality and to mainstream action with reference to these issues across its policy and practice. The toolkit has been widely disseminated across the sector in England, Scotland, Northern Ireland and Wales. It is too soon to tell what its impact has been. However, informal evidence and feedback suggests that it has been widely read. It is also increasingly being used by a range of HEIs in reviewing and evaluating their operations and the practices of departments, schools and whole institutions. We are also aware that the toolkit has had some impact outside the sector with organisations such as those in the voluntary sector, social inclusion partnerships and equality organisations. There has also been interest from individuals and institutions outside the UK who have found the toolkit helpful in addressing parallel issues in different national contexts.

References

Bhavnani, Reena (2001) *Rethinking Interventions in Racism*. Stoke on Trent, Trentham Books.

Bird, John (1996) *Black Students and Higher Education: Rhetorics and Realities*. Buckingham, The Society for Research into Higher Education and the Open University Press.

Bonnet, Alistair (2000) *Anti-Racism*. London, Routledge.

Carter, John, Steve, Fenton and Tariq Modood (1999) *Ethnicity and Employment in Higher Education*. London, Policy Studies Institute.

Commission for Racial Equality (1991) *A Question of Merit: A Report of a Formal Investigation into Lecturer Appointments in Leicestershire*. London: Commission for Racial Equality.

Essed, Philomena (1991) *Understanding Everyday Racism: An Interdisciplinary Theory*, Newbury Park, London, Sage Publications.

Gillborn, David (1995) *Racism and Antiracism in Real Schools: Theory – Policy – Practice*. Buckingham, Open University Press.

Hall, Stuart (1992) 'The West and the Rest: Discourse and Power' in *Formations of Modernity*, Cambridge, Open University Press: 275-320.

Law, Ian (1996) *Racism, Ethnicity and Social Policy*. London, Prentice Hall.

Macpherson, William (1999) *The Stephen Lawrence Inquiry Report of an inquiry by Sir William Macpherson of Cluny*. London, HMSO.

Major, Lee Elliot (2002) 'Incredible islands: A disturbing report shows universities must tackle race issues' in *The Guardian*, Tuesday January 15, 2002.

Modood, T. (1992) *Not Easy being British: Colour, Culture and Citizenship*. London; Runnymede Trust and Trentham Books.

Modood, Tariq (1997) ''Difference', Cultural Racism and Anti-Racism', in Werbner, Pnina and Tariq Modood (eds.) *Debating Cultural Hybridity*. London, Zed Books: 154-172.

Neal, Sarah (1998) *The Making of Equal Opportunities Policies in Universities*. Buckingham and Bristol, USA, The Society for Research into Higher Education and the Open University Press.

Ross, K. (2000) 'Race' and Ethnicity. In D. Woodward and K. Ross (eds.) *Managing Equal Opportunities in Higher Education: A Guide to Understanding and Action*. Buckingham: Open University Press.

CHAPTER ELEVEN

Transforming the Curriculum?
The problem with multiculturalism

Sanjay Sharma

The promise of multiculturalism – living with difference – belies its agonised, paradoxical status. Can equality and difference be reconciled? Does multiculturalism mean the dismantling of Western universalism or is it the ally of ethnic particularisms. Is there something that can be called a multicultural curriculum? Contestations over the meanings and purposes of multiculturalism do not simply reflect existing ideological conflicts – they are constitutive of its ambivalent political praxis.

In Britain, education has been the principal arena of debate about multiculturalism. Structured by political ambivalences they have focused primarily on race and ethnicity in schooling. They have not resolved a public understanding of multiculturalism, nor its pedagogical efficacy. While discussions have shifted beyond education and acquired broader currency, institutions of higher education have essentially ignored this issue. Whether the contested discourse of multiculturalism has operated in an compensatory or transformatory educational mode, the challenge of multiculturalism remains astonishingly unacknowledged for the practices of teaching and learning in British Universities.

Burgeoning accusations of institutional racism against these universities have evoked a predictable defensiveness couched in the language of liberal tolerance, promotion of the equality of opportunity and cultural diversity. The failure to expose and combat the normalising culture of whiteness in universities should not be reduced to the institutional inertia of these organisations. The Race Relations (Amendment) Act 2000 might – if anything does – affect university policies and possibly practices of staff employment and student recruitment. But the everyday activities of learning and teaching are a more complex issue for the realisation of a multicultural university. Under the purview of educational quality assurance the curriculum has increasingly been subjected to scrutiny, yet this managerialist response to educational development and pedagogy excludes an interrogation of the politics of knowledge and difference for universities today.

This chapter makes such an interrogation, identifying what is at stake in transforming the university curriculum. To critically examine issues of multiculturalism means confronting the ethics and aporia of cultural difference. Any benevolent shifts towards multi-culturalism should not be celebrated as a progressive educational move. Neither should it be understood solely in terms of the juridico-legal pressures of the recent legislation. Multiculturalism as currently on offer articulates a neo-liberal agenda that acknowledges and values cultural differences while its hegemonic operations seek to regulate these dif-ferences. Moreover, the role of the contemporary university in a knowledge economy is compelling them to compete in the market-place of global knowledge production. The knowledge about Otherness – ways of life, cross-cultural hybridities and geographies, emerging markets, technologies and communications – has become vital to producing a new 'information-rich, self-reflexive' educated class of 'flexible workers' for the needs of transnational capital (Zavarzadeh and Morton, 1994). The multicultural curriculum needs to resist both the demands of a 'global multicultural capitalism' (Žižek, 1997) and concomitant universalising Eurocentrism.

There is no blueprint for a multicultural curriculum and pedagogy. Instead there are some materials and content which are in one way or another marked by ethnic/racial dif-ference. The inclusion of differences of Others is what characterises the curriculum as multicultural. But an educational praxis that seeks merely to include 'other knowledges' or reveal the truth about 'other cultures' is doomed to failure, as it ultimately serves to reproduce existing hegemonies of cultural authority and racialised knowledge. Although refusing to specify a universal multicultural teaching method I do not reproduce a facile postmodern denouncement of totalising knowledges and practices. My position is animated by concrete pedagogic concerns that reckon with the 'irreducible political antagonisms' of multiculturalism (Hesse, 1999) and offers an alternative conception of how we may hink through the ethical grounds[1] of a multicultural curriculum.

Contested multiculturalisms

The vision of a multicultural curriculum in higher education means putting into question the historical role which the Western university has played since Renaissance in the develop-ment of European thought. It is one thing to recognise the implication of universities in the colonial mission which set out to civilise and conquer the non-European world. It is quite another to recognise this as part of the process of decolonisation, the whole paradigm of the Western university is being challenged by the counterflow of populations and ideas from South to North, East to West. (Cohen, 1995)

The first steps towards a multicultural university for the 21st century is the eradication of its historic elitism and Eurocentrism. Such a de-centring of Western knowledge is intimately tied with what Phil Cohen calls as the 'counterflow' of non-European ideas and peoples. The encounter with cultural difference outside of domination, appropriation or assimilation, however, eludes the hegemony of contemporary liberal multiculturalism. Although the goals of multicultural education in Britain have generally included attempts to broaden the curriculum by taking into account cultural diversity, little has been done to deconstruct its own regimes of knowledge. Acrimonious debates over university education in the US are on somewhat different lines.

What has been dubbed as the 'culture wars' fought in US campuses, primarily over the content of the curriculum, have thrown into question the status and relevance of the universality of the Western canon[2]. The very identity of the university and its contemporary role in multicultural societies are under challenge. There has been no such equivalent war over the canon nor a challenge to the racial formation of the university curriculum in Britain. One reason might be the relatively small presence and influence of minority academics and students on British campuses, compared with the US. While this situation is slowly changing, minorities in Britain still remain racially marginalised in an educational sphere which has at best sustained a compensatory liberal multiculturalism. This illustrates the significance of how issues of multiculturalism have been politically mobilised in higher education. Gerard Delanty highlights the impact of the politics of identity and difference in the US:

> The university was allegedly based on only one culture, the common heritage of humankind. The politicisation of multiculturalism has destroyed the illusion of universality. Nowhere has the onslaught on liberal multiculturalism been more apparent than in the curriculum. The debate in the humanities on the western canon and the debate on hidden histories in history and the social sciences has transformed the teaching programmes of the leading American universities. (Delanty, 2001)

He suggests that in the US the politics of ethnicity have been privileged over class. Current debates over university access and inclusion appear to acknowledge class inequalities in Britain, but issues of racialised exclusion remain epiphenomenal.

The entanglement of multiculturalism and education has been connected to schooling, not higher education, perhaps because this is where the contention of minority children and parents has been most acute (Tomlinson, 1985). Although higher education has its own specific concerns, debates about multicultural schooling can be used to broadly situate the problematic of educational multiculturalism in Britain.

Educating reason
Multicultural education and schooling has been a site of power struggles – an ideological battleground between liberal (multicultural), radical-left (antiracist) and neoconservative (monocultural) educationalists and activists. Traditionally, identifiable political perspectives have determined the accounts of multicultural education along these ideological fault-lines. These oppositional positions are, however, inadequate – conceptually and politically – for developing new educational thinking, as they are for analysing the cultural conditions of late modernity (Donald and Rattansi, 1992; May, 1999b). The battles between the three positions appeared to have ended in the late 1990s. The narrative about progressive forms of multicultural education in Britain would end in the de-legitimation of its projects.[3]

One key limitation on developing progressive approaches and, potentially more empowering educational practice, has been the lack of a theoretical interrogation of their epistemological and political discourses. The dominant academic research tradition in education in the UK has tended to be empirically driven, especially in relation to the messy realities of teaching and learning in the classroom. As David Buckingham (1996) points out, some of this has taken place in the context of local struggles in schooling; and committed teacher interventions and Black parental demands have been pivotal in challenging the liberal notions of a neutral curriculum. Buckingham argues that critical pedagogy work in the US has lacked an engagement with the complexities of classroom life. He charges US work with 'theoreticism'. But we should learn from the attempt to address questions of multiculturalism and difference from a critical standpoint,[4] whereas such concerns are still theoretically under-developed and educationally marginalised in the UK.

Interrogating the modernist foundational principles and practices of progressive education has however increased over the last decade in Britain (see especially Donald and Rattansi, 1992; May, 1999a; Rattansi and Reeder, 1992a). Ali Rattansi and David Reeder have argued that the crisis of legitimation within progressive educational movements has reflected a growing suspicion of traditional belief in 'Enlightenment thought'. The authors identify 'a distinctly postmodern distrust of the simplistic grand narratives and scenarios for change' through the vehicle of a modernist education as so far constituted (Rattansi and Reeder, 1992b:14). They argue for the necessity of re-evaluating some of the key conceptual and political suppositions of progressive and radical educational thinking.

Rattansi and Reeder (1992b) point to the de-legitimation of educational approaches from a postmodern perspective. By accommodating a range of political and epistemological perspectives and embodying a variety of discursive frameworks postmodernismisn still a useful term. As a cultural condition it is often conflated with the more philosophically orientated umbrella term of poststructuralism. Michael Peters (1996) identifies a common trajectory of thought in the scepticism towards the project of the Enlightenment. He cites Lovibond:

> The Enlightenment pictured the human race as engaged in an effort towards moral and intellectual self-realisation, and so the subject of a universal historical experience; it also postulated a universal human reason in terms of which social and political tendencies could be assessed as 'progressive' or otherwise... Postmodernism... rejects the doctrine of the unity of reason. It refuses to conceive of humanity as a unitary subject striving towards the goal of perfect coherence (its common stock of beliefs) or a perfect cohesion and stability (in its political practice). (Lovibond, quoted in Peters, 1996:1-2)

Liberal education is founded upon Enlightenment thinking: the 'modernist dream of 'educating reason' based on a universal education' which supposedly applies to all nations and cultures (Peters, 1996:2). The critique of subject-centred reason is a challenge to education based upon Enlightenment ideals. It is not surprising that Peters turns to Jean Francois Lyotard's *The Postmodern Condition* (1984) as a key critique of Enlightenment reason. Lyotard infamously proclaimed that the postmodern condition represents 'an incredulity towards metanarratives': the rejection of any forms of 'totalising thought' such as the Enlightenment belief of rational and liberatory knowledge produced by science, philosophy and education, or the emancipation of the unified rational subject of reason. These grand discourses of Western society are seemingly no longer viable, and acted to only legitimate a Eurocentric narrative and mode of being purporting to be globally universal. For Lyotard, postmodern knowledge and education is against metanarratives and foundationalism. It celebrates heterogeneity, dissent and difference over homogeneity, consensus and universality. His contentions need not be embraced un-critically, but he draws attention to the possibility that we are witnessing a terminal decline of the intellectual and political authority of Enlightenment metanarratives such as Liberalism and Marxism, which are the very narratives that have underwritten pro-gressive and radical education projects.

The de-centring of these grand narratives also suggest the decline of the cultural hegemony of the West in a postcolonial world. Robert Young characterises post-modernism 'as European culture's awareness that it is no longer the unquestioned and dominant centre of the world' (1995:19). This links with the intellectual and political de-centring of 'Man' as the subject of Western liberal humanism 'whose identity depended on the othering of subordinate class, racial, gendered and sexual subjects who were ... marginalised from the democratic right to a political subjectivity' (Mercer, 1994). This 'de-centring' has engendered and legitimated a broad range of oppositional minority dis-courses and cultural practices, accompanied by a new politics of representation, found in both liberal and radical forms of multiculturalism. New kinds of cultural and political identities are expressed through various forms of identity politics, for example in Black, women's and gay movements; and also a politics of difference that recognises the forma-tion of new political groupings based on categories such as race, gender or sexuality, but also the intersubjective and discursive conditions of identity production (Hall, 1991).

While these de-centrings open up ambiguously to a variety of expressions of identity politics and difference, they are nevertheless, as Stuart Hall argues:

> matched, from the very heartland of cultural politics, by the backlash: the aggressive resis-tance to difference; the attempt to restore the canon of Western civilisation, the assault ... on multiculturalism; the return to the grand narratives of history, language and literature (the three supporting pillars of national identity and national culture); the defence of ethnic absolutism, of a cultural racism that has marked the Thatcher and Reagan eras; and the new xenophobias that are about to overwhelm fortress Europe. (Hall, 1992b:25)

The neo-conservative backlash against challenges to the Western canon is emblematic of the wider response to the breaking down of old political certainties, national-cultural borders and the centred white male subject. At the heart of this conflict is a struggle over culture which is 'intertwined with the issues of power, representation, and identity' (Giroux, 1994:67).

Contemporary rethinking of British multiculturalism points to fundamental theoretical and pedagogic concerns, and the need to refigure culture for education (Donald and Rattansi, 1992). Culture has been the critical site through which the ideological divisions between liberal multicultural and antiracist educational perspectives have been ex-pressed, although the crisis of representation was expressed most emphatically in the lan-guage of culture in Britain a century ago. As Maria Koundoura (1998) points out, critics such as John Stuart Mill and Mathew Arnold argued that (élite) 'men of culture' could 'unite classes' and prevent the debasement of culture by the political enfranchisement of the working class. Arnold in particular argued that 'the state should represent its citizen's 'best self', and since the 'men of culture' are the representatives of this self, the state should represent culture' (Koundoura, 1998:69). These claims should not be under-estimated, adopted as they were in the first government report on the teaching of English in British compulsory state-funded education – the *Newbolt Report* of 1921. A literary education was championed as a pedagogy capable of diffusing class antagonism and pro-ducing social cohesion by recognising a shared investment in the national culture (Bhattacharyya, 1991). The production of national unity by staging a common culture which can class antagonisms and other cultural differences has been reproduced in the discourse of liberal multicultural education. As Koundoura (1998:70) writes: 'Such is the history ... from which multiculturalism as an educational policy – with its agenda of *representing* and *teaching* cultural difference – arises' (emphasis added).

Cultural diversity has been the dominant motif in the representation and teaching of dif-ference in contemporary liberal multiculturalism, for both schooling and university education. From a neo-marxist antiracist perspective, this approach has been proble-matised for reifying culture and ethnic group identity at the expense of examining power relations in society (May, 1999b). While ostensibly a convincing critique, the antiracist approach mistakenly entailed rejection of ethnicity or culture, rather than examining the cultural politics of representation (Rattansi, 1992; Rattansi, 1999). The ideology of cultural diversity has helped to manage cultural/racial differences within the nation. But as suggested by Homi Bhabha (1990), it has also sought to control and repress cultural difference:

> Although there is always an entertainment and encouragement of cultural diversity, there is always a corresponding containment of it. A transparent norm is constituted, a norm given by the host society or dominant culture, which says that 'these cultures are fine, but we must be able to locate them within our own grid' ... a containment of cultural difference. (Bhabha, 1990:20)

Bhabha's contentions alert us to the danger of notions pertaining to the construction of a unitary or common culture, whether in crude conservative sense of the exclusive nation or the liberal sense of diversity within unity. It is this transparent, white norm which is erased in accounts of liberal or benevolent multiculturalism. As Peter McLaren has asked: 'Who has the power to exercise meaning, to create the grid from which Otherness is defined, to create the identifications that invite closures on meanings?' (McLaren, 1995:213).

The containment of cultural difference constructs culture epistemologically as an 'em-pirical object of knowledge', and compels it to be understood as a discrete category that can be discovered, observed, evaluated and contextualised – though always governed by a transparent norm (Bhabha, 1994). In reifying culture, liberal multiculturalism ignores the operations of power that produce culture as a knowable anthropological object in the first place. The project of multicultural education, the appreciation and knowledge of other cultures, or the encouragement of cultural diversity in curriculum practices can only manifest itself through an absolute or relative difference against an invisible Euro-centric frame of reference. At the heart of this compensatory multiculturalism there exists an acknowledgement of otherness as only a balkanised or domesticated Other. The act of making ethnic otherness a knowable object of knowledge can be understood as making the Other the same. That is, the relationship or encounter with the Other is one of appropriation or domination (cf. Chow, 1998; Nealon, 1998).

The problem of educational multiculturalism is exacerbated by the problem of otherness. The domination of sameness over otherness – the overcoming of difference and poly-vocality – has defined the 'Western knowledge project' (Scheurich, 1997). This project has been best understood in terms of the Enlightenment quest of accumulating universal knowledge, exemplified by the idea of the university (see Delanty, 2001). James Sheurich (1997), echoing the work of postcolonial theorists such as Gayatri C. Spivak, contends that the 'will to power' of Western knowledge is connected to the drive to appropriate, order and conquer. Thus, the educational praxis of simply including know-ledge about 'other cultures' into an existing curriculum masks the epistemic violence of the binary division of Same/Other. Moreover, the supposedly more sensitive multi-cultural representation of other knowledges or identities in their pluralities does not over-come the problem of otherness. The totalising project of Western knowledge encounters difference by transforming (reducing) it to the Same, otherwise difference remains unknowable, exterior to universalist frameworks of understanding and interpretation – beyond the grasp of the curriculum.

The Western domination of otherness should not be conceived as operating outside of history. The expansion of global capitalism has recently embraced otherness, and ethnicity has becoming a driving force in the development of new markets in food, fashion, tourism, literature etc. As Michael Hardt and Antonio Negri (2000) contend, in our present condition of Empire, a neo-racism of 'differential inclusion' is operating which actively acknowledges ethnic differences and 'hybrid subjectivities', yet pacifies them against a normalising whiteness.[5] The 'turn to the Other', in both the economic and academic arenas, is always fraught with producing and reproducing relations of domination and control.

But we must not conclude that an encounter with alternative non-Western systems of knowledge and ways of life is impossible. If multicultural curriculum has any political value we would need to pursue it in relation to exploring an ethical relationship with the Other outside domination and appropriation (Nealon, 1998). To deny this possibility is to deny the diversity of human existence. Differences have arisen because of the multi-plicity of open-ended cultural encounters and dialogic exchanges. It is when these dif-ferences are arrested and domesticated that the domination of otherness arises (Falzon, 1998).

Beyond culture

It is scarcely surprising that few schools have adopted multicultural initiatives. Multi-culture persists in its marginality, especially for those schools in 'all white areas' (Jones, 1999) as cultural diversity has been defined as of relevance only to other ethnic groups. Furthermore, the common practice of using non-white children as a multicultural resource has not been possible in such schools (Gaine, 1988; 1995). So an exegesis of the politics of whiteness has never been explored. The majority of developments have concentrated on correcting teacher attitudes and introducing cultural diversity to a mono-cultural school curriculum (Jones, 1999). Failing to examine the culture of whiteness within the liberal tradition of multicultural education has not been an oversight but an outcome of its own reductive conception of culture and the denial of an exnominated normative whiteness.[6]

Similarly, it could be argued that multicultural developments in the university curriculum have largely been necessitated by the increasing presence of minority students, as well as the need to address wider socio-economic implications of globalisation. Only when the racialised bodies of these students and staff enter into the white spaces of the university might issues of cultural or racial difference become concrete pedagogical concerns. While the disciplinary and theoretical imperatives of a non-Eurocentric, globalised curriculum have been significant for recent developments in the academy – not only in the social sciences and humanities – these political-intellectual imperatives have not been the driving force for legitimating an academic multicultural praxis. More tellingly, confronting the normalising whiteness of the academy in relation to curricular innovations is still profoundly muted. In the rare instances of engaging issues of pedagogy to expose university racisms, curriculum developments are habitually reduced to matters of content and disciplinarity[7] The responses to the demand for a multicultural curriculum generate agitated questions: 'What are these non-Eurocentric ideas and bodies of cultural knowledge that should be taught to our students? What should be included?' and an anxiety that 'there are not enough black authors on our reading lists'. These additive forms of inclusion regulate multicultural curricular developments, yet they are structured so as to produce a domesticated otherness that fails to challenge existing Eurocentric frameworks of knowledge.

What gets constructed as multicultural knowledge needs to be refigured in terms of the emergence of a particular cultural formation – how an identity or knowledge of otherness is constituted. To interrogate the possibility of non-Eurocentric knowledge means questioning how systems of colonial governance and knowledge have maintained a manichean divide between the Same and the Other – the 'West and the Rest' (Bhabha, 1994; Hall, 1992a; Said, 1987). In relation to the colonial encounter between Europe and its abject Other, Bhabha observes that the 'problem of cultures' most intensely emerge at their boundaries, at points of political conflict and crisis. He extends this argument to the contemporary postcolonial situation, asserting that it is at this boundary that meanings and values are lost or misread in the contestation

> ...of everyday life, between classes, genders, races, nations. Yet the reality of the limit...of culture is rarely theorised outside well-intentioned moralist polemics against prejudice and stereotype, or the blanket assertion of individual or personal racism – that describe the effect rather than the structure of the problem. The need to think the limit of culture as a problem of enunciation is disavowed. (Bhabha, 1994:34)

Such a consideration of culture counters the liberal multicultural myth that cultural diversity emerges through an accumulative process of synthesis and accretion of difference (Papastergiadis, 1997). Bhabha offers an alternative to the account that cultural differences are irrevocably connected to or ordered by the principle of identity. The dif-ferences that mark current borders of identity – such as gender, race, sexuality, religion, nation – are not where Bhabha locates the problematic of cultural difference (Johnson and Michaelson, 1997). He contends that the articulation of cultures is possible because they are a 'signifying or symbol forming activity' lived out through forms of repre-sentation which can never be complete in themselves. Cultural difference is a 'process of translations' which '...opens up the possibility of articulating different, even in-commensurable cultural practices and priorities' (Bhabha, 1994:211).

Bhabha points to the hybridity of culture, which is not dependent on accretive processes of unmediated exchange based on 'the illusion of transferable forms and transparent knowledge' (Papastergiadis, 1997:279). It is at the borders that these already de-centred cultural practices are contested, and hybridity as a form of cultural difference 'gives rise to something different ... a new area of negotiation of meaning and representation' (Bhabha, 1994:211). He contends that this limimal space has the potential for new struc-tures of counter-authority and political initiatives that may not fit into our conventional and educational frames of reference.

The space of cultural hybridity is, however, not a ground of identity or a border site in which differences are to be 'crossed over' (Johnson and Michaelson, 1997) or simply assimilated. What is significant is the conditions of emergence of a culture, which is always marked by an 'undecidability' in the advent of its arrival (Bennett and Bhabha, 1998). This is not to say that judgements cannot be made or differences cannot be marked. Rather, it is to say that there are no anterior unambivalent grounds of cultural authority that determine which identity-differences are to matter. What gets represented as other cultures is thus a political-pedagogic act of knowledge production. Cultural dif-ference should not be conceived as the impossibility of meaning/knowledge or a slide into forms of curricular cultural relativism. Neither does it engender a pedagogy of 'teaching the conflicts', as advanced by Gerald Graff (1992). In his humanist-ethical perspective he asserts that 'conflicts' are an inherent part of life and constitutive of the formation of knowledge. It is through mutual dialogue and conversation that students may be exposed to conflictual discourses and learn to take account of divergent outlooks and 'live with difference'. Graff apparently recognises the possibility of vastly discordant knowledges, but he disingenuously offers a dehistoricised notion of conflict as an innate attribute of the condition of knowledge – which disavows the Western 'will to power'. Against such a neo-liberal pluralism which diffuses the social force of conflicts, the irreducible antagonisms of cultural difference need to be politically located in struggles over meaning and representation. As Mas'ud Zavarzadeh and Donald Morton state:

> The meanings of the signs of culture are produced, in [the] curriculum, through social struggles along the lines of class, gender and race and the state's power to subjugate. Signs are neither eternally predetermined nor panhistorically undecidable: they are rather 'de-cided' or rendered as 'undecidable' in the moment of social conflict. (1994:180)

Bhabha's proposition that the articulation of a culture is an incipiently hybrid process is important against positing any simple (anti-)essentialist notions of cultural and identity formation. The study of other cultures based on their content is no longer viable. The conditions in which a particular culture, identity or knowledge emerge, and the constant negotiations, dissonant exchanges, and operations of power which mark those conditions and inscribe particular differences would have to underwrite multicultural pedagogies. Educational multiculturalism cannot be reduced to the consensual unity of a shared culture or conflictual cross-cultural dialogues or the banality of pluralised knowledges. Critical multiculturalism inhabits the entangled political terrain of possibly discordant and disruptive cultural encounters. To practice critical multicultural pedagogy would mean risking antagonistic exchanges in a seminar, as the range of points of view and knowledges will not be diffused in the moment of their expression. And teacher authority and epistemological frameworks are at risk of coming under scrutiny and being challenged. Yet it is a committed pedagogy which seeks to open up new ethical possibilities of social understanding.

Towards a multicultural curriculum

The challenge of a radical multicultural curriculum is immense. It fundamentally questions the praxis of education. The conventional focus on content has eclipsed questions of how it may be taught. Progressive pedagogies claim that the aim should be to teach students how to think critically, rather than decide what they should think. However, as David Lusted (1986) points out, in the act of pedagogy, one cannot simply separate form and content. What we teach is tied to how we teach. Not only does this shift us beyond content, it also shows that the Enlightenment desire of educating reason is antithetical for a critical pedagogy which rejects the universality of knowledge and culture. The pedagogical interdependence of the what and the how means there are 'no pedagogies in general' (Hall, in Lusted, 1986). So we cannot advance a universal multicultural pedagogy. A critical multicultural standpoint would resist the present university educational market-place, which increasingly demands a packaged curriculum often defined by rationalistic learning outcomes.

Contrary to standardising university teaching and instrumental modes of learning, a multicultural pedagogy needs to be considered both as a site-specific and a tactical activity. It is site-specific because it always takes place in particular concrete teaching contexts. How multiculture is engendered and mobilised is contingent upon the regimes of power/knowledge operating in the space of pedagogy. To unravel such a contested space is difficult and risky because it is likely to disrupt the cultural authority of our existing pedagogies (Gore, 1993). But it is a necessary risk if we are to seriously engage the aporia of cultural difference. A multicultural context conceives that the unknowable or the unrepresentable is as significant as what we do know or can represent in the curriculum. An ethical relation to other knowledges cannot be prescribed or determined in advance – it is an open-ended, site-specific political relation which is constantly remade. As a corollary, a non-universalist pedagogy will be 'tactical' (Chow, 1993; Sleeter and McLaren, 1995) because it acknowledges there is no one master narrative of understanding, interpretation or liberation. A critical multicultural curriculum would attempt to respond to the contemporary conditions of knowledge production – conditions in which university institutional racisms remain an everyday reality of teaching and learning.

Notes

1   The notion of 'the ethical' in this chapter does not refer to a universal, prescriptive set of foundational rules to follow, or the banality of the liberal aphorism of 'we must respect Others'. Rather, we shall discover that ethics is conceived as a grounded *social relation* subject to power (Nealon 1998).

2   Key texts which have defined this debate have been Bloom (1987) *The Closing of the American Mind*, D'Souza (1991) *Illiberal Education* and Kimball (1990) *Tenured Radicals: how politics has corrupted Higher Education*.

3   The de-legitimation of multicultural education has taken place on a number of fronts. During the reign of Margaret Thatcher, many forms of progressive education came under fierce attack, especially from the neo-conservative New Right, (Gordon, 1989). However, from critical left perspectives, antiracist education was also problematised, especially after the publication of the Macdonald Report (1990) *Murder in the Playground*, concerning the death of an Asian schoolboy. According to Rattansi (1992:11) it was 'widely interpreted as signalling the failure of the antiracist project in education'.

4   The British-based theorists, May (1999c) and Rattansi (1999), highlight that one of the most productive sites of work around multiculturalism has emerged in North American critical educational debates, especially by theorists such as McLaren (1995; 1997) and Giroux (1992; 1994).

5   See Sharma and Sharma (2003) for an extended discussion of neo-racism and otherness in the age of *Empire*.

6   It is in the educational fields of media and cultural studies where we can identify some engagement with whiteness in schooling and higher education, for example, see Cohen (1987; 1991).

7   More disturbingly, there has been an unrelenting rise of an educational market-place determining the types and content of university courses (Giroux, 2000; Zavardzadeh and Morton, 1994). Political questions of multiculturalism are increasingly becoming more difficult to raise in this era of a corporate academe.

References

Bennett, D. and Bhabha, H. (1998) 'Liberalism and minority culture: reflections on 'culture's in between", in D. Bennett (ed) *Multicultural States: rethinking identity and difference*, London: Routledge

Bhabha, H. (1990) 'The Third Space: interview with Homi Bhabha', in J. Rutherford (ed) *Identity*, London: Lawrence and Wishart

Bhabha, H. (1994) *The Location of Culture*, London: Routledge

Bhattacharyya, G. (1991) 'Cultural education in Britain; from the Newbolt report to the National Curriculum', *Oxford Literary Review* 13(1): 4-19.

Bloom, A (1987) *The Closing of the American Mind*, New York: Simon & Schuster

Buckingham, D. (1996) 'Critical Pedagogy and media education: a theory in search of a practice', *Journal of Curriculum Studies* 28(6): 627-650.

Chow, R. (1993) *Writing Diaspora: tactics of intervention in contemporary cultural studies*, Bloomington and Indianapolis: Indiana University Press

Chow R. (1998) *Ethics after Idealism, Bloomington and Indianapolis*, USA: Indiana University Press

Cohen, P. (1987) *Racism and popular culture: a cultural studies approach*, London: Centre for Multicultural Education

Cohen, P. (1991) *Monstrous images, perverse reasons: cultural studies in antiracist education*, London: Centre for Multicultural Education University of London Institute of Education

Cohen, P. (1995) 'The Crisis of the Western University', in P. Cohen (ed) *For a Multicultural University, Vol. Working Paper 3*, London: New Ethnicities Unit, University of East London

Delanty, G. (2001) *Challenging Knowledge: the university in the knowledge society*, Buckingham: SHRE and Open University Press

Donald, J. and Rattansi, A. (1992) *'Race', culture and difference*, London: Sage/Open University

D'Souza, D (1991) *Illiberal Education: the politics of race and sex on campus*, New York: Free Press

Falzon, C. (1998) *Foucault and Social Dialogue*, London: Routledge

Gaine, C. (1988) *No Problem Here: a practical approach to education and 'race' in white schools*, Repr. with revisions. Edition, London: Hutchinson

Gaine, C. (1995) *Still No Problem Here*, Rev. Edition, Stoke-on-Trent: Trentham

Giroux, H. (1992) *Border Crossing: cultural workers and the politics of education*, London: Routledge

Giroux, H. (1994) *Disturbing Pleasures: learning popular culture*, London: Routledge

Giroux, H. (2000) *Impure Acts: the practical politics of cultural studies*, London: Routledge.

Gordon, P. (1989) 'The Educational New Right', *Multicultural Teaching* 8(1): 13-14

Gore, J. (1993) *The Struggle for Pedagogies: critical and feminist discourses as regimes of truth*, London: Routledge

Graff, G. (1992) *Beyond the Culture Wars: how teaching the conflicts can revitalize American eduction*, New York: Norton

Hall, S. (1991) 'Old and new identities, old and new ethnicities', in A. King (ed) *Culture, Globalization and the world-system*, London: Macmillan

Hall, S. (1992a) The question of cultural identity, in S. Hall (ed) *Modernity and its Futures*, Buckingham: Open University Press

Hall, S. (1992b) 'What is this 'Black' in Black popular culture', in G. Dent (ed) *Black Popular Culture*, Seattle: Bay Press

Hardt, M. and Negri, A. (2000) *Empire*, London: Harvard University Press

Hesse, B. (1999) 'It's your world: discrepant M/multiculturalisms', in P. Cohen (ed) *New Ethnicities, Old Racisms?*, London: Zed Books

Johnson, D. and Michaelson, S. (1997) 'Border secrets: an introduction', in D. Johnson and S. Michaelson (eds) *Border Theory: the limits of cultural politcs*, London: University of Minnesota Press

Jones, R. (1999) *Teaching racism, or tackling it?: multicultural stories from white beginning teachers*, Stoke-on-Trent: Trentham Books

Kimball, R (1990) *Tenured Radicals: how politics has corrupted Higher Education*, New York: Harper and Row

Koundoura, M. (1998) 'Multiculturalism or multinationalism?' in D. Bennett (ed) *Multicultural States: rethinking identity and difference*, London: Routledge

Lusted, D. (1986) 'Why Pedagogy?' *Screen* 27(5): 2-14

Lyotard, J. F. (1984) *The postmodern condition: a report on knowledge*, Manchester: Manchester University Press

Macdonald, I. (1990) *Murder in the playground: the Burnage report*, London: Longsight Press

May, S. (ed) (1999a) *Critical multiculturalism: rethinking multicultural and antiracist education*, London: Falmer

May, S. (1999b) 'Critical multiculturalism and cultural difference: avoiding essentialism', in S. May (ed) *Critical multiculturalism: rethinking multicultural and antiracist education*, London: Falmer

May, S. (1999c) 'Introduction: towards a critical multiculturalism', in S. May (ed) *Critical multiculturalism: rethinking multicultural and antiracist education*, London: Falmer

McLaren, P. (1995) *Critical pedagogy and predatory culture: oppositional politics in a postmodern era*, London: Routledge

McLaren, P. (1997) *Revolutionary multiculturalism: pedagogies of dissent for the new millennium*, Boulder, Colo.; Oxford: Westview Press

Mercer, K. (1994) *Welcome to the Jungle: new positions in black cultural studies*, London: Routledge

Nealon, J. (1998) *Alterity Politics: ethics and performative subjectivity*, London: Duke University Press

Papastergiadis, N. (1997) 'Tracing Hybridity in Theory', in P. Werbner and T. Modood (eds) *Debating Cultural Hybridity*, London: Zed Books

Peters, M. (1996) *Poststructuralism, politics and education*, Westport, Conneticut ; London: Bergin and Garvey

Rattansi, A. (1992) 'Changing the subject? Racism, culture and education', in J. Donald and A. Rattansi (eds) *'Race', culture and difference*, London: Sage/Open University

Rattansi, A. (1999) 'Racism, 'postmodernism' and reflexive multiculturalism', in S. May (ed) *Critical multiculturalism: rethinking multicultural and antiracist education*, London: Falmer

Rattansi, A. and Reeder, D. (eds) (1992a) *Rethinking Radical Education: essays in honour of Brian Simon*, London: Lawrence and Wishart

Rattansi, A. and Reeder, D. (1992b) 'Introduction', in A. Rattansi and D. Reeder (eds) *Rethinking Radical Education: essays in honour of Brian Simon*, London: Lawrence and Wishart

Said, E. (1987) *Orientalism*, London: Penguin

Scheurich, J. (1997) *Research method in the postmodern*, London: Falmer

Sharma, S. and Sharma, A. (2003) 'White Paranoia: Orientalism in the age of Empire', *Fashion Theory* 7(3/4)

Sleeter, C. and McLaren, P. (1995) 'Introduction: exploring connections to build a critical multicultura-lism', in C. Sleeter and P. McLaren (eds) *Multicultural education, critical pedagogy and the politics of difference*, Albany: State University of New York Press

Tomlinson, S. (1985) 'The 'Black Education movement', in M. Arnot (ed) *Race and Gender: equal opportunities policies in education,* Oxford: Pergamon Press/Open University

Young, R. C. (1995) *Colonial Discourse: hybridity in theory, culture and race*, London: Routledge

Zavarzadeh, M. and Morton, D. (1994) Theory as Resistance: politics and culture after (post) structuralism, London: Guildford Press

Žižek, S. (1997) 'Multiculturalism, or the Cultural Logic of Multinational Capitalism', *New Left Review* (225): 28-51.

CHAPTER TWELVE

The Equality Challenge Unit and the Race Relations (Amendment) Act 2000:
A Developmental Approach to Implementation in Higher Education

Joyce Hill and Emmanuell Kusemamuriwo

Introduction

n this chapter, the Director and the Ethnicity and Policy Adviser of the Equality
Challenge Unit describe how the ECU has worked with the Higher Education
Institutions (HEIs) in England, Scotland and Wales to implement the Race Relations
(Amendment) Act 2000. Their approach throughout has to be supportive and developmental. HEIs are legally autonomous bodies, individually answerable to UK law. The Act
is uniformly applicable in England, Wales and Scotland, despite the different time-frame
set by the Scottish Parliament, but does not apply in Northern Ireland, which has a different framework for equalities legislation.

The Equality Challenge Unit

The Equality Challenge Unit was set up by and for the UK Higher Education sector in
2001, and became fully operational on 1 August, although not quite all staff appointments had been made by then. Joyce Hill is the Director and Emmanuell Kusemamuriwo
is the Ethnicity and Policy Adviser. There are six sponsors, who contribute funds on a
pro-rata basis: the Higher Education Funding Council for England (HEFCE), the Higher
Education Funding Council for Wales (HEFCW), the Scottish Higher Education Funding Council (SHEFC), the Department for Employment and Learning in Northern
Ireland (DELNI), and the two HE representative bodies, Universities UK (UUK) and the
Standing Conference of Principals (SCOP), which are both membership organisations.
The staff of the ECU hold their contracts through Universities UK, which provides some
of its sponsorship in kind, but the Unit is not operationally part of Universities UK. It is,
rather, answerable to its sponsors through a representative Group. The arrangement may
seem awkward, but in practice it has the huge advantage that the ECU does not belong
either to the heads of the institutions (through SCOP or UUK) or to the funding bodies.

At the same time there is a genuine ownership by both the funding bodies and the sector's institutional heads. This gives the Unit access to the major sources of leadership and leverage, but also the freedom to address the issues in all their complexity, since the unit is bound by no one point of view. In this respect, it is positioned quite differently from the Commission on University Career Opportunity (CUCO), which was in some respects our predecessor body, and which operated from 1995-2000 as part of Universities UK.

The setting up of the ECU was prompted by the growing needs identified from within the sector, together with an awareness of the challenge of the then impending UK and EU legislation. There was also increasing public awareness that action was needed in Higher Education, since several reports on the sector in the late 1990s identified areas of apparent concern in relation to equality of opportunity, particularly in HE employment. These included *The National Committee of Inquiry into Higher Education* (the Dearing Report, 1997), the *Independent Review of Higher Education Pay and Conditions* (the Bett Report, 1999), and a study of ethnicity and employment in higher education (Carter, Fenton and Modood, 1999). Government took up the theme, with the then Secretary of State for Education, David Blunkett, forcefully stating in a speech at the University of Greenwich in February 2000 (p. 27, 92) that: 'Higher Education has not made sufficient progress on equal opportunities for its employees in the past. In fact the situation is frankly deplorable'.

Questions were also being posed by Trade Union research and by the Equality Commissions. In parallel, the EU, through legislation and other policy initiatives, was giving equality issues greater prominence, which increasingly required real action rather than fine phrases and was producing studies which indicated that problems evident in the UK were also apparent in other Member States. Significant among these were studies on mainstreaming gender equality in science (ETAN Working Group, 2000) and the participation of women in the TMR Marie Cure Fellowships scheme (Ackers, 2001). So the ECU was established by and for the sector, as a pro-active response to the clearly identified challenges, with a large mission and a wide-ranging set of aims. The mission is to improve equal opportunities for all who work or seek to work in the UK Higher Education sector. The unit's aims are:

- to work with all stakeholders to raise the awareness and profile of equal opportunities,

- to provide specific advice to institutions to help them secure improvements in equal opportunities,

- to help specify appropriate data to institutions to support equal opportunities monitoring,

- to monitor performance at sector level,

- to support HEIs directly in developing appropriate institutional benchmarks and standards that will help measure progress,

- to develop and disseminate good practice, looking to experience from within and outside the sector, in this country and abroad,

- to commission research to underpin the development of policy and practice.

The Unit serves the whole of the UK and all grades and categories of staff. Students are not included in its remit, although where equalities legislation embraces students as well as staff (as with the RRAA), it offers generic advice on student issues, since the polices and practices on which we are advising and commenting are essentially indivisible, even though HEIs have relationships with and responsibilities towards employees and students which are differently defined. However, the ECU is not a statutory body, and has no inspectoral powers. It can inform, advise, warn, encourage, and otherwise support the development of better practice (for example by working with national bodies to achieve a coherent approach and set of standards), but the autonomy of HEIs is paramount: each is individually answerable for their practices in fulfilling the requirements of the law and in promoting equality of opportunity within the framework of their own mission and aims.

The following account of the ECU's developmental approach to the implementation of the RRAA in UK Higher Education should be understood in the light of the Unit's broader mission. Nevertheless, since our foundation in the summer of 2001, the implementation of the RR(A)A has taken up the greater part of our resources. This would probably have been necessary in any case, given the scale of change the Act requires and the challenges it poses, but it is also a factor of our extremely small size, since a concerted effort in one area has an immediate and adverse impact on our capacity in others. At the outset we were set up as a team of four: one Director, two Policy Advisers, and one Administrator,[1] although we were able to obtain special funding for a specialist in media and communications from November 2001, initially for two years. It quickly became evident – ever more acutely as the Unit established itself and as the level of demand from HEIs continued to grow – that we needed more staff, or a radically scaled-down remit. The sponsoring bodies, recognising the problem, commissioned an external review in the summer of 2002, with the result that, as from 2003/4 academic year, the Unit has had a phased programme of additional appointments, and a new operational structure. The Unit is set to continue to 31 December 2005, but there may be a further review in 2005 to reassess sectoral need, which could possibly lead to some extension. Our largest undeclared aim, however, is that we eventually make ourselves redundant.

The RRAA: facilitating a developmental approach
(i) The RRAA in the larger context: opportunities and synergies
The General and Specific Duties of the RRAA, set out in the Statutory Code published by the Commission for Racial Equality, issued in May 2002 for England and Wales and November 2002 for Scotland, require a clearly identified race equality policy, together with plans for implementation – effectively an action plan. However, race equality does not exist in isolation from gender, disability, sexual orientation, religion or belief, age, student status, contractual mode of employment, or any other area which might be the basis for conscious or unconscious unequal treatment or unequal opportunity, whether expressed at institutional or individual level. Promotion of equality of opportunity, which is one of the RRAA's general duties, is a universally applicable responsibility and is

always multi-dimensional, even if – as the RRAA requires – there are times when we have to focus on one dimension as the 'lead area'.

The ECU's approach, reinforced by its broader remit, has thus always been to emphasise the extent to which the Statutory Code's descriptions of frameworks for implementation, and procedures and practices for eliminating unlawful racial discrimination, promoting good race relations, and promoting equality of opportunity provide a good practice guide that can serve as a template for actions supporting the integration and mainstreaming of improved equality of opportunity. It should be inclusive of race, but reach beyond it. This is not to say that difficult areas such as race should be hidden under the comforting guise of diversity or equality. Problematic issues which individuals and institutions find difficult to address need to be subjected to focused and challenging scrutiny in the public domain and with measurable steps for improvement identified. This is why the Statutory Code is explicit about requiring a clearly defined race equality policy and implementation plan. But it is to say that the Statutory Code, if read in a positive spirit rather than as a series of bureaucratic impositions, is capable of prompting changes of policy and practice throughout the whole area of equality of opportunity. The major institutional benefit that will result is that racial equality is addressed within its necessarily multi-dimension context, and that the challenges posed by other defined equality areas – where legal requirements are increasing – are met in a coherent and integrated way, more economically and more successfully than if they are treated as a series of hurdles that have to be dealt with one by one as a cumulative administrative burden.

In advocating this inclusive approach to the standards set by the RRAA, we have therefore consistently argued for a concerted reassessment of all relevant policies, practices, operational frameworks and administrative support mechanisms, together with a re-appraisal of the location of management responsibility and institutional leadership, so that we achieve an agreed and coherent standard for the whole of the institution's activity, bearing in mind the need to implement current and impending legislation effectively and efficiently.

Responding to the developing legislative agenda, we published a document with the Joint Negotiating Committee for Higher Education Staff (JNCHES) entitled *Partnership for Equality: Action for Higher Education* in February 2003 (available electronically at http://www.ecu.ac.uk/publications/). This provided guidance and recommendations on the application in HE of all present and prospective legislative requirements relating to equality in employment. It was endorsed by the Secretary of State for Education and Skills, the Minister for Education and Life-Long Learning in the Welsh Assembly Government, the Minister for Enterprise, Transport and Lifelong Learning in the Scottish Executive, and the Minister with Responsibility for Employment and Learning, Northern Ireland. Their joint foreword stressed the need for embedding and mainstreaming, and welcomed 'the sector's commitment to bring about a step change in its human resource management' (p.2).

The sector now has further support and encouragement from the increased emphasis on equal opportunity issues in the annual grant letters, and from the requirements placed upon them by the Funding Councils to produce strategically focused human resource strategies. There is some variation in the way the different Funding Councils have gone about this, but the development is generally underpinned by a range of practical support, including conferences, workshops and seminars, consultancy advice, and documentary guidance. In raising the profile of such matters as monitoring and target-setting, staff development, the management of poor performance, and equal pay for work of equal value, the Funding Councils have made a major and timely contribution to the larger context in which the RRAA is being implemented, providing yet more opportunities for wider institutional development.

(ii) The RRAA as catalyst

The RRAA is undoubtedly a catalyst for change. No other equal opportunities law in the UK has gone so far in setting out the positive duty and in specifying, as a set of minimum standards, the practical actions to be taken to achieve implementation. The step-change can be encapsulated by comparing the RRAA with the Race Relations Act (1976), Section 71, which it amends. The 1976 Act, like other earlier equalities legislation, set a requirement that had no practical specifications for implementation, and which focused on not discriminating on the grounds of race. The amended Act, in sharp contrast, sets minimum implementation standards (the Specific Duties for the various bodies and authorities bound by the Act in different ways), interprets what these mean in practical terms (in the Statutory Code and in supplementary guidance provided by the CRE), and as the legal lynch-pin defines general duty as requiring pro-active engagement in three areas: the elimination of unlawful racial discrimination; the promotion of good race relations and equality of opportunity. The specification of active responsibility, by contrast with the earlier Act's standard of not discriminating, marks the step-change. Radical re-thinking is now required about how policy might be appropriately conceived and put into action.

With this change demanded by the RRAA, and with the challenge to planning and practice, the implementation of equal opportunity standards should surely move on. Practical plans are called for in the RRAA, a pro-active approach is demanded, monitoring is required, impact assessments must be carried out, and the results must be published. The whole cycle of activity is in the public domain, with outcomes being assessed in relation to hard evidence. The Act is thus not simply a major development in the field of race relations but a watershed, a catalyst for change across all areas of equality and diversity with which it interacts. This message is central to the ECU's work in facilitating the implementation of the RRAA in the UK Higher Education sector.

(iii) Policy development in Higher Education

The ECU's first public activity was to organise UK-wide conferences in the summer of 2001, in London (twice) and Leeds. These events predated our operational launch in August, but we saw the the Act as so important that we used what staff we had to prepare the sector and to explore with practitioners what the key issues might be. That September, we also presented a paper to the annual conference of Vice-Chancellors, circulated a version of it to heads of SCOP institutions and began to feature the RRAA in presentations to professional groups. But, like everyone, we were limited in the practical advice we could offer because the consultation version of the CRE's Statutory Code was not issued for England and Wales until just before Christmas (with Scotland issuing a consultation version of the Code later, in accordance with its initial deadline of 30 November 2002 for publication of policies and plans). From then until the initial English and Welsh deadline of 31 May 2002, demand from the sector rose inexorably. We organised conferences and workshops, visited HEIs to make presentations to governing bodies and senior staff, issued documentation, responded to individual institutional enquiries by phone and email, and commented extensively on drafts of policies and action plans that colleagues asked us to read. We also issued a model race equality policy structure for HEIs in England and Wales, translating what was then available from the CRE only as generic guidance into a language and structure tailored for Higher Education. The structure remains available on our website, http://www.ecu.ac.uk/race/. There were those who wished we had written a model policy rather than a structure, but we deliberately decided not to do so. We were conscious of the detailed and targeted action required in the new policies and action plans, and we were – and are – convinced that the level of engagement needed as the first step in a major process of change could only be achieved if each HEI undertook its own analysis, worked on identifying its own responsibilities, and translated them into policies and plans that were owned outright by the institution. No single generic policy could have catered for the diversity of the sector or for the different positions in which institutions found themselves in relation to the requirements and expectations of the RRAA.

At the same time, we advised and worked with HEFCE and HEFCW in Bristol and Cardiff to develop their Race Equality Schemes and Action Plans. These too had a publication deadline of 31 May 2002 and, once published and implemented, would be an important element in defining the context within which HEIs would be operating. Funding Councils' Race Equality Schemes were partly concerned with their functions as employers. But the key challenge in each case was to define the race equality-relevant functions in the Funding Councils' interaction with HEIs and to determine how these could on the one hand meet the pro-active requirements of the RRAA, while on the other keeping within their contractual relationships with universities and colleges, which are autonomous and individually answerable to the law. It was a delicate line to tread, and needed careful explanation to the CRE, since the relationship between the Funding Councils and HEIs is unique in public authority areas. Following extensive discussion, the CRE accepted that the Funding Councils have no applicable enforcement or sanctioning powers under the 1992 Education Act. And since there are no over-arching statutory inspectoral bodies for HE, the CRE recognised that it would need to keep a closer watch on the sector than they would if inspectorates could exercise monitoring responsibilities under the Act. This position is reflected in the CRE's Education Policy, for which the ECU was one of the advisory bodies.

Since statistical monitoring is a key element in implementing the Act at both sectoral and institutional level, we also provided advice to the Higher Education Statistics Agency as it deliberated how best to revise its categories and develop a staff record which covered all employees. Other successful interactions included the agreement, through JNCHES, that race should be a dimension in the framework for conducting equal pay audits, and that the appraisal scheme of clinical consultants with joint NHS/University contracts should explicitly include their responsibilities under the RRAA. Behind the scenes interactions such as these are crucial in supporting implementation, since it is by harmonising and mainstreaming the requirements of the Act across the sector's activities that the necessary procedures and standards will be embedded.

Following the May publication deadline, we participated in conferences held by the two Funding Councils in England and Wales to consult further on their Race Equality Schemes. Working first with HEFCE and later with HEFCW, we embarked on a major project of reviewing and advising on HEIs' Race Equality Policies and Action Plans. Each project was intended to be developmental and supportive for its own institution, while at the same time allowing the Funding Councils to satisfy themselves, under the terms of their Race Equality Schemes, that each HEI had an appropriate policy and plan on which to build for the future. Detailed analytical reports on the individual policies and action plans were sent in confidence to each HEI, and the ECU took responsibility for providing follow-up advice, supported by further conferences, which we organised jointly with the CRE. Within England, HEFCE decided to ask institutions which had weaker policies and plans to submit a revised version by 31 May 2003 for further confidential analysis and recommendations, again managed by the ECU. HEFCW operated the same iterative and developmental review process to a different timetable, with the ECU providing institutional-level advice, supplemented by conferences tailored for Welsh HEIs.

In Scotland, where the initial deadline for publication was 30 November 2002, the ECU's main period of activity began that May. We held two conferences in Edinburgh for both HE and FE, one focusing on the RRAA and the preparation of policies and plans and the other on targets and monitoring. We also sent a substantial information pack to each HEI and, as for England and Wales, circulated a Model Race Equality Policy Structure (which can be consulted on the ECU website http://www.ecu.ac.uk/race/). Sponsored by SHEFC, we provided four half-day workshops in Edinburgh, Inverness, Glasgow and Dundee in September 2002. And in the weeks leading up to 30 November we visited several Scottish HEIs, responded to enquiries by phone and email, and commented on draft documentation. The Scottish Higher and Further Education Funding Councils together engaged in a review of race equality policies and implementation plans. The ECU served on the Steering Group and was responsible for providing supportive developmental feedback to institutions in the HE sector. Follow-up regional workshops in Scotland, to which the ECU contributed, were offered jointly to HE and FE. In common with England and Wales, institutions with weak policies and plans were asked to revise and resubmit them for further review and advice.

In all three countries, the review exercise was concerned only with the written documentation and this could be seen as a serious limitation. But the publication of policies and plans is a Specific Duty, without which the Act cannot begin to be fulfilled. Ensuring that the sector has met this requirement and has its foundations in place is thus not a matter of mere documentation; it is an essential first step in a complex and continuing process. In working with the ECU on a systematic developmental programme of the kind described, the Funding Councils provided considerable support to the sector and demonstrated willingness to meet this challenge.

Further changes to the Race Relations Act 1976 and thus to the amendment Act, based on the EU Race Directive, came into effect on 19 July 2003, and we provided an *Update* for the sector on these (*Update* 07/03 http://www.ecu.ac.uk/updates: see also *Update* 06/03 on dealing with racism on campus). The principal elements of the amendments derived from the EU Race Directive are:

*   new definitions of unlawful discrimination

*   new definitions of harassment

*   changes to the definition of victimisation during and after employment

*   extension to the period during which a claim for harassment can be brought

*   a shift in the burden of proof from the complainant to the respondent in a court or tribunal, provided that the complainant has established a *prima facie* case of un-lawful discrimination or harassment.

Since these elements are to be a standard feature in other equalities legislation (e.g. sexual orientation, religion or belief, age) it can be hoped that their incorporation into race equality keeps the various strands of legislation in close alignment, and assists in mainstreaming through the existence of common standards.

(iv) Areas for action

The template devised by the ECU for the reviews of policies and implementation or action plans provided for a discursive analytical overview of six main areas:

*   evidence for pro-active engagement with the General Duty

*   definition of relevant functions and the integration and mainstreaming of racial equality through these functions

*   plans for a communication strategy and continuing consultation

*   procedures for analytical target setting and monitoring

*   procedures for impact assessment and regular review, together with definition of responsibilities for further action, and procedures for publication

*   plans for support and training, including needs-analysis where necessary.

Under each heading, an indication was given of any additional work required, followed by a summary of recommendations. A more detailed tabular analysis was also provided, from which the analytical overviews and recommendations were derived. The templates for England and Wales were the same with some minor adjustments were made for the Scottish review.

Significant progress has clearly been made by the sector but certain areas need further attention. These include:

- strengthening links between policy aims and objectives and the specific activities identified in the action plans, for example by improving the structure of the documents, refining timescales and being clearer about objectives or targets

- improving the communicability of policies and plans so they are practical, accessible documents, useful for all staff, all actual and prospective students and the general public

- defining and prioritising race-equality functions more clearly across the full range of the HEI's activity

- developing systematic and wide-ranging consultation and communication strategies, to inform the implementation and further development of policy and practice

- embedding race equality objectives into all forms of collaborations, partnerships and contractual engagements, including procurement, together with measures to check compliance and the specification of action to be taken where matters are unsatisfactory

- full integration of students, including international students, into policies and plans[2]

- clarifying complaints and disciplinary procedures relating to violation of institutional policies and the law

- determining success criteria for measuring progress which is essential for annual impact assessments

At the time of writing some HEIs have some way to go in monitoring and collecting baseline data. A few continue to subsume race issues within a wider equal opportunities/social inclusion agenda but although this may be understandable, specific demands on public bodies made by the RRAA include a clearly defined policy and implementation plan for race, the elements of which must be easy to identify and to monitor. In developing advice on integration and mainstreaming, we are therefore using professional meetings and discussions at institutional level to examine ways in which HEIs might most effectively carry out a review of all policies and plans which have actual or potential equal opportunities dimensions, and to consider ways in which overarching equal opportunities policies might be fully responsive to the increasing array of specific legal requirements.

Six months after the initial May deadline for England and Wales of May 2002, the CRE commissioned the Schneider-Ross consultancy to undertake a baseline survey of the nature, extent and quality of the response by public bodies to the RRAA. *Towards Racial Equality* (Commission for Racial Equality, 2003) reports on their findings. The ECU represented Higher Education on the Advisory Group and provided detailed advice about devising a questionnaire for the education sector which could be fairly answered by HE as well as FE and schools, given that HE has significantly different legal status, internal structures, and range of functions and responsibilities. Responses were voluntary, but the

HE response-rate was far higher: the highest (58% compared with 38% for FE and 20% for schools). Predictably, perhaps, the best rate of response was from central government (66%) and criminal justice and policing (65%). Given the HEFCE/ECU process of policy review which was already in hand in England, the HE sector naturally scored high in answer to the question of whether they had a policy in place, and it was pleasing to learn that 80% of the FE/HE respondents believed that work on the Race Equality Policies had produced positive benefits. As with all public authority areas surveyed, the report identified some points of relative weakness in HE. These closely echoed those listed above, although there was less detail in the Schneider-Ross report.

The report concludes with recommendations from the CRE for each of the main public authority sectors, based on the findings of the survey. Only England and Wales were included in the survey, but for HE the recommendations are UK-wide (p. 147) and state that the Higher Education Funding Councils in England Scotland and Wales should:

- undertake in 2004 a survey of higher education institutions' implementation of the duty to promote race equality with a particular focus on delivering race equality outcomes;

- amend the Annual Operating Statement for Higher Education Institutions to include, from 2004, a requirement for higher education institutions to report annually on achievements in implementing the public duty to promote race equality through inclusion in the Annual Operating Statement.

In fact, the two Funding Councils that were by then in a position to do so had already anticipated elements of these recommendations, since both HEFCE and HEFCW required annual information from HEIs with effect from July 2003; and HEFCE and the ECU had already announced plans for a survey in England in 2004, with a focus on implementation.

(v) Projects in higher education

The review of policies and action plans described above was principally aimed at assisting individual HEIs, but it has also allowed the ECU to identify areas in which further support and guidance are needed. The unit has consequently set up a number of collaborative ventures to explore the issues and produce further assistance for higher education. Dissemination will include conferences and workshops where appropriate, but in all cases there will also be written guidance, published in various forms and made available through our website: www.ecu.ac.uk.

- *Implementation Project*: this is a practical two-year project in which the ECU and the CRE, in collaboration with a number of HEIs representing the diversity of the sector across England, Wales and Scotland, will identify opportunities and problems in implementing the RRAA at institutional level. In the first year of the project, the focus is on the individual HEIs; in the second year, it will shift to dissemination across the sector.

- *Consultation Project*: For this project in the 2003/4 academic year, the ECU is in partnership with the Joint Negotiating Committee for Higher Education Staff, representing management and trade unions. The purpose is to find out how best to achieve the wide range of meaningful consultation the RRAA requires, both within the HE community and beyond, and to produce written guidance. This will be based on experience in working with HEIs which are not involved in the Implementation Project, but similarly reflect the diversity and geographical spread of the sector.

- *Communications project*: This project, funded by HEFCE and led by the ECU, will produce a brief publication designed to be a helpful, easily accessible guide for communication officers within higher education on best practice in promoting equal opportunities. The audience for this are press and public relations officers – those dealing with external relations, marketing and similar functions.

- *Guidance on Equality in HE Procurement*: In July 2003 the CRE published *Race Equality and Public Procurement: A guide for public authorities and contractors*. This responds to requests for further advice on how to implement the requirement that race equality be embedded in contractual relationships, including procurement. The ECU was represented on the Working Group. More work will clearly be needed by the HE sector in thinking through the complexities of how to achieve race equality-proofed contractual relationships with academic partners such as schools, work-placements and partner institutions in the UK and abroad, franchised work, and the many contractual relationships with other public authorities, notably the Teacher Training Agency, and the National Health Service in medical, dental and health education. In the more narrowly defined area of procurement the ECU was instrumental in setting up a working group which produced the *Equality in Higher Education Purchasing (EHEP) Toolkit*. For HE purchasing officers who have access, this is available on their professional website: (http://www.jppsg.ac.uk/guidance/categoryview.asp?GuidanceCategoryID=17&CategoryTitle=Equality+in+Purchasing)

- *Guidance on monitoring*: Although the CRE has provided guidance on what should be monitored under the RRAA, there is a clearly articulated need for further help in mapping this advice onto HE activity, developing practical frameworks, and achieving good response-rates when information depends upon individual cooperation. The ECU is collaborating with HEFCE on this project but the guidance, when issued in 2004, will be available throughout the sector. This project will also consider monitoring requirements of other equality areas.

Conclusion

The RRAA is ground-breaking legislation. It requires major changes in all our public bodies, a difficult and often disturbing process. Sometimes progress will be slow and erratic. But we know that in higher education the foundations are now in place and we can build on them. The *Building the Anti-Racist HEI Toolkit*, for which we served on the Steering Group, has been a valuable resource thus far, and will continue to be so as the focus shifts from developing policies and plans to making a real difference through actual outcomes.

Notes

1   The Athena project, which was established in 1999, was incorporated into the ECU when the Unit was set up. Its mission is to promote the advancement of women in science, engineering and technology in higher education and a significant increase in the number of women recruited to top posts. The project has operated in synergy with the ECU, but has continued with its defined area of activity. Originally, the project end-date was March 2003, but special funding from the OST allowed the two part-time staff to be employed for a further defined period in order to carry forward their dissemination programme.

2   'International' is interpreted widely to include EU students as well as those from beyond the EU, despite the common restriction of 'international' within HE to refer only to students who pay international rather than UK/EU fees. The tendency in several policies and plans to focus more attention on staff than on students, as noted by one of the consultants who was contracted to carry out reviews in England on behalf of HEFCE and the ECU, may be accounted for by what was then the relatively recent emphasis on human resource strategies and the work undertaken as a result.

References

Ackers, L (2001) *The Participation of Women Researchers in the TMR Marie Curie Fellowships 1994-1998 Science*, European Commission: Research Directorate General

Blunkett, D. (2000) *Modernising Higher Education: Facing the Global Challenge*, Department for Education and Employment, DfEE Publications

Carter, J., S. Fenton, and T. Modood, (1999) *Ethnicity and Employment in Higher Education*, London: Policy Studies Institute

Commission for Racial Equality (2003) *Towards Racial Equality: an evaluation of the public duty to promote race equality and good race relations in England and Wales*, London: CRE

ETAN Expert Working Group, (2000) *Science Policies in the European Union: Promoting Excellence through mainstreaming gender equality,* European Commission: Research Directorate General

Independent Review of Higher Education Pay and Conditions (Bett Committee), (1999) London: Stationery Office

The National Committee of Inquiry into Higher Education (Dearing Committee), (1997) London: Stationery Office

PART FOUR
THEORISING PERSISTENT RACISMS

CHAPTER THIRTEEN

Discourse on Institutional Racism: the genealogy of a concept

Barnor Hesse

We listen for it, we take it by surprise, we sniff it out, we follow it, lose it, find it again, shadow it, and every day it is more nauseatingly exposed. Oh! *the racism* of these gentlemen does not bother me. I do not become indignant over it. I merely examine it. I note it, and that is all. I am almost grateful to it for expressing itself openly and appearing in broad daylight, *as a sign.* Aim Césaire[1] (emphasis added)

Introduction

When the public inquiry into the racist murder of the Black teenager Stephen Lawrence published its findings in February 1999, it seemed a propitious event. The Macpherson report made not just the familiar charge of racism in Britain, but the provocative indictment of 'institutional racism'; and that from a former judge with impeccably conservative credentials. The concept of institutional racism had entered a public domain that had no specification of a history or cultural formation in which it could be located: consequently there was no institutional policy and political discourse with which it could be shown to be associated. Although these theoretical questions have not attracted much curiosity, it is troublingly evident that the absence of considered responses has long undermined the debate about institutional racism.

In his reflections on the police Macpherson defined institutional racism as:

> The collective failure of an organisation to provide an appropriate and professional service to people because of their colour, culture or ethnic origin. It can be seen or detected in processes, attitudes and behaviour which amount to discrimination through *unwitting prejudice, ignorance, thoughtlessness* and racist stereotyping which disadvantage minority ethnic people. (Macpherson, 1999, para 6.34)

Much has been said about this definition, but I am more concerned that this was not the first time a public inquiry led by a senior judge had made a public statement about institutional racism. In 1981 following the civil disturbances in Brixton, Lord Scarman led an inquiry to investigate the nature of police/black relations. Scarman (1981) concluded that institutional racism did not exist in Britain. But he did concede:

If however, the suggestion being made is that practices may be adopted by public bodies as well as by private individuals *which are unwittingly discriminatory* against black people, then this is an allegation which deserves serious consideration, and where proved, swift remedy (my emphasis). (cited in Macpherson, 1999, para 6.10)

The Macpherson/Scarman juxtaposition offers significant insights into British institutional racism. Notice, firstly, the contrast in the sites to which they allocate the actual and possible allegation. Where Macpherson has taken institutional racism to be institutionally specific (e.g. the police), Scarman has understood it as socially generic (e.g. Britain). So we have a *low threshold* institutional specific application of the term and a *high threshold* socially generic attribution. Secondly, it is remarkable that the terms upon which Scarman locates the unwitting discriminatory practices of public bodies outside the definition of institutional racism are the very terms which Macpherson attributes to similarly unwitting practices of institutional racism. Hence we have intentionalist and consequentialist accounts of institutional racism. Thirdly, although Scarman and Macpherson suggested very different understandings of institutional racism, they do agree that whatever the incidence of racism in British institutions, whether institutional or individual, the racism was characteristically unwitting. So from opposite poles comes a shared concept of racism as aberrant. Fourthly, despite the apparent parochialism of this British debate, the reference to an African American concept forged during the Black Power movement in the late 1960s alerts us to the significance of a postcolonial interrogation. The Macpherson/Scarman convergence around the idea of racism as aberrant runs concurrently with the pronounced liberal hegemony of opposition to fascism (antifascism) in the United States and Europe following the Second World War. So we also have a concept of racism where contested international dimensions are unmarked if not disavowed. In this chapter, I consider what might account for these regularly subjugated or routinely disqualified considerations (Foucault, 1977). I argue that the failure to examine their conceptual and social implications conceals the governmental dimensions and colonial inheritances of western racism. What I present here is therefore a genealogy of institutional racism seen as a concept located in our troubling postcolonial era.

International antiracism
There is more to a genealogy than a narrative historical account. It begins not with the past but from an analysis of the present, identifying something as particularly problematic which has traditionally not seemed so. The task is to develop a historical investigation, a genealogy, of what has given rise to that un/problematic present (Bartelson, 1995). Let us consider the contemporary international concept of racism disseminated by the United Nations. Concerted international attention to the issue of racism occurred during the first week of September 2001. On that occasion the United Nations held its World Conference against Racism, Racial Discrimination, Xenophobia and Related Intolerance in South Africa. The purpose was to discuss and agree a global declaration against racism. However, after three decades of the United Nations urging member national governments to respond to racism, we might be forgiven for asking: what is this racism that the United Nations urges us all to oppose, redress and prevent?[2] If we turn our attention to the thirty seven page declaration that finally emerged from the Durban con-

ference, what is meant by racism appears to be universal and global, as well as particular and historical. It is envisaged as located everywhere, since nowhere in particular is identified. At the same time, particular populations are identified as victims of racism. These include people of African descent, indigenous peoples, people of Asian descent, migrants, refugees and asylum seekers. The declaration identifies five distinct historical and structural sources of racism: transatlantic slavery, colonialism, apartheid, genocide and 'xenophobia against non-nationals, particularly migrants, refugees and asylum seekers' (Unesco, 2000: 4). Referring mainly to 'racial discrimination' and 'xenophobia' as their contemporary social forms, the declaration insists racism consists of 'any doctrine of racial superiority, along with theories which attempt to determine the existence of so-called distinct human races' (Unesco, 2000: 3). Racism is in effect an ideology, associated with objectionable political regimes and inhuman social circumstances that somehow survive, residually translated against the internationalist humanitarian grain into the world of human rights and liberal-democracies.

There are two points I want to make about this, both of which suggest a distinctive genealogy for the declaration's concept of racism. Firstly, it assumes that only societies in exceptional historical circumstances produce racist ideologies or that racist ideologies are produced in societies which are exceptions to some prescribed cultural rule. Secondly, because racism is construed as an exceptionalist ideology based on ideas of biological superiority, it has no direct relation to the institution of rights-based discourses and liberal-democracy.

There is a particular history from which this international conception of racism as disseminated by the United Nations derives its conceptual meaning. This is the history of the European intellectual and political reaction to Nazi Germany and the Holocaust after the Second World War. The modern international concept of racism, which evolved during the 1930s and emerged fully-fledged in the post-1945 period, was not greatly influenced by the models of slavery or colonialism or even apartheid. It was constructed in a relation of proscription to the discourse of racism exemplified by the racialised state of Nazi Germany. Viewing other experiences of racism through this conceptual lens formed in the post-war/postcolonial period may have impoverished our capacity to understand the longevity and structural features of racism. The history of the concept of racism as an extremist ideology as proposed in the discourse of the United Nations is of one that has traditionally privileged the social experiences of the Holocaust within the war torn dislocations of Europe during 1939-1945. This means that the colonial history of the experiences subsumed under that concept of racism cannot be located in its conceptual horizon.

Liberal/colonial racism

If we go back to a time before the United Nations came to define our internationally publicly acceptable sensibilities, we can consider the political culture in which its failed precursor, the League of Nations, was implicated. So what was the international position before the universal condemnation of racism we take for granted these days? A contrast can be drawn from the experience of Japanese diplomats at the 1919 Paris peace conference, following the First World War. Japan had earned the right to participate as a major power. Since its military defeat of Russia in 1905 it had increasingly drawn the imperial world's attention to its modernising credentials, which included an industrial economy that rivalled France in 1919, an impressive infrastructure of communications systems and educational institutions, and a formidable military force with 'one of the world's three or four biggest navys' (MacMillan, 2001: 315). However, the so-called Great Powers (United States, British Empire and French Empire) were racially ambivalent about the presence of the Japanese, choosing to include or exclude them from particular discussions almost at whim. Throughout the conference the Japanese were aware of the reluctance of the West to accept them as international equals. This made their determination to have a 'clause on racial equality written into the covenant of the League of Nations' (MacMillan, 2001: 322) challenging and intriguing.

During the discussion of the articles of covenant, the consideration of a clause on religious liberty gave the Japanese the opportunity to propose an amendment to extend this to questions of race. The 'racial equality clause' called for 'equal and just treatment in every respect, making no distinction, either in law or in fact, on account of their race or nationality' (Furedi, 1998: 42). The Japanese felt that as a world power their citizens should be treated with respect outside Japan. The racist reaction by white Californians to Japanese immigrants was a particular concern. Race equality however was opposed by the western powers and particularly vehemently by the delegation from the British Empire. The western powers had no interest in defining the international issue of race as morally or politically contestable (MacMillan, 2001).

The debate on race equality can be read to highlight significant features of the institutional morphology of race in international relations during 1919-1939, before it partially morphed into the configuration of the much later United Nations condemnations of racism. Firstly, the reluctance and opposition of the West to race equality, defended the colonial formation of western and non-western relationships through race insofar as this sustained the West's economic, legal and political privileges in the international order. Secondly, the subsequent League of Nations enshrined both a liberal and imperial conception of a world order in which race expressed their conceptual and political unity in a regime of 'racial historicism' (Goldberg, 2000). This was evidenced in its mandate system which divided the colonised world into A, B and C categories. These were arranged in descending order of readiness for self-government, depending on the colonised's perceived fitness for independence and self-determination or the need to be under a more civilised form of governance. The mandate system, an obligation assumed by the Western powers to rule within agreed imperial reason, symbolised the liberalisation of imperialism insofar as the colonised 'native' was construed as being capable of civilised elevation. This 'internationalisation of the principle of civilisation' can be credited with creating a 'new international environment within which colonial administration was to be conducted' (Keene, 2002: 133). Even these so-called liberal aspirations to assimilate the natives to the imported western designs of representative democratic institutions could be abandoned in circumstances that resisted assimilation and replaced by 'new doctrines of separate development for different races, segregation and colour bars' (Mazower, 1999: 57).

Thirdly, although no condemnation of racism was articulated through the League of Nations, there was the development and affirmation of an influentially overarching concept of race relations. It is important to emphasise that despite the domestic scenario with which we have come to associate race relations in our post-imperial nationalist political cultures, it was and still is part of a western imperial discourse of segregation and colour bars. According to Frank Furedi race relations evolved during the early 20th century as a political and policy framework, in conjunction with explicit colonial imperatives to defend the western imperial system against non-western resistance. The concept of race relations was developed in the form of civil governance after the First World War as a way of alleviating western imperial anxieties about the possibility of its 'global decline'; thus was race relations consolidated 'as a discipline' (Furedi, 1998: 2). Race relations in its western designed settings involved surveying, studying, regulating and intervening diplomatically or militarily among colonised and racially segregated populations in order to undermine their formulation of a critical consciousness of racial domination. Here, international relations were imperial relations, and they in turn were the imprimatur of race relations. So we can begin to see the specific formation of racism that has largely remained eclipsed by the hegemony of 20th century Eurocentric conceptualisations.

Eurocentric concept of racism

As Robert Miles (1989) has pointed out, the first time the term racism is consistently used and applied is during the 1930s in connection with the relation established between nationalism and antisemitism in Nazi Germany. The first sustained exposition is by Magnus Hirschfeld in his book *Racism*, originally published in 1934 in German and then posthumously in 1938 in English. I choose to focus on this text, not because it is or ought to be the first or last word on the Eurocentric understanding of racism, but because of the exemplariness of its conceptual formulation. In Hirschfeld's analysis it is evident that his concept of racism is predicated on condemning any mobilisations around the idea of race as drawn from detestable, illiberal ideologies. That such an early formulation should correspond to contemporary liberal thinking in international relations and the dominant discourses of Western social scientific community is striking.

Hirschfeld was reflecting on the concerted politics of antisemitism as race hatred in Europe, and how legislation against Jewish Europeans in the 1930s was inscribed in the public policies of the Nazis and their social eugenics programmes. So the discursive contours that establish this early concept of racism follow the impress of that 'paradigmatic experience' (Hesse, 2004) through which it was traced. Hirschfeld described the objective of his work as to examine 'the racial theory which underlines the doctrine of race war' (Hirschfeld, 1938: 35), a war conducted between the antagonistic discourses of liberalism and fascism. This theory identifies four main features of racism. Firstly, the objectionable doctrine is exceptional in having been translated into a persecutory practice. Secondly, it is a doctrine which defines human populations according to a tabulation of a distinct hierarchy of races and corresponding attributes. Thirdly, it identifies the mobilisation of a doctrine that results in discrimination, exclusion and extermination. Finally, this doctrine is conceived as exclusively fascistic and anti-liberal. Much of this is broadly recognisable as racism, as is its subsequent institutionalisation in what has become known as the 'Racial State' (Goldberg, 2000).

Certainly, from the 1930s to the 1950s this idea of racism assumed international status within an oppositional (antiracist) discourse, principally directed against ideas associated with race, whether they are seen as superstition or fallacy. Ruth Benedict's book *Race and Racism* (1942) elaborated the concept of racism as it would be understood in the post-1945 period, following the revelations of the Holocaust. It was taken to designate relations of ascribed biological superiority and inferiority. It formed part of the understanding enshrined in the United Nations' Universal Declaration of Human Rights in 1948, which was shaped principally by an opposition to fascism, the consolidation of liberalism and the retention of imperialism. In the latter half of the 20th century, critiques of western populist articulations of racism highlighted their political recoding from biology to culture, from 'inegalitarian racism' to 'differentialist racism'. But even those critiques of a 'new racism' involved in nationalist opposition to the presence of minorities and migrants, was conceptually indebted to the foundational 'paradigmatic experience' of the Holocaust (Hesse, 2004). In relation to the idea of human rights, racism has long been defined primarily in Eurocentric terms. This is so not only where colonialism and liberalism are seen as no longer central to shaping the experience of racism in the West, but also because whatever passes for racism has been traditionally depicted as a codified ideology rather than a routine social practice.

The Eurocentric concept of racism universalises the particularity of a distinctive western liberal concern with racialised fascism and obscures the cultural relation between liberalism, colonialism and racism (Hesse, 2004; Sayyid, 2003). Its Eurocentrism, in forming the basis of a hegemonic template in European social science, has led in the direction of combating and researching racism in terms of ideology and exceptionalism. The latter variously includes the pseudo-scientific ideas of race, racial discrimination, racial segregation, extremist nationalist ideology and the racial state, all of which are generally associated with illiberalism, especially fascism. However, in treating racism principally as a radical deviation from the enlightenment of the West, it precludes asking whether the European colonial formation of racism is, or ought to be, reducible to that conceptualisation. What accounts for the ineradicable Eurocentrism in this concept of racism is a universalised insistence that whatever corresponds to the template of the racism of the Nazi era must be a highly aberrant development, the characteristics of which can only be construed within the discourse of exceptionalism, that is to say, outside the legitimacy of western hegemony.

The problem of exceptionalism

What does it mean to regard racism as a form of exceptionalism? Giorgio Agamben suggests a 'relation of exception' exists where the force of law, authority or regulation defines itself against what it has rendered 'exterior' to it (Agamben, 1998). In these terms any hegemonic assemblage (e.g. western liberal-democracy) represents its integrity and legitimacy by removing from identification with itself whatever threatens to place its universalised values into disrepute (e.g. western fascism/racism). The formal exclusion of the removed is at the same time the creation of the exception, that which is formally declared to be an unwarranted excess, outside the accredited western culture. What made the idea of race and its juridical elaboration of fascism unacceptable in the West were the persecutory and genocidal excesses of the Nazi era. These excesses broke unequivocally with imperial conventions of international law that had facilitated the design of racially specific practices for regulating the colonial realms of non-Europe as distinct from Europeans in Europe (Keene, 202: 136-137). The western powers were confronted by such racist excess in the Holocaust that they threatened western culture's claims to civilisation and humanism. Although the post-war international establishment of the United Nations symbolised liberal-democracy's victory over Nazism, it procured a return to the international rule of law without effectively disestablishing the prevailing imperial/liberal system of 'racial rule' (Goldberg, 2002). Fascism/racism was proscribed as exceptionalism through a form of political 'interdiction' (Agamben, 1998), thus removing it from the sacraments of an unquestioned western hegemony, if not western history.

Because the principle of western hegemony is predicated on the imperial organisation of consent to its international rule of law, it involves both imposing its culture of rule and popularising its rule of culture; therefore the exception must also be understood as that which cannot be represented, that which has had the sanction of the law removed from it (Agamben, 1998). This helps to explain how and why in the imperial/liberal reason of western polities after 1945, the indictment of fascism/racism as exceptional involved the view that it could effectively be proscribed and removed. And because 'the relation of exception is (also) a relation of ban', what is banned is not 'simply set outside the law and made indifferent to it, but rather abandoned by it' (Agamben, 1998: 28). However, I need to distinguish between positive and negative senses of abandonment. Positive abandonment is juridical (see Agamben, 1998); it can be seen as the basis for the United Nations and Western governments banning nationalist-fascist racism through proscription. However, in being proscribed the meaning of fascism/racism is at the same time affirmed as a coherent, even though objectionable, formation. Negative abandonment involves denial of any meaning or existence: so some forms of racism remain unacknowledged and ignored. Historiographic abandonment is evident where liberal-colonial racism cannot be readily assimilated to nationalist/fascist racism and where it is exposed as an exception to western hegemony. Its conceptual resistance to being assimilated and distorted in this way renders it dismissable within the hegemonic gaze of the west (Hesse, 1999). So it is not surprising that a historical case still has to be made in politics for how we understand the institutional relation between colonialism, liberalism and the persistence of contemporary forms of racism.

Post-war racism and the United Nations

The United Nations was established in 1945 to avoid the outbreak of large scale warfare and to protect weaker states against aggression (Falk, 1998). However, the principles underlying it, and particularly its Universal Declaration of Human Rights in 1948 were directly influenced by the Nazi atrocities of the Second World War and hence by a Eurocentric concept of racism[3]. This meant that subsequent UN resolutions became the basis for nationally sanctioned critiques or condemnations of racism, to the extent that the latter could be demonstrated as a 'denial of the principles of the Charter of the United Nations' and a 'violation of human rights and fundamental freedoms proclaimed in the Universal Declaration' (UNESCO, 2001: 294). But this left intact the conceptual and political problem of addressing the coloniality of racism. According to Talal Asad (2003) not only did the Declaration refrain from taking into consideration the 'question of national rights on which human rights inevitably depended', it also excluded from its theorisation the 'constitutional structures of empire' (Asad, 2003: 136, 137). Firstly, the significance given to national sovereignty suggests that those fully accommodated within the nation, with racially accredited citizenship had a more legitimate basis for their human rights as individuals. Whereas those marginalised by nationalism or excluded through immigrant status from the authenticity of the nation, those communally occupying a racially second class citizenship, could be open to greater abuses of their human rights and lesser recognition from the national government (e.g. the post-1945 history of racist attacks in Britain). Secondly, the Declaration, in assuming a direct convergence between the rule of law and social justice, relied too closely on the 'power of the state to identify, apply and maintain the law'. There was 'no explicit recognition that what is allowed by the law may be unjust and therefore intolerable' (Asad, 2003: 138). This suggests that policies of western social institutions, though lawful, eminently liberal or unquestionably democratic, could nevertheless sustain practices which traditionally privileged the concerns, perspectives, rights and livelihoods of white European and American citizens without directly disparaging others (e.g. the post-1945 history of racially inflected immigration law and practice in Britain).

Racism experienced by the racially disparaged 'non-white' or colonially dominated 'non-European' could not be adequately addressed by this framework. Only a form of judicial denial was possible. Also disavowed was the contested international meaning of racism raised by anticolonial struggles and revolutions that implicated subordinated populations across Asia, Africa, Cuba, the US, Palestine and Iran against Western and/or white hegemony, in protracted movements for decolonisation, national liberation and freedom. The critical passion and popular force of these agitations also involved profound interrogations of the parochial meanings attached to the racism that had attracted so much criticism in the West. Given the great western moral revulsion against racism in the postwar period, why did racially segregated peoples in the US and South Africa, and the colonised in European empires have to wage such major struggles and revolts against the resistant racism of western powers? Is it not time we questioned the myth of a mass conversion to antiracism in the West from the late 1940s onwards? Did the West really experience the organic resumption of a temporarily interrupted western democracy on the way to consensual global hegemony? Such self-serving historiography fails to explain why colonial racist practices were sustained and elaborated by Spanish, Portuguese, American, British, French and Dutch polities for over two centuries prior to and following Nazism. If it is unquestionable that the political issues posed by race and racism had changed in the world since the defeat of Nazism, the more perplexing question is why?

Western democracy or western racism?

What has been the relationship between western racism and western democracy following the Cold War? The idea of representative democracy that underpinned western ideals of superiority in the postwar period was defined as much by anti-communism as liberalism (Mazower, 1999). What problematised the image of democracy in international relations were the challenges of anticolonialism/antiracism from disenfranchised populations in Africa, Asia and the United States, and the role of the Soviet Union in ideologically exploiting these recurrent inconsistencies to indict western racism. Significantly, the response of the US throughout the early stages of the cold war was to try and 'prevent the emergence of race as an issue in the United Nations' (Furedi, 1998: 192). Both the US and Britain adopted similar approaches to those deployed during the second world war: trying to 'minimise racial consciousness and depoliticise race' (Furedi, 1998: 192). The concern for the West was the possibility that exposure of its racisms might persuade nations in the Third World to align with the Communist bloc. So domestic race relations was increasingly bound up with ostensibly unrelated foreign policy relations.

Although the post-war rebuilding of Europe is not usually associated with questions of colonialism and racism, nonetheless the Cold War made them relevant. Policy initiatives undertaken by the US, as part of the Cold War realignment, including the establishment of Nato, the Marshall plan and the Truman doctrine, not only bolstered European colonialists, but also 'indirectly funded those governments' efforts to preserve white rule against indigenous independence movements in Asia and Africa' (Borstlemann, 2001: 53). Throughout the 1950s and the 1960s, US mobilisation against the external threat of communism had a far higher priority for Federal administrations than the assault on the internal atrocities of racism (Borstlemann, 2001). In Britain there was little Government interest in the need to address racism, other than the desire to exclude fascism from the political mainstream. Concerns with an imploding Empire and induced economic migration from the Caribbean, Africa and South Asia, had more to do with national prestige, public order, criminality, assimilation and community relations than anything that could be construed as racism. All of which continued to beg the question, just what was the relation between western racism and western democracy?

The experience of the US is illustrative of at least three ways in which we can understand the meaning of this relationship and how it has been sustained. The first concerns the conditions under which and the reasons why the West began to address subaltern interrogations of racism. During the 1960s the civil rights movement's capacity to internationalise itself and socially expose the racial duplicity and exclusivity of American democracy was so powerful that 'federal government action on civil rights' became 'an aspect of Cold War policy making' (Dudziak, 2000: 15). What the Cold War revealed in relation to civil rights legislation was how the western state's domestic antiracism had as much to do with sustaining an international image of western democracy, as a counter to Communist or antiwestern propaganda, as the liberal righting of publicly castigated wrongs (see Borstlemann, 2001; Gerstle, 2001).

The second way in which democracy and racism became related concerns the impact the Cold War had on forms of racism that were mobilised to represent the dehumanising and disenfranchised conditions of subordinated non-white/non-European populations. In the US the Cold War supplied the terms of realpolitik that influenced the politics and discourses of civil rights activists. Here, racism was condemned by using the vernacular associated with the Eurocentric concept of racism, thereby attaining the status of a legitimate public indictment. Penny Von Eschen insightfully refers to this instrumentality as the 'rewriting of racism':

> Some civil rights activists equated racism with Nazism in order to legitimate their struggle. Throughout World War Two black Americans had portrayed Nazism as one consequence of imperialism and one manifestation of racism, seeing antifascism as a critical component of democratic politics but not to the exclusion of anticolonialism. *Now Nazism became the standard of evil, and antiracist struggles appealed to the similarities between racism and Nazism for their legitimacy* (Von Eschen, 1997: 153; emphasis added).

Where it became influential, the Eurocentric rewriting of colonial racism had three telling consequences for what was to be considered a democratically acceptable and accredited discourse of antiracism in the field of western public reason. Firstly, racism was understood outside of the particularities of western history and defined as an aberrant yet universal phenomenon; an ahistorical evil, exemplified in the racially segregated Southern States and apartheid South Africa, both of which could be ranked along side the exceptionalism of Nazi Germany. Secondly, the anticolonial critique, particularly with the passage of civil rights legislation (and the formal dissolution of Empire) was now foreclosed and replaced by Cold War liberalism; shifting the analysis of racism from the colonial political economies of dominant institutions to the social psychology of prejudices and race relations. Thirdly, with the impact and formation of racism no longer so readily depicted in its global governmentalities[4] it was increasingly associated with extremist forms of domestic nationalist ideologies (Hesse, 2004).

Majorities and minorities

The passage of civil rights legislation and the antiracist traditions surrounding it were not merely cynical endeavours. But, despite the range of moral and political motivations involved, the inherited antiracist tradition in the development of public policy has obscured the coloniality of the relationship between racism and democracy. During the Cold War period of legal desegregation and formal decolonisation, western nations like the US and UK were confronted with having to adjust their national representations and institutional commitments to take account of discredited racial formations. For the first time the western nation was forced to reconsider the formal assumption that its natural citizenship was exclusively white. This was symbolised in the change of policy language from colonial descriptions of the so-called Negro problem or the coloured problem or the immigrant problem, to the liberal terminology of racial minorities and ethnic minorities in the idiom of race relations, multiculturalism and colour blind societies (Hesse, 2000; Goldberg, 2000; Brown *et al*, 2003). However, as Asad points out, the 'notion of minority sits uncomfortably with the secular Enlightenment concept of the abstract citizen' (Asad, 2003: 174). Citizens who comprise a liberal-democratic state share an abstract equality, in which each citizen is significant as an individual. In western democracies the idea of minority conflicts with this formal equality, as ethnic or racial 'minorities are defined as minorities only in hierarchical structures of power' (Asad, 2003: 175). Long regarded as incarnating foreignness and otherness, their equal political inclusion and social participation within the western antiracist nation is dependent on their communal identities assimilating to a national discourse which precludes their particular ethnicisation of feelings, memories, concerns and historical commentaries. In this way, the individuality of minorities is burdened and diminished by being negotiated through the social inequalities of their communities' representation within the nation. It is a 'burdened individuality' inscribed in the routinisation of being 'equal and inferior' (Hartman, 1997).

Contemporary western democratic nations do not question the constitution of a racial majority's claim to the state as its national representative or its arrogation of the right to embody the nation's heritage, identity and history. It is difficult to imagine how this could be so unless precepts and practices of coloniality form a crucial, undisturbed part of the western democratic tradition. This is a tradition in which the ideal of a racial majority in permanent authority remains sutured to the disavowed colonial history of the imperial western nation which made possible its 'racial rule' (Goldberg, 2000). Because of the routine, everyday ways in which a racial majority can be invoked democratically as popular opinion or the national way of life, racial minorities find their place in a colonial relation, as politically dependent subjects and unofficially second class citizens. In this scenario the relation between democracy and antiracism experienced by the racial minority is one where a nationally proscribed racism conforms to that which the representatives of the postulated racial majority are prepared to indict. This returns us to the basis from which the Eurocentric concept of racism has drawn and cultivated its hegemony since the end of the Second World War.

The denouement of institutional racism

So what has been the relation between colonialism and racism in the postwar/ postcolonial era of the late 20th century? Mainstream European and American social science traditions have not considered racism to be a central part of western societies either during or after colonial regimes. Western social sciences have generally understood colonialism more through tropes of law and legislation than culture and regulation, particularly where the formal disestablishment of colonial regimes and the racisms they expressed are concerned. Within sociological discourse for example, the end of European empires and US racial segregation are considered as resembling discrete legal terminations of superceded historical periods. Racism is accounted for in terms of residuum and exceptionalism rather than continuity and conventionality. This is partly due to the failure to understand the western political culture of colonialism, both its historical continuities and contemporary specificities. For example, what is known as the problem of cultural diversity, or the question of multiculturalism in Europe and the US, derives its unsettling meanings from western colonial and imperial projects in which designated non-Christian/non-European/non-white others were constituted as subordinate racial subjects in western polities (Mignolo, 2000). The dominant western response to the multicultural, given its racialised terms of reference, has never been devoid of colonialism. The colonial relation involved western powers in governing culturally diverse 'non-European' otherness by coercing or inducing its acceptance of a normalised white rule, which meant their succumbing to western authority, representation, classifications, epistemologies and regulations. Although western governments were forced to begin contemplating changes in their imperial remit, given the expansion of liberal-democratic governance in the post was period, this has not damaged the culture of colonialism which has become as significant a part of western ways of being as secularism, humanism or speaking English.

In Europe migrants (and their descendants) from Africa, Asia and the Caribbean had their historic relations of dependency and subordination reconfigured when entering the terrain of the European nation: the 'classic postcolonial' transition (Hall, 2000). So how is the coloniality of racism both continued and denied in Western democracies? Firstly, following formal decolonisation, racial relations of coloniality continued, though often signified in culturally different ways and new political instances, and so thoroughly westernised as to be considered unremarkable (e.g. ideas of racial harmony or good and bad race-relations, see Hesse, 2000)). Secondly, there was a socially developed process of colonial displacement and denial (i.e. colonialism is seen as affecting the past not the present); marked unmistakably by a 'collective amnesia about and systematic disavowal of empire' (Hall, 2000: 218), leaving the culture of coloniality influential in social design (e.g. immigration regulations) but silenced in social representation. Thirdly, in relation to the newly democratically incorporated citizens, the migrants from the former colonies, the 'encounter was interpreted as a new beginning'. Longstanding Europeans began to look at these 'children of empire' as if they could not envisage from where they had come or what relation they could possibly have with the European nation (Hall, 2000: 218). The European nation became an imagined community with an ever present nationalist history and an ever distant colonial past. Yet what constantly interrupted the idea of an effective postcolonial transition in places like Britain was the persistence and recurrence of complaints, accusations and mobilisations against racism. Where the incidence of racism could not be successfully represented by the state in Eurocentric terms, or where these terms were refused by critics, the compatibility of racism and liberal-democracy was exposed, if not explained.

A concept is born

On both sides of the Atlantic this raised the question of what concept of racism could be extracted from these paradoxes and dilemmas of western democracy's retreats from and yet definite intimacies with coloniality? (see Lowe, 2004). This question engaged the work of WEB Du Bois (1947), Aime Cesaire (1955), and Frantz Fanon (1956) during the late 1940s and 1950s in the convergence between the immediacy of the post Second World War period and the urgency of the anticolonial and civil rights movements. Reading their critical examinations of western democracy, even from this historical distance, obliges us to question whether it is anachronistic to talk about coloniality after the end of empire and racial desegregation. Is there a need to reject 'the assumption that the world has been decolonised' (Grosfoguel, 2002: 204)? It was from this form of interrogation that the concept institutional racism first appeared as a bold formulation in the work of Stokely Carmichael and Charles V. Hamilton during the late 1960s. What is most remarkable and generally overlooked in Carmichael and Hamilton's famous text *Black Power: The politics of liberation in America* is the incredulity of the opening which establishes the premise for the analyses which follow. They begin by asking:

> What is racism? The word has represented daily reality to millions of black people for centuries, yet it is rarely defined – perhaps just because that reality has been such a commonplace. By racism we mean the predication of decisions and policies on considerations of race for the purpose of subordinating a racial group and maintaining control over that group (Carmichael and Hamilton, 1967: 3; my emphasis).

What makes this intervention so challenging was their insistence twenty years after the establishment of the United Nations and the Universal Declaration on Human Rights, and following the passage of the 1964 US Civil Rights Act, that racism was something that still had to be defined. The historical continuity of American racism and the routine ways it has been precluded from definition led to the suggestion that institutional racism 'has another name: colonialism' (Carmichael and Hamilton, 1967: 5). This is an extremely insightful and radical move away from the Eurocentric concept of racism.

I do not suggest that Carmichael and Hamilton's initial formulation of institutional racism should be treated as foundational or even original. Bearing in mind the circumstances of activist political struggle in which that text was written and the fact that conceptual analysis was hardly the main focus of their intervention, it is understandable that theirs is neither the most sophisticated nor elaborate version of this concept. Nevertheless, it has profound implications for the analysis of the relation between western racism and western democracy which many proponents and critics have, with a few exceptions (e.g. Blauner, 1972; Goldberg, 2002) generally failed to develop. They see institutional racism as emphasising practices of racial governance, not the ideological codifications of race that so concerns the Eurocentric approach. In suggesting racism comprises a regime of practices, they locate the rationale and coherence of that regime in the colonial relation between white and black (i.e. non-white), European and non-European, west and non-west; rather than in the nationalist relation between majorities and minorities, or citizens and immigrants.

Carmichael and Hamilton are alluding to a liberal-democratic/colonial assemblage[5] that is coherent in terms of its continuities yet traditionally disavowed and unexamined in western political culture. It is in that conventional context rather than in the so-called exceptionalist circumstances of legalised racial segregation that we are asked to understand that racism can be both 'overtly' individual (e.g. racist attacks) and 'covertly' institutional (e.g. racist housing allocation policies). Although how to understand the relation between the two forms is not always clear, it is argued that 'institutional racism relies on the active and pervasive operation of anti-black attitudes and practices', where a 'sense of superior group position prevails' and it is envisaged that 'blacks should be subordinated to whites'[6] (Carmichael and Hamilton, 1967: 5). What is at stake here is whether we understand the framing of institutional racism in the systematic terms of ideological discourse or in the routine pragmatics of racist governance. For Carmichael and Hamilton the concern is overwhelmingly with racist practices and their racially governmental or regulatory conventions[7]. The significance of their approach turns on what meaning we give to 'covert' in relation to these institutional practices. The weak sense of the term treats covert as indirect, subtle, adumbrated or perhaps unwitting; however this runs the risk of diluting the institutional dimension, it lacks a systematic quality and is imbued with a strangely individual and idiosyncratic orientation. The stronger sense of 'covert', is more institutionally inflected, and can be described as that which is concealed, hidden, disguised, unacknowledged, denied but which is consistent in its impact or strategic effect[8]. In this sense it is the colonial dimension of the liberal-democratic/colonial assemblage that has a covert institutional presence, underwritten by a 'hidden transcript', euphemised by the 'official transcript' (see Scott, 1990). Institutional racism, unlike the ideological racism associated with so-called 'overtly racist regimes' (Fredrickson, 2001), is contextualised by liberal-democratic culture, it 'originates in the operation of established and respected forces in the society and thus receives far less public condemnation' (Carmichael and Hamilton, 1967: 5). That is the challenge which still confronts us.

Conclusion

Although the idea of institutional racism is far from secure either politically or conceptually in the West, understanding the concept's genealogy from the perspective of the postcolonial era compels us to ask questions of racism which are routinely ignored. Foremost among these is whether coloniality shares a family resemblance with liberalism in being constitutionally unwritten into our western democratic institutions. The limitations of the Eurocentric concept of racism are obvious. It takes its major concerns from the discredited fascist excesses of nationalism. Institutional racism is best described as a de/colonial concept (Hesse, 2004)[9] that finds its concerns in the obscured inadequacies of western decolonisation and the disavowed continuities of its liberal/colonial practices. It is important to turn our attention to examining the relation between western coloniality, democracy and racism. The future of race relations is now at stake. We need to recall that the idea of race relations exhibits, symbolically and practically, the 20th century history of its coloniality. Even the liberal idealisation of racial harmony or racial integration does not lie outside socially regulating and managing the interface between Europeans and non-Europeans, though this now takes the apparent democratic form of white majority and non-white minorities. Historically the task of maintaining good race relations was always to avoid making non-Europeans racially conscious of their subordination and exploitation by eliminating European public displays of racist sentiment. Such diplomatic comportment has been called the 'silent protocol' of race relations (Furedi, 1999).

The public expression of racism in front of the colonised and racially subjugated was to be studiously repressed. Liberal/colonial practices of racism were to be sustained through covert rather than overt discourses (Furedi, 1999). If this is part of our western cultural inheritance, then perhaps another name for institutional racism is race relations[10]. I should like to thank Bobby Sayyid for his patient insights and Ian Law for his insightful patience.

Notes

1 This essay is written in homage to Aimé Cesaire's famous *Discourse on Colonialism*, an unsurpassed poetic and political critique of the cultural and violent formations of modernity introduced by western imperialisms; including the latter's disavowals of the racisms and devastation its so-called civilising missions produced. The text is also important, though lesser known for one of the earliest uses (among anti-colonialist writers during the 1950s) of the newly internationalised concept, racism. Cesaire de-privileges its association with Nazism and insists on its prior attachment to European humanism.

2 This was not the first conference of its kind. In 1978 and 1983, the United Nations had organised World conferences to 'Combat Racism and Racial Discrimination'. Each was planned within a policy framework of 'three decades of Action to Combat Racism and Racial discrimination'. The first decade covered, 1973-1983, the second, 1983-1993 and the third 1993 – 2003. The Durban conference, though attended by delegates from all over the world, including those representing NGOs, seemed to attract little media attention in relation to the question of racism in the 21st century. The media publicised resolutions concerning demands by African, African American and Caribbean delegates for reparations for Atlantic slavery and the proposition by various Arab and Muslim delegates that Zionism be equated with racism. For a while this threatened to derail the conference. Yet despite the eventual withdrawal of the delegations from the US and Israel and the initial resistance of the British, French and Dutch delegations to recognising Atlantic slavery as a crime against humanity, the conference managed to sustain its proceedings. So despite the potential for disagreements and failures to resolve polarised positions, the Durban conference went ahead as planned. The persistence of this conference, together with the heritage of the previous two, suggested that racism, even if not effectively tackled or addressed, was nonetheless widely recognised as a social phenomenon (see Unesco, 2001).

3 The planning conference for the UN held at Dumbarton Oaks, Washington DC in September 1944, with the US, Soviet Union, England and China in attendance as the allied major powers. China's proposal that the pending United Nations charter include a clause on racial equality was unambiguously opposed. The principle of racial equality was not something the Allies were prepared to accept and China was persuaded that it was not in its international interests to pursue that direction. As with the earlier Japanese proposal on race equality in 1919, the Chinese proposal in 1944 questioned the colonial formation of international relations and its analogue in western domestic race relations (Gallicchio, 2000).

4 It is beyond the scope of this essay to discuss the importance of Michel Foucault's ideas on 'governmentality' for understanding questions of race and racism. The intention here is simply to highlight the latter's formation as governmental phenomena designed in deployment within western imperial settings. Governmentality describes the social penetration of institutional practices of governing and their institutional mentalities of governing. Foucault suggests that, from the late 18th century onwards, distinctive conceptions of government, population and political economy develop in combination to produce a new social arena of intervention and regulation. Although coloniality is not one of Foucault's concerns, his ideas bear a family resemblance to the global way in which race is constituted in the colonial framing of such a social arena. In this sense the colonial governmentalisation of race (the practices and emphases of racism) can be said to comprise: 'The ensemble formed by the institutions, procedures, analyses, and reflections, the calculations and tactics that allow the exercise of this very specific albeit complex power' (Foucault, 1994: 219). These ideas are developed further in Hesse and Sayyid (forthcoming, 2005).

5 Political concepts drawn from western tradition (e.g liberalism, democracy, nationalism) tend to exclude or diminish any constitutive reference to its colonial dimensions. The challenge is to develop analyses which are both incorporative and contextual regarding the colonial. For example Martin Shaw (2000: 104) has argued 'the heyday of the nation-state (roughly 1870 – 1945) was also that of the modern European empire'. The implications of this are striking where he also argues that the 'dominant form of the state was not, therefore, simply a nation-state, but the nation-state-empire within an interimperial system'. In a related manner David Goldberg (2002: 7) has made a compelling case that the racial state was not an aberration in the western tradition, but a central formation, 'modern states and racial states are deeply intertwined, the conditions of the latter bound up with the possibilities of the former'. My use of the Deleuzian term 'assemblage' (see Patton, 2000) is intended to suggest that the unity of political regimes may be constituted by the composition of apparently disparate (e.g. liberal, colonial democratic) forms of power, relationships and knowledge, which somehow remain unseen within interpretive traditions that disavow the possibility of particular unities.

6   It is important not to mistake this description of a colonial relation for the suggestion that racism is simply what 'whites' do to 'blacks'. This criticism (see Miles and Brown, 2003) fails to see that racism within the European/ American colonial relation designates hegemonic white and subjugated non-white constituencies. In that context western nation building has encountered different forms of resistances from these various so-called 'non-white' constituencies, which have often developed political and cultural traditions that emphasise their own exclusive resistances. It also means that Black people, like other 'non-whites' in the colonial relation, can embody the particularity and symbolise the universality of the racist experience.

7   Robert Miles (1989; and Brown et al, 2003) has argued that concepts of racism which emphasise the Black/White relation (in my terms the colonial relation) are reductive and commit the sin of 'conceptual deflation'; while concepts of racism that accentuate practices or institutions, beyond the centrality of ideologies commit the greater sin of 'conceptual inflation'. However because Miles has privileged as universal what I have parochialised as the Eurocentric concept of racism, anything that is conceptually less or more than that can only be seen as a deviation from what he clearly takes to be foundational. It is only within the realm of policing concepts that they can be seen as under threat. An alternative view, pursued here, suggests concepts can be neither inflated nor deflated, only be contested by the production of qualitatively different concepts (see Deleuze and Guattari, 1994).

8   At the beginning of this essay I referred to high and low thresholds of citation concerning the incidence of institutional racism. Correspondingly it may be said that where there is a high threshold of citation for the pervasiveness of institutional racism, it is the stronger sense of 'covert' which is stressed.

9   The de/colonial describes an imperative to decolonise the failures, unevenness and incompleteness of western decolonisation. It suggests three things in particular. Firstly, as a concept, it draws attention to the formal postcolonial era as the horizon within which frustrated movements towards decolonisation (e.g. antiracism) and contextually different continuities of coloniality (e.g. racism) are fused and imbricated in undecidable ways. Secondly if postcolonialism can be seen as comprising those discourses which comprehend and challenge the incompleteness of decolonisation in the western hegemony of globalisation, the de/colonial is concerned with the forms decolonisation can take in that liberal-democratic context of disavowal. Thirdly, because western racism is symptomatic of coloniality and the failures in decolonisation, de/colonial concepts of racism are concerned with the genealogy and specificities of its colonial forms and governmentalities (see Hesse, 2004; Hesse, 2000)

10   The similarity of race relations to what Foucault has identified as disciplinary power. We can think of the colonial evolution of race relations as cultivating 'methods which made possible the meticulous control of the operations of the body, which assured the constant subjection of its forces and imposed upon them a relation of docility-utility (that) might be called disciplines" (Foucault, 1979: 137). Race relations as a colonial discipline of the early 20th century was very much the imperial supplement to the liberalisation of 'racial historicism' (the belief in the capacity of the lesser races to improve through the civilising qualities attributed to the imperial state, see Goldberg, 2002). In the latter half of the 20th century, its initiatives and programmes continued to be based on projected concerns with racial conflict that might be directed against perceived racial domination. Racial integration within liberal-democracy implies the political and cultural docility of the racially minoritised body. The managing of good race relations means minimising the grounds for threats to racial authority or eliminating the perception of racial domination, rather than challenging racial domination.

References

Agamben, G. (1998) *Homer Sacer – Sovereign Power and Bare Life*, Palo Alto: Stanford University Press

Asad, T. (2003) *Formations of the Secular – Christianity, Islam and Modernity*, Palo Alto: Stanford University Press

Bartelson, J. (1995) *A Genealogy of Sovereignty,* Cambridge: Cambridge University Press

Blauner, R. (1972) *Racial Oppression in America*, New York: Harper and Row

Borstlemann, T. (2001) *The Cold War and the Color Line – American Race Relations in the Global Arena,* London: Harvard University Press.

Brown, M.K., Carnoy, M., Currie, E., Duster, T., Oppenheimer, D.B., Shultz, M.M. and Wellman, D. (2003) *White-washing Race – the myth of a Color Blind society,* Berkeley: University of California Press

Carmichael, S. and Hamilton, C.V. (1967) *Black Power – The politics of liberation in America*, New York: Vintage books

Cesaire, A. (1955/1970) *Discourse on Colonialism*, New York: Monthly Review Press

Deleuze, G. and Guattari, F. (1994) *What is Philosophy?,* London: Verso

Dudziak, M.L. (2000) *Cold War Civil Rights – Race and the image of American Democracy,* Princeton: Princeton University Press

Eschen Von, P.M. (1997) *Race against Empire – Black Americans and Anticolonialism 1937-1957*, Ithaca: Cornel University Press

Falk, R. (1998) 'The United Nations and Cosmopolitan Democracy: Bad Dream, Utopian Fantasy, Political project' in D. Archibugi, D. Held and M. Kohler eds. *Re-imagining Political Community*, London: Polity Press

Foucault, M. (1994) *Michel Foucault – Power: essential works of Foucault 1954-1984, Vol. 3*, London: Penguin Books

Foucault, M. (1979) *Discipline and Punish – The birth of the prison*, New York: Vintage books

Furedi, F. (1998) *The Silent War – Imperialism and the changing perception of race*, London: Pluto Press

Gallicchio, M. (2000) *The African American encounter with Japan and China – Black Internationalism in Asia 1895-1945*, Chapel Hill: University of North Carolina Press

Gerstle, G. (2001) *American Crucible – Race and Nation in the Twentieth Century*, Princeton: Princeton University Press

Goldberg, D.T. (2002) *The Racial State*, New York: Blackwell

Grosfoguel, R. (2002) 'Colonial Difference, Geopolitics of Knowledge, and Global coloniality in the Modern/Colonial Capitalist world-system', *Review*, Vol. XXV, No.3

Hall, S. (2000) 'The Multicultural Question' in B. Hesse ed. *Un/settled Multiculturalisms – Diasporas, Entanglements, Transruptions*, London: Zed Books

Hirschfeld, M. (1938) *Racism*, London: Victor Gollancz

Hesse, B. (2004) 'Im/plausible Deniability: Racism's Conceptual Double Bind', *Social Identities*, Vol. 1, Issue 10, January

Hesse, B. (2000) 'Introduction: Un/settled Multiculturalisms' in B. Hesse ed. *Un/settled Multi-culturalisms – Diasporas, Entanglements, Transruptions*, London: Zed Books

Hesse, B. and Sayyid, S. (forthcoming, 2005) *Paradoxes of Racism – western governmentalities in culture and politics*, London: Pluto Press

Lowe, L. (forthcoming, 2004) 'Intimacies of Four Continents' in A.L. Stoler ed. *Tense and tender ties: North American History and postcolonial studies*, Durham: Duke University Press

Macmillan, M. (2001) *Peacemakers – The Paris Conference of 1919 and its attempt to end War*, London: John Murray

Mazower, M. (1998) *Dark Continent – Europe's Twentieth Century*, London: Allen Lane/Penguin Press

Miles, R. (1989) *Racism*, London: Routledge

Miles, R. and Brown, M. (2003) *Racism, Second edition*, London: Routledge

Mignolo, W.D. (2000) *Local histories/Global designs – Coloniality, Subaltern knowledges and Border thinking*, Princeton: Princeton University press

Patton, P. (2000) *Deleuze and the Political*, London: Routledge

Sayyid, S. (2003; second edition) *A Fundamental Fear: Eurocentrism and the emergence of Islamism*, London: Zed Books

Scott, J. (1990) *Domination and the Arts of Resistance – Hidden Transcripts*, New Haven: Yale University Press

Shaw, M (2000) *Theory of the Global State – Globality as an unfinished revolution*, Cambridge: Cambridge University Press

Stoler, A.L. (2002) *Carnal Knowledge and Imperial Power*, Berkley: University of California Press

CHAPTER FOURTEEN

Slippery People: the immigrant imaginary and the grammar of colours

Salman Sayyid

Eight men are in a warehouse, some are sitting some are standing. Joe Cabot sits in front of them on a table, behind him is a blackboard with a drawing of a jewellery store. Joe Cabot lectures the group on the need for anonymity in case of capture, to preserve their anonymity all men (who with the exception of his son and himself do not know anyone else in the group) will be given an alias. Joe Cabot gives the following aliases: Mr Brown, Mr White, Mr Blonde, Mr Blue, Mr Orange, Mr Pink. The following dialogue ensues:

Mr Pink: *'Why can't we pick our own colour?'*

Joe Cabot: *'I tried that once – it didn't work. You get four guys fighting over who is going to be Mr Black. Since nobody knows anybody else, nobody wants to back down. So forget it, I pick. Be thankful you're not Mr Yellow.'*[1]

Introduction

The problem of colour coding as a marker of identity often confronts ethnicised minorities. Colour is the mark which distinguishes some ethnic groups from other unmarked i.e. colourless or white ethnicities. The process by which ethnic marking occurs is not the way that Mr Pink would prefer. Ethnic minorities cannot chose their designation, they cannot have a self-ascribed identity. Cabot's method of picking the aliases for the gang indicates the link between identity formation and the exercise of power. It is this relationship that I wish to explore in the context of how the identities of those who are considered to be ethnically marked and unmarked are constructed.[2]

The exchange between Mr Pink and Cabot is an example of a wider discussion of identity politics. Mr Pink would like to pick his own colour, to work under a self-ascribed identity. The scenario Joe Cabot seems to fear is, that left to their own devices the gang would disintegrate into war of 'all against all' as each gang member would fight to have the coolest alias. For Cabot '[t]he political danger resides not in the closure of identity and but in the hell of infinite difference'.[3] The political process is about the construction and maintenance of identities. From mundane administrative policies to statements of grand politics, the process of identification is central. It involves the exercise of power.

The formation of identities of ethnically marked populations is part of a political process. If ethnic identities are ascribed in the manner of Joe Cabot, by some leviathan, this has an effect on those who end up bearing such subjectivities. The ascription of an identity involves more than a designation of a label. It involves the establishment of a variety of ways in which identity is regulated and policed. The ascription of identities has major social, economic, political and cultural effects. It is through the articulation of identities that social relations are constructed and maintained and acted upon. The way certain population clusters are articulated has a major effect on their life chances. The history of the people of colour, or ethnically marked communities, in Britain can to some extent be told as a history of the way in which various designations have been deployed over time to fit them into the landscape of British identity. The current subject positions organised around labels such as Asian, Black and Muslim which populated Britain's ethnoscape have emerged through complex interactions and struggles.[4] How the various colours were formed, how their fuzzy edges were policed is part of the history of postcolonial settlement. This chapter does not offer a historical narrative of the various trans-formations in the identity of ethicised minorities but focuses on the conditions and pos-sibilities of being ethnically marked.

Deploying the immigrant imaginary

All western plutocracies operate with definitions of citizen and foreigner as a means of determining the membership of a political community. The notion of citizen requires the notion of foreigner; without it the concept of citizen would have no value. The immigrant occupies an unresolved position between citizen and foreigner. Consequently the im-migrant disrupts the closure of the nation. The presence of the immigrant points to the way in which a 'foreign' element is located within the citizen body. The internal 'foreigner' who is a non-citizen because she is foreign may also enjoy some rights. The discourse of post-imperial immigration and settlement of Europe provides a reservoir of highly mobile tropes, which have been used over time to mark out various groups of ex-colonial settlers.[5] This is the discourse of the immigrant imaginary which explicitly or implicitly provides a lexicon through which ethnicised minorities are managed, through which their foreignness is domesticated but not eradicated.

It is possible at the analytical level to distinguish four key features of this discourse. First, the immigrant imaginary sees an ontological distinction between host society and im-migrants. This difference is marked in various ways. The immigrants' food smells, their music is loud, their family structures are anarchic or oppressive, their everyday conduct differs from that of 'normal people'. Where the host society has networks, immigrants have kinship; whereas the host society has modernity, immigrants are tradition-bound. Consider how settler communities have so often been considered as outside the pale of proper politics. It is thought that their activities can be explained in terms of factionalism or machinations of egotistical community leaders.[6] The difference between host and settler becomes overdetermined by metaphors culled from two-hundred year old scholastic traditions. Disciplines such as anthropology often mark out this division between the settlers and the hosts, and police it.

Secondly, immigrant experiences are read from either an exoticised or banalisied register. The exotic celebration finds popular expression in steel bands and saris, the banal in the homilies to colour blindness. The immigrant imaginary is able to incorporate the tension between exoticisation and banalisation in its articulation of immigrants. The tendency to exoticise treats the immigrant as incarnating exceptionality: a manifestation of difference, expressed in signifiers of ritual, dress, and life in general. This is countered by the seemingly opposite tendency to make the immigrant the Same. The bland sameness produced by banalisation empties the Other of any particularity and instead emphasises more general structures such as genetic make-up or their evolutionary development into the essence of what is human.[7] So beneath their skins, immigrants are no different from the ethnically unmarked. There is nothing distinctive about them. The exoticisation of the immigrant works by treating every aspect of the immigrant experience as distinct. The banalisaton of the immigrant works by considering the immigrant to be indistinct. Both modes of appropriating the immigrant, despite their superficial opposition, are based on the assumption that the ethnically unmarked provide the norm by which the immigrant is to be judged. The ethnically unmarked represents the quintessential human.

Thirdly, the immigrant imaginary assumes that with the passage of time the ontological distinction between immigrant and host will be eroded as the host society consumes the immigrants.[8] It assumes that over time immigrants will integrate into the host culture. The degree of integration ranges from uncritical assimilation, in which the immigrant disappears without trace into host society, to equally untheorised hybridisation in which the immigrant ends up as a hyphenated and hybridisied member of the host community – adding colour and cuisine to the host society. Whatever route they take, the immigrants will find that all roads lead to their eventual elimination as distinct populations. Furthermore, the act of consumption by the host will not substantively transform the host – the host remains the same and it is the immigrants who are chewed up and digested. This trope finds itself in politicians' speeches and opinion-makers' commentaries as exhortations to immigrants to hasten the process of assimilation by eliminating whatever practice is considered to cause moral panics, for instance arranged marriages, matriarchal households, cultural schizophrenia or youth delinquency.

Fourthly, the form of integration can be represented in discrete and successive stages called generations. A generation is one of the key units of analysis of narratives of this type. Generations are considered to be permanent units by which the immigration experience can be accounted for while maintaining the status of immigrants. Generational differences are articulated as the crystallisation of changes that immigrants are supposed to go through over time. Each generation marks progress towards integration into the host community. The immigrant imaginary presents a picture analogous to how tadpoles, over time, turn into frogs. Using the concept of generations within the immigrant imaginary performs two functions. First, it prevents the completion of the process of immigration. The prefixing of 'first', 'second' or 'third' to 'generation' defers the moment when the immigrants can be considered settlers, part of the society in which they reside. The ethnically marked ex-colonial settlers become permanent immigrants. This act of freezing the immigrant to the moment when they get 'off the plane or boat', reinforces the essentialisation of the immigrant, since regardless of how many generations have passed the immigrant remains an immigrant. The process of immigration has no end; the moment of assimilation is continually deferred. Thus the immigrant relationship to the society they reside in remains that of a newcomer. Second, the concept of generation works to de-historicise immigrants, to remove them from the currents of history and thus exclude any political dimension of their experience. Generations are deployed as a temporal category that removes any political dimension from causal explanation. So the differences between the first and second generations are narrated as due to differences in assimilation into the host society and not as changes in historical context. The immigrant is to be transformed over time into a member of the host society but the transformation is constantly deferred.

The immigrant imaginary has wide circulation in both academic and popular culture. It provides the tools by which the identity of immigrants can be regulated and disciplined. It makes available the subject positions open to the immigrant communities and the conditions that underlie that opening. It is through the use of the idea of the immigrant imaginary that the usual stories about 'ethnics' in European plutocracies are written and disseminated. Issues of cultural schizophrenia are read as forms of generational conflict, the notion of dual allegiances – for example the problem of being Muslim and Western, cruelty to animals, domestic violence and arranged marriages all provide policy-makers, professional provocateurs such as Richard Littlejohn, Julie Burchill or David Blunkett and academics with a steady supply of horror stories. The immigrant imaginary is essentialist, teleological, and ultimately xenophobic . While ostensibly it has prided itself in its ability to narrate the transformations arising out of the migration process, its ontology subverts its epistemological ambition. It is a paradigm of social change that can only account for change as teleology. It is an attempt to understand social identities, which rests upon a pre-given 'whatness' that is immutable and that determines the behavior of both immigrants and hosts. It is an imaginary that is about the Other, but remains grounded in Western supremacist discourse.

Slavoj Žižek points out how cynically ideology operates. He argues that we are often aware that we are being manipulated by messages we get from advertising or state propaganda we do not believe them but we act as though we do. By this detached acting we fulfil the ideological function and make it true. So you know that particular brand of soap powder won't wash whites whiter – but you still buy it. Cynical reasoning comes about when a discernible split develops between the official version and the unofficial view.[9] The immigrant imaginary produces a bifurcated representation, but the split is along the racial hierarchy, between the ethnically unmarked and ethnically marked. The immigrant imaginary limits the ability of those who are ethnically unmarked to transcend their socialisation and become aware of the postcolonial context of the ethnically marked settlers. The ethnically unmarked tend mostly to experience the imaginary without irony and cynicism. The ethically marked tend mostly to experience the imaginary more ironically, but there are limited alternative narratives to account for their experiences. When they play the part of native informants they are often compelled to resort to its grammar, since no other discourse is available. As I shall demonstrate the immigrant imaginary is inadequate to account for the complexities of Britain's postcolonial ethnoscapes.

Postcolonial interruptions

Generally, the postcolonial refers to a set of features that include the following: indirect Western rule, formation of ex-colonies into polities ideally patterned on the Westphalian template with its isomorphism between territory, population and government, growth of indigenous capitalist elites linked to global networks of culture and influence, and the internalisation of the metropolitian-colony hierarchy within the ex-colony.[10] Chronologically, the postcolonial denotes a temporality after the colonial European empires when direct European rule over large parts of the non-European world has been dismantled. For the nation-empires of Britain and France the postcolonial starts with end of the second Thirty years war, 1914-1945. Other European states have other dates for instance for Portugal it is after the revolution of 1975, for the USSR 1989-1991. The postcolonial varies from place to place so cannot be precisely dated.

At the conceptual level, however, what is key to the postcolonial is the erosion of the binaries which defined colonialism[11], of the West and the Rest dyad in which the world is hierarchically arranged in terms of a superior west and inferior rest. We must be clear about what the blurring of the distinction between the colonised and the coloniser means. The postcolonial interrupts the relationship between the coloniser and the colonised without erasing it. To use Derrida's expression, the postcolonial puts the colonial under erasure.[12] The postcolonial marks the end of the colonial, but also recognises that the present is haunted by the end of the colonial. The colonial era may have ended but we have not arrived at a new beginning. It is this transition between the ending of colonialism and the beginning of something new that cannot be fully identified that the postcolonial seeks to denote.[13]

The postcolonial refers to the socio-economic, cultural and political conditions that arise from the 'de-centring of the West'. This has opened the space for two main projects. Firstly, a project aimed at resisting the process of de-centring the west by normalising the western enterprise[14]. Secondly, a project aimed at trying to re-centre the west by closing the gap created between the idea of the universal and western identity[15], which can be called Eurocentrism.[16]

Borderlines

The immigrant imaginary is based on the redeployment of the colonial discourse from the periphery to the centre, to the interior of the European formation. This redeployment is not only a matter of biographical detail in which six degrees of separation connect colonial administrators, anthropology professors and race relations experts. It is more seriously a product of the way colonial governmentality is re-tooled to provide the regulatory regimes which police the ethnically marked populations of the ex-colonies: the immigrants. The presence of colonial tropes within the immigrant imaginary does not mean that it is a hangover from previous times. The imaginary is articulated both in the context of, and awareness of, postcolonialism. It can be seen as a rejection of the postcolonial by drawing on the residues of the colonial past and relocating it within the discourse of Eurocentrism or Westerness. The immigrant imaginary has a difficult relationship with postcolonialism. On the one hand it clearly rejects the postcolonial, by articulating signifying practices that are derived from colonialism, while on the other hand its necessity arises out of major sources of the postcolonial including the migration of people from ex-European colonies. The mass settlement of ethnically marked ex-colonial subjects in the former imperial heartlands is a graphic illustration of the phenomena of the postcolonial. The postcolonial undermines the immigrant imaginary by throwing its foundations into question. Thus the relationship between postcolonialism and the immigrant imaginary is what Derrida would call undecidable. This undecidability generates the petty paradoxes and convolutions of the immigrant imaginary that makes it inadequate for coping with Britain's complex ethnoscapes. But this also indicates why it is still the only officially sanctioned way of addressing the ethnically unmarked.

Postcolonial critique of the immigrant imaginary

Postcolonialism is based on the deconstruction of colonial binaries. The founding assumption of the immigrant imaginary is the ontological distinction between host and immigrant. This distinction is based on a larger distinction between the west and rest. The postwar immigration and settlement of Britain meant the relocation of people of the rest into the west. This has eroded the difference between these areas and has made it difficult to maintain the ontological distinction between host and immigrant societies. Postcolonialism points to the way in which the categories of host and immigrant are constituted through the inability to maintain the strict border between the west and rest. The slogan: 'We are here because you are there' captures the link between the constitution of the metropolitan host and the peripheral immigrant. Consequently the relationship between host and immigrant is not between two fully formed positive identities but rather the product of an articulatory practice. Therefore, one cannot take the notion of host/immigrant as a given. The erosion of the ontological distinction between host and immigrant entails the abandonment of the cognates of this relationship and the theoretical hierarchy which sustains them.

The use of the banal or the exotic to try and capture the immigrant experience becomes increasingly unsustainable as postcolonialism draws attention to the way these descriptions support a view of immigrant life as pathologically arising from the cultural features of immigrants. The effect is to exclude the operations of racism from the way in which immigrants are defined and determined. Instead, we look for pathologies in their culture. The pathologies of racism and those induced by racism are relocated as pathologies of the immigrant, arising from some internal factor. This was provided historically by biological accounts and now by sociological and cultural accounts. According to postcolonialism, the banal and the exotic are seen as two sides of the same coin of racist discourse which constructs some populations as both ethnically marked and minoritised ethnicities.

By interrogating the hierarchy between host society and immigrants, postcolonialism also questions the way chronology is used as a substitute for causality. Time seems to act upon only the immigrant. This depoliticises the experiences of immigrants, since any changes they undergo are already hardwired into their being. The political as a process of instituting social relations is absent from the immigrant imaginary, since most of the transformations immigrants experience are given. The narratives that tell of a more or less unproblematic transformation of the immigrant into the host are located within Westerness, with the interruption of Westerness it is difficult to imagine that the immigrant will simply disappear into the host. The politicisation of the immigrant transforms the notion of generations from a subject of temporality to an agent of history. What becomes significant is not generations but the experiences that groups encounter and how they transform their identities. The experience of being a generation becomes less relevant than the constitution of a particular subject position, which may be organised through age cohorts or the experience of coming into metropolitan societies. So for example the assumption that progressive secularisation would take place amongst second and third generation Muslim settlers has proved wrong. Developments in the world have produced the conditions which have awakened Muslim subjectivity, not weakened it, thus contradicting the expectations of progressive generational secularisation and assimilation.

The capacity of the immigrant imaginary to govern the ethnically marked, while still formidable, is under frequent stress. In Britain for example a distinct Muslim subjectivity has emerged which has disrupted the attempt at containment by the immigrant imaginary of the ethnically marked by the labels of 'Black' and 'Asian'. The Muslim subjectivity manifested itself despite great hostility and made itself felt, for example in the provision of grant maintained Muslim schools, the moral panic over Muslim terrorists and the impossibility of continuing to manage the ethnically marked through the labels of 'Black' and 'Asian'. The emergence of a distinct Muslim subjectivity in Britain is due to developments within the Muslim global ummah, which could not be controlled or regulated from the UK. The establishment of a Muslim diasporic identity demonstrates how events and processes associated with postcolonialism and the erosion of the frontier between the west and rest, and between the host and immigrant, can transcend the framings of the immigrant imaginary.

Postcolonialism will not dispel the immigrant imaginary in a puff of logic. It will not slink off into the waste bin of history, nor take its rightful place on our bookshelves along with alchemy, or astrology. The immigrant imaginary continues to recuperate postcolonial interruptions. Opinion makers are still haunted by the presence of the inalienable aliens that the immigrant imaginary articulates. The chain of paradigmatic associations that bind asylum seekers, terrorists, immigrants, Yardies and Islamic fundamentalists may be configured in different registers, but it still remains beholden to the immigrant imaginary.

What are the factors that support the immigrant imaginary? Why does it persist and why is it continually deployed by policy-makers, opinion-formers and academics? Why does it continue to be institutionalised and resourced? Even when the pictures on our television screens tell us a different story, the commentary reassures 'us' that the post-colonial has not arrived. The immigrant imaginary needs greater energies expended to shore it up. Like a boat with a large hole, the immigrant imaginary keeps afloat as long as the water coming in is less than the amount the crew can pump out. To explain this persistence requires exploration how the challenge of the postcolonial condition has affected European and English-British identity.

Re-thinking colours

The persistence of the immigrant imaginary lies in its supplemental relationship to British white identity. This cannot be fully developed here but only outlined[17]. The emergence of modern forms of governance overlaps with the formation of Western racism following the appropriation of the Americas and establishment of a world order centred on Europe. Many of the technologies associated with governmentality find their initial deployment in the colonies. Governmentality, with its emphasis on the regulation of bodies resonates with development of the discourse of racism. Consequently it is possible that the modern form of governmentality was racialised. Racial logic may be hard-wired into the contemporary state. Racism here is not auxiliary to the modern state, nor is it incidental to the construction of European identity. A key feature of European colonialism which sets it apart from other forms is the deployment of the racial frontier. This frontier successfully overcame one perennial problem of empires, the phenomenon of proconsuls identifying with local populations and seeking independence from the imperial centre.[18] European colonialism, directed at managing relations between Europeans and those subjugated by them, was dominated by the discourse of racism[19]. The narration of a common Roman-Christian heritage provided a pan-European unity in the face of non-Western subject positions.[20] This narration of Europe as a white, Christian, scientific and modern formation, whose roots can be traced from Ancient Greece onwards (the so-called Plato-to-NATO sequence), privileges place in the history of the world and is central to the construction of European (including English-British) identity.

Note that the immigrant imaginary is not a neutral representation of the lives and experiences of immigrants. It is the means by which the identities of the ethnically marked are constructed. Through the construction of the ethically marked, the ethnically unmarked white European English identity is articulated. Postcolonialism poses a challenge to the essential homogeneity of English-British and European ethnic identity, as it seeks to re-narrate these identities in terms of their contingency. The abandonment of the immigrant imaginary requires a decolonisation of the institutional ensemble comprising British state and society. This necessitates a deep uprooting of everyday assumptions through which ordinary European men and women account for themselves and their place in the world. The figure of the immigrant continues to guarantee European privilege in a post-European age. The constructions of the immigrant imaginary allow the colonial drama to be played out in the absence of Empire, thus permitting the idea of *Festung Europa* as an exceptional cultural formation to persist.

Despite the heavy investment in the immigrant imaginary, it is increasingly difficult to disguise its inability to master the complexities of postcolonial ethnoscapes. It cannot adequately account for how the ethnically marked end up being over-represented in prisons, sink estates, among the unemployed and underemployed while being under-represented in senior levels of higher education, parliament, board rooms and among the affluent and well-connected. The immigrant imaginary does not provide a vocabulary by which the racial aspect of the relationship between the ethnically unmarked and marked populations can be brought into focus.

Beyond the immigrant imaginary

Alternative ways of articulating the identities of the ethically marked are beginning to proliferate as the ability of the immigrant imaginary to rule these alternatives out of order wanes. By questioning the exceptional status of the Western enterprise the postcolonial condition makes it possible to move beyond treating the immigrant experience as a series of pathological reactions in an otherwise normal universe. It makes it possible to de-naturalise the colonial narrative and unravel its relations of power/knowledge which attempt to sustain, through colonial derived representations, a construction of the immigrant as continuation of the colonial subject in metropolitan settings.

The immigrant imaginary continues to seek colonial solutions to postcolonial dilemmas. For example, one of the constant themes in trying to explain the riots among mainly Muslim youths in northern England was in terms of their cultural exclusion from the mainstream of British society. Commentaries were replete with the usual metaphors of the immigrant imaginary. But a common feature of communities is that they take a territorial form.[21] Territiorialisation will motivate the young of that region to protect their territory from perceived threats such as those posed by white supremacists.[22] Policies based on the tropes of the immigrant imaginary are irrelevant to lives and experiences increasingly shaped by logics of the postcolonial condition and all that it entails. The narratives of causality that are deployed to account for immigrant behaviour are de-contextualised by the postcolonial condition. The understanding of diversity has to move away from accounts structured around the binaries of colonial discourse. The de-construction of the immigrant imaginary means a re-accounting of the history of our species away from verities of westerness. Such a task is immense but it has begun in many fields. The choice then is whether to build upon these interventions to produce an account of the world which no longer ontologically privileges the Western enterprise. At the level of ethnic studies this means not only the recognition and investigation of white ethnicity, but also the deliberate abandonment of the key features of the immigrant imaginary. We can then develop a better understanding of the ways in which the contemporary division of diversity between the ethnically marked and unmarked continues to colour contemporary society.

Conclusion

The ethnic marking and colour coding of individuals can provide a powerful means of regulating identities and managing social relations. Returning to the opening example in this chapter, Mr Pink did not want to be called Pink because of its associations with effeminacy, but Cabot required all members of his criminal enterprises to bear names based on colours. So all Mr Pink could do to assert his identity was to try and opt for another colour. Cabot's colour coding provided the grammar which regulated the representation of identities. The immigrant imaginary similarly provides the grammar of ethnic relations in Britain. It is the means by which the identities of both ethnically marked and unmarked populations are articulated. For while the focus of the immigrant imaginary is on the ethnically marked, its ability to sustain itself is based on the way it perpetuates colonial tropes in the context of the postcolonial. This has helped to preserve a decontested notion of European/English-British identity. The immigrant imaginary is one way by which English-British national identity is imagined, an identity that has yet to be decolonisied. This is a profoundly political issue, since the articulation of identities ultimately involves the exercise of power, as Mr Pink learned when Cabot threatened him into accepting the name he had been given.

Notes

1   Quentin Tarintino, *Reservoir Dogs*.

2   I am drawing on the distinguish in semantics between marked and unmarked terms, where lexemes which are marked (for example, by edition of suffix) are more restricted than unmarked terms which tend more general context of use.

3. Connoly, 1991, 59

4   See Brah (1996).

5   A discourse can be articulated from a variety of sites, it has no final fixed form and maintains a systemic and non-random relationship with other statements within its field.

6   E.g. Werbner(1991).

7   Exoticisation is often recognised as essentialising, whereas as banalisation is often considered to be outside this essentialising impulse. Such a conclusion, however, is only possible by misunderstanding what is involved in essentialism.

8   This consumption is not purely metaphorical, for the commercialisation of aspects of the immigrant experience particular in areas of cuisine, costume are often cited as examples of how immigrants are being integrated into society, since their food and clothes are being sold to the general public.

9   Sloterdijk (1988: 218)

10 Hall, (1994)

11 Hall, (1994)

12 Derrida refers to 'under erasure' as recognisably inadequate but having no suitable replacement. Thus it is both incorrect (hence crossed out) and still necessary (hence it remains). The crossing out shows its limits, its presence shows its necessity. Stuart Hall deploys this concept in his discussion of the postcolonial.

13 The postcolonial is the recognition of the light at the end of the tunnel of the colonial. But does it belong to an oncoming train?

14 Hall, 1996; Hesse (2000).

15 See Sayyid, 1997, for further elaboration of this argument.

16 Sayyid, (2000).

17 For a fuller exposition of this argument see Hesse and Sayyid (forthcoming).

18 M. Mann identifies this problem as one of the main obstacles for imperial continuity: the tendency of proconsuls to 'go native'.

19 See Hesse, (this volume) for a genealogy of the category of racism. Here I am using racism generically.

20 See Frank Furedi's *The Silent War* for the role this unity played in the regulation and maintenance of international colour lines.

21 See Mann (1986) for the way in which territorial fixing compels communities to organise for defence.

22 See Hesse et al (1994) for a study of the linkage between racist violence and what he calls 'white territoriality'.

References

Asad, T. (2003) *Formations of the Secular – Christianity, Islam and Modernity,* Palo Alto: Stanford University Press

Ballard R. (ed.) (1994) *Desh Pardesh,* London: Christopher Hurst

Banks, M (1996) *Ethnicity: Anthropological Constructions,* London: Routledge

Brah, A (1994) *Cartographies of Diaspora,* London: Routledge

Frankenberg, R. (1993) *White Women, Race Matters: the Social Construction of Whiteness,* London: Routledge

Furedi, F. (1998) *The Silent War – Imperialism and the changing perception of race,* London: Pluto Press

Goldberg, D.T. (2002) *The Racial State,* Oxford: Blackwell

Hall, Stuart, 'When was the 'the post-colonial'? Thinking at the limit'. in Iain Chambers and Lidia Curti (1999), *The Postcolonial Question: Common Skies, Divided Horizons.* London: Routledge

Hesse, Barnor, *et al.,* (1994) *Beneath the Surface,* Aldershot: Averbury

Hesse, Barnor 'White Governmentality: Urbanism, Nationalism, Racism.' In Sallie Westwood and John Williams (1997) *Imagining Cities: Scripts, Signs, Memory.* London: Routledge

Hesse, B. and Sayyid, S. (forthcoming, 2005), *Paradoxes of Racism – western governmentalities in culture and politics,* London: Pluto Press

Mann, Michael (1986) *The sources of social power Vol 1.* Cambridge: Cambridge University Press.

Mazower, M. (1998) *'Dark Continent – Europe's Twentieth Century',* London: Allen Lane/Penguin

Miles, R. (1989) *Racism,* London: Routledge

Modood, T. (1994) 'Political Blackness and British Asians' *Sociology* Vol. 28 No.4 November

Sayyid, S. (1997) *A Fundamental Fear: Eurocentrism and the emergence of Islamism,* London: Zed Books

Shaw, M (2000) *Theory of the Global State – Globality as an unfinished revolution,* Cambridge: Cambridge University Press

Werbner, P.(1996) 'Essentialising the Other: a critical response' in Terence Ranger, Yunus Samad and Ossie Stuart (eds.) *Culture, Identity and Politics,* Aldershot: Avebury

Notes on Contributors

Les Back is Professor of Sociology, Goldsmiths College, University of London.

Colin Clark is Lecturer in Sociology and Romani studies in the School of Geography, Politics and Sociology, University of Newcastle upon Tyne.

William Gulam is Senior Lecturer in the Revans Institute for Action Learning and Research, Salford University

Barnor Hesse is Senior Lecturer in Sociology, University of East London.

Joyce Hill is Director of the Higher Education Equality Challenge Unit and Visiting Professor in the School of English, University of Leeds.

Shirin Housee is Senior Lecturer in Sociology, University of Wolverhampton.

Ozcan Konur is a social researcher. His recent study was into the emerging public policy issues on access to higher education by disabled students.

Emmanuell Kusemamuriwo is Ethnicity and Diversity Policy Adviser in the Equality Challenge Unit.

Ian Law is Director of the Centre for Ethnicity and Racism Studies and Senior Lecturer in the Department of Sociology and Social Policy, University of Leeds.

Deborah Phillips is Deputy Director of the Centre for Ethnicity and Racism Studies and Senior Lecturer in the Department of Geography, University of Leeds.

Andrew Pilkington is acting Head of Social Studies, University College, Northampton

Nirmal Purwar is Senior Research Fellow in the School of Social Studies, University College, Northampton

Jacques Rangasamy is Lecturer in the School of Art and Design, University of Salford

Salman Sayyid is University Research Fellow in the Department of Sociology and Social Policy, University of Leeds

Sanjay Sharma is Lecturer in the School of Cultural and Innovation Studies, University of East London.

Laura Turney was a Research Fellow at the University of Leeds working on the Institutional Racism in Higher Education Toolkit Project in 2001-2003. She is presently a Principal Researcher with the Scottish Executive.

David Tyrer is a social researcher who recently completed his PhD on 'Institutionalised Islamophobia in British Universities' at the Institute for Social, Cultural and Policy Research, University of Salford.

Author Index

Subject Index